HOW TO WRITE A PLAY

How to Write A Play

by
Raymond Hull

Writer's Digest Books

Cincinnati, Ohio

Dedicated to
FRED HILL—actor, director, impresario, all-around
man-of-the-theatre.
Fred, it was your advice and encouragement that set me writing
for the stage. A thousand thanks!

INTRODUCTION

Back around 1965 I began teaching night school courses in—among other subjects—play writing. I looked for a textbook to recommend to my students, a book they could work with after our ten two-hour class sessions were done, but I couldn't find one that I liked. Compared with other literary forms, plays seemed to have been neglected by the how-to writers.

So I wrote the book myself, and *Profitable Playwriting* was published in 1968. That little book stayed in print for fourteen years. Still, it wasn't quite good enough to live forever.

After the final curtain was rung down on *Profitable Playwriting* I undertook, for Writer's Digest Books, a bigger, better book on the same subject.

I know more about play writing now than I did in 1968. I have read, seen, and written more plays; I have talked with and worked with more actors, actresses, directors, scene painters and producers.

I have retained the basic theory of the former book in this one. It's essential; it's timeless; without it you cannot properly understand old plays, or write new ones. But this book is much thicker than the old one; here I have ample space to demonstrate all major technical points with quotations from plays famous and obscure, to adorn them with my own comments, and to drive them home with exercises designed to set readers writing.

I was also able to add a lot of new material interesting and useful to playwrights—some things that I thought of myself, and some that were recommended by the learned, tactful editors of this company. To them I hereby express my hearty thanks.

TABLE OF CONTENTS

CHAPTER ONE
The Playwright's Business 1
An audience *pays* to see a play; they expect it to give them a satisfying emotional experience. Success or failure in this is the criterion of good or bad playwriting. The spectator is always right.

CHAPTER TWO
History and Conventions of the Theatre 9
Since 535 B.C. the play has developed from a stylized religious ceremony to a multi-form public entertainment; some of the ancient conventions persist today.

CHAPTER THREE
Dramatic Structure................................25
Here is the rule of the Six C's. It has worked for all the great playwrights; it will work for you, too.

CHAPTER FOUR
Conflict..51
Conflict is what audiences want to see; you must base your play upon some kind of conflict—maybe sublime, maybe ridiculous, but *always* conflict.

CHAPTER FIVE
Characters 79
Stage characters ought to be more interesting than the Toms, Dicks, Megs, and Jills of everyday life. Yours is the power to create them.

CHAPTER SIX
Characters II: Dialogue 95
Stage dialogue must be more meaningful, more concentrated, and more interesting than the day-to-day chit-chat of home, store, and office. Here's how to write it.

CHAPTER SEVEN
Characters III: Action 131
The spectator has eyes, as well as ears. Give your stage characters plenty of interesting, significant actions.

CHAPTER EIGHT

Complications 151

An audience keenly enjoys *suspense* and *surprise*. Complications are the plot techniques through which you provide those delightful emotions.

CHAPTER NINE

Crises 163

One uniform emotional pitch maintained throughout the play would bore an audience. Feed them a series of events, each with its own crisis—like the well-timed punches of a skilled boxer.

CHAPTER TEN

Catastrophes 169

Catastrophe—the turn of events for better or worse by which you resolve each point of intense emotional involvement. Whether or not you create surprising, yet credible catastrophes largely determines the success of your play.

CHAPTER ELEVEN

Conclusions 175

Each scene, act, and play needs a good conclusion, one that will leave your audience with that "satisfied" feeling. Effective conclusion is not just a halt in the action: it's a well-planned winding up of all threads in the plot.

CHAPTER TWELVE

The Stage and Its Equipment 179

You are writing, not primarily for the printed page, but for the theatre; so familiarize yourself with the construction and the technical apparatus of the theatre.

CHAPTER THIRTEEN

Actors, Directors, and Spectators 187

Your script is just a series of marks on paper—until *people* transmute *script* into *performance*. The more you know about actors, directors, and spectators, the better your chances of *successful* performance.

CHAPTER FOURTEEN

Writing the Play 199

The play—radically different in form and purpose from the story or novel—presents some problems in the writing. Here are hints on avoiding or solving the problems.

CHAPTER FIFTEEN

Special Forms 209

Technical and artistic tips on writing melodramas, farces, and absurd plays.

CHAPTER SIXTEEN

Production and Publication...................221

A script cannot really be called a play until it has been performed. Here are hints on how to get your plays performed and how, after that, to get them published so as to earn money.

CHAPTER SEVENTEEN

How to Build a Writing Career...................225

Why sit tapping away unsuccessfully in the lonely attic? There are ways to achieve *success*—to write copiously and sell often, to be recognized, to be in demand, as an accomplished, prolific playwright.

CHAPTER EIGHTEEN

Glossary of Theatrical Terms 229

Are you an *angel?* Is someone *featherbedding* you? Do you have any broken *props?* Are your *wings* big enough? These and lots more theatrical expressions defined. Read this, and talk fluently to theatre people.

Recommended Reading...........................234

Index...236

CHAPTER ONE

The Playwright's Business

IF YOU WANT TO WRITE for the stage, this book will show you how. If you are not a writer, this book will lead you to a better understanding of the playwright's methods and problems. Whether you are a writer or not, it will lead you to greater satisfaction from reading playscripts and seeing plays acted.

There are about 175,000 groups regularly performing plays in North America alone. They produce a lot of old favorites, but they are looking for new plays, too—plays that are fairly inexpensive and simple to produce, yet stimulating for actors and audiences alike.

DIRECTIONS FOR PERFORMANCE

First, realize that writing plays is radically different from writing for the printed page—stories, poems, novels, articles and nonfiction books. These are finished literary works designed to convey your thoughts directly to a reader. A playscript is not!

Always be on guard against putting into your plays things that cannot be portrayed on stage. In one published play, written by a famous novelist, is the stage direction: *A wasp settles on the peaches.*

An effective touch, maybe, in a story; but useless in a play! Where do you get a trained wasp? And even if you could train the wasp, your audience would not be able to see it!

True, some people do sit at home, or in school, and *read* plays, but that is only a secondary use. A playscript is primarily *a set of instructions for a performance.*

You, as a playwright, are expected to develop your theme, not necessarily so that it reads well on paper, but so that, when acted, it will give the audience a satisfying emotional experience.

PERSONAL INVOLVEMENT

A writer may spend years successfully turning out stories, books, poems or articles without ever stepping inside a publisher's office or a book bindery.

One may write without ever speaking to an editor or a typesetter, without ever seeing a linotype or a printing press. (I'm not recommending this detached style of operation, but it can be done.)

I remember sitting in the audience at a lecture on play writing. One listener asked, "Would it help me, as a would-be playwright, to go to the theatre and see a play?"

The lecturer said that it would.

I think I would have replied, "No! One visit to the theatre won't help make you a playwright, any more than dipping one toe in the water will help make you a swimmer. You are entering a new medium—the theatre. You must immerse yourself in it *often, for long periods of time,* if you want to adapt yourself to it."

I say it here, near the front of my book, and I shall keep hammering away at the point: you have little hope of success as a playwright unless you make yourself familiar with the theatre, on both sides of the curtain. Later on I shall offer some specific suggestions on how to do that.

START SMALL

You should not expect to rush straight into the costly, complicated business of Broadway production, any more than a student architect would expect to begin a career by designing a Pentagon or a World Trade Center.

Small-scale play producers, because their expenses are low, can afford to gamble on unknown writers. In small-scale theatre you can meet the actors, scene-painters, lighting and sound-effects people who are going to transform your script into a performance. These contacts are precious. Ask questions, listen, take notes. You will learn more than you could discover from taking any course or reading any book (even this one), techniques concerning *your* play, being produced in *these* particular circumstances!

Moreover, in a small theatre you may find an opportunity to direct your own play—and what an education *that* will be! Directing is an unequalled means of learning the innumerable details of play production that you need to understand if you expect to write successful plays.

THE AUDIENCE

All this behind-the-scenes study and work is only a preliminary to the test of your play—performance before a paying audience. Performance gives you the chance to check and correct your work. If the spectators are interested, they will sit still and silent; if they are amused, they will laugh; if they are pleased, they will applaud.

But they never flatter. If they are bored, they will show it by squirming in their seats, coughing, etc. John Dryden said, concerning the first performance of his *Don Sebastian, King of Portugal,* ". . . the watch often drawn out of the pocket, warns the actors that their audience is weary."

So, by watching your audience you can discover which parts of the script are good, and which are bad. What fails in one production can be removed or improved for the next.

WHAT'S IN A RULE?

A number of rules are offered in this book for the guidance of writers. These are not inviolable laws; they simply describe methods that many competent playwrights have found to be effective. Such methods are the easiest for a beginner; they are most likely to lead him on to success. When, with the aid of the rules, he has thoroughly mastered his craft, that will be the time to risk breaking them.

EXERCISE 1:1
Go and see a play (or think back to a play you saw recently).
Write a 500-word review of it—the sort of piece you might write for a local newspaper.
Tell enough about the situation, characters and action to make your piece comprehensible to a reader who has not yet seen the play; yet do not reveal so much as to destroy the suspense for a reader who plans to see it later.
Write what you and the rest of the audience liked or disliked about the show. Try to analyze your feelings a little more closely than would the average spectator. Specify the merits or demerits of sets, lighting, sound effects, costumes and music. Name the cast members who gave particularly good or bad performances.
If you knew the play in advance, through having seen other productions of it, or by having read the script, give your opinion as to how well or how poorly the company carried out the playwright's intentions.

EXERCISE 1:2
After you have written your own review, compare it with what the theatre critic in your local paper had to say about the same production.
Even if you can't see many plays, make a habit of carefully studying the theatre reviews, especially reviews of plays by local writers. What are the typical faults of the plays? What are the strong points most often mentioned? What do these comments suggest to guide you in your own writing?

FROM THE HORSE'S MOUTH

Bronson Howard (1842-1908) was the first American who succeeded solely as a professional playwright—that is, he was not also earning money as an actor or producer.

A few of his better-known plays were *Saratoga, Diamond, Moorcroft, Lilian's Last Love, Peter Stuyvesant.* He adapted several of his plays for the

English stage *(Saratoga,* for example, became *Brighton),* and scored great successes with them in London.

Howard once remarked: "The ideal of a playwright is a happy blending of writer and stage carpenter."

He means that the playwright should have an intimate, and preferably a practical knowledge of the wood and cloth, the nails and paint, the struts and braces, the lights and curtains—all the physical apparatus that creates the visual impression of the play.

He means that it is not enough to think only of the words the characters will speak: you must be aware of the entire spectacle that the audience will witness.

I follow Howard's prescription. I'm writing this page on a Friday. Yesterday morning I was helping two other people from my drama group build the set for a play we are producing. Every morning of next week we shall continue the set construction. The actors will have their last few rehearsals in the finished set, then the play opens the following Thursday.

I don't mean to imply, by the way, that stage carpentry is the only possible "blending" ingredient. Costuming, makeup, lighting, prompting, sound effects—participation in any behind-the-scenes activity is helpful to the playwright.

So, get yourself involved somehow with the practical side of play production. Don't tell yourself that such personal involvement can wait till you have a few playscripts written and ready for performance. I'm saying, emphatically, that it can't wait!

Personal experience on, or behind, the stage will help you avoid most of the impracticalities, physical and financial, that keep the scripts of many aspiring playwrights from being acted.

THE EXEMPLARY DOZEN

This book contains numerous excerpts from other writers, a few of them famous, others obscure. Some of the nineteenth-century plays I've quoted are by American playwrights whose work deserves to be better known and appreciated by American readers. But you can use more than I have space to offer.

Borrow or buy a dozen printed plays. You can include a couple of old ones if you like (Shakespeare, Goldsmith, Molière and the like). Two or three nineteenth-century plays would be useful, but at least half the collection should be fairly modern—say thirty years old or less. Include several of the kind of plays that you want to write.

You need not spend a lot of money on this collection. Browse around used bookstores and see what you can pick up cheap. Consult play-publishers' catalogues in your library; you may want to send off for copies of a few plays that you can't find in books.

This "Exemplary Dozen" need not be plays that you already know. It will be better, in fact, if a few of them are completely new to you. Especially valuable will be plays that you can later see performed on stage.

Consider that all these twelve, old and new, familiar and unfamiliar, are examples of successful playwriting. They have attracted producers and audiences; they have found publishers. That's what you want to do with your plays.

Scattered through this book are exercises based on these plays that you select. You will analyze them for the qualities that helped them succeed. You will learn to look at a printed play with the actor's, the director's and the producer's eye. You will learn to judge dramatic strengths and weaknesses. You will begin as you read to see plays in your mind's eye, as they will appear in performance.

So if, as I suggested, you choose some of your kind of plays, these Exemplary Dozen exercises will become personalized instruction, aimed at *your* needs and interests.

THE BUSINESS SIDE

This collection of playscripts will also give you some information about the business side of play writing and production.

Bear this in mind from the start: success with a play is not a magical process that transports you from your typewriter to a crowded theatre on opening night where the audience gives you a standing ovation.

Play production often involves personal negotiations, some of them quite delicate. There are necessary business procedures—hall rentals, printing of posters, programs and tickets, sales campaigns, press interviews, and so on. More about that later. Some of the items in the next exercise deal with the business side; it's useful to set yourself thinking along these lines right from the start.

EXERCISE 1:3
On a separate sheet of paper for each, write at the top the title of one of your Exemplary Dozen plays.

Don't try to read all the plays through at this stage: just write down a few technical details. N.B. All the answers may not appear in all of the scripts. Then it would be instructive to look elsewhere, perhaps in a biography of the author.
1. The author.
2. Date of writing.
3. If the play is an old classic, who (if anyone) translated, edited or otherwise worked on it, to bring it to the form you now see?
4. Who, if anyone, owns the copyright? Who must be consulted for performing or public reading permissions?
5. Is the play classified as tragedy, comedy, farce, sketch, melodrama, etc.?
6. Who first produced the play on stage? When? Where?
7. Has it been adapted for film or TV? If so, by whom?

8. Who first published the edition you are reading? When?
9. What reprintings, if any, have been made?
10. Is the author alive? If not, when did he or she die?

SUMMARY

The playscript: directions for a performance. Get personally involved with the theatre. Start small; if possible, learn to direct.
Audience reaction: the real test of a play.
The ideal playwright: writer-*cum*-stage carpenter. Study the kind of plays you want to write.
Play production: an art *plus* a business.

CHAPTER TWO

History and Conventions of the Theatre

MOTION PICTURES and television are newfangled forms of entertainment; they have their own rules and regulations. The theatre, on the other hand, has a 2,500-year history. It has undergone considerable transformation, but it has retained a lot of conventions, some obviously useful and others that seem a bit silly. You will be able to write more easily for the stage, and will stand a better chance of getting your plays produced, if you understand something of that history and those conventions.

GREEK ORIGINS

The stage play as we know it in the Western world had its origins, and much of its development, in religion. Dionysus, also known as Bacchus, was a Greek nature-god, credited with instructing mankind in the arts of growing grapes and making wine. This high-ranking god was honored at Athens in annual spring festivals. A chorus of fifty, costumed as satyrs (half man/half goat), danced around an altar chanting hymns of praise, called dithyrambs.

In or about 535 B.C., a radical change took place: the poet Thespis began writing dithyrambs to be performed by a solo singer and chorus alternately—that is, a form of dialogue. (It is in commemoration of this pioneer playwright that actors are sometimes referred to as "Thespians.")

The next 120 years saw extraordinary developments in the new art of playwriting. The ancient Dionysian rites turned into something recognizably similar to the theatre we know. Characters walked, talked and acted on a raised stone stage, before an audience on rows of stone seats. The chorus, below and in front of the stage (like a modern theatre orchestra), sang intermittently a musical commentary on what the actors were doing.

Such plays were all performed outdoors, in unroofed auditoriums, by daylight. There was no means of artificial lighting adequate for the indoor performances that we have come to accept as the norm.

Among the famous names in the period of dramatic experimentation are the tragedians Aeschylus (525-456 B.C.), Sophocles (495-406 B.C.), and

Euripides (480-406 B.C.), and the comic playwright Aristophanes (448-380 B.C.).

Playwrights of that period were prolific. Aristophanes wrote more than forty plays. Aeschylus wrote seventy-two, and Euripides, more than ninety!

Here is an excerpt from Aeschylus's *Prometheus Bound*, judged by some critics to be his greatest work. Prometheus, according to Greek legend, was a Titan who stole fire from heaven and gave it to mankind on earth. In punishment for this, Zeus had him chained to Mount Caucasus.

In this scene, a chorus of sea nymphs converses with the hero.

CHORUS
Hard as these chains, and cold as all these rocks
Is he, Prometheus, who withholds his heart
From joining in thy woe. I yearned before
To fly this sight; and, now I gaze on it,
I sicken inwards.

PROMETHEUS
To my friends, indeed,
I must be a sad sight.

CHORUS
And didst thou sin
No more than so?

PROMETHEUS
I did restrain besides
My mortals from premeditating death.

CHORUS
How didst thou medicine the plague-fear of death?

PROMETHEUS
I set blind Hope to inhabit in their hearts.

CHORUS
By that gift thou didst help thy mortals well.

PROMETHEUS
I gave them also fire.

CHORUS
And have they now,
Those creatures of a day, the red-eyed fire?

PROMETHEUS

They have: and shall learn by it many arts.

CHORUS

And truly for such sins Zeus tortures thee
And will remit no anguish. Is there set
No limit before thee to thine agony?

PROMETHEUS

No other: only what seems good to Him.

The translation, by Elizabeth Barrett Browning, gives us a fair idea of the stately verse style in which the tragedies of this era were written.

EXERCISE 2:1

Imagine a present-day situation. There have been allegations about cruel treatment of prisoners in the penal system of some state. A committee of would-be reformers is touring a penitentiary. They interview a prisoner who has a life sentence for some serious offense against the government. He or she eloquently tells them his or her side of the story. (For exactly what happened, where and when, exercise your imagination. This exercise will get you started expressing abstract concepts, e.g., treason, in specific, human terms.)

If you particularly want to, you can write the scene in verse.

EXERCISE 2:2

Now develop the theme. Make it richer, more interesting, more instructive. Don't let all the committee passively accept everything the prisoner says. Have one of them hostile to the prisoner. Consider how he will challenge and oppose the prisoner's narrative; work out how he will criticize his fellow-members for being so gullible.

Finally, let this hostile member *do* something, or at least *announce* that he is going to do something, to bring the scene to a strong, decisive conclusion.

ROME

Romans, like the Athenians, had old established rites of singing and dancing in honor of their gods. Around 360 B.C. some crude forms of dialogue were added, but Romans saw no real plays until 240 B.C., when Livius Andronicus began translating Greek plays into Latin.

Over the following two centuries, the theatre grew in popularity, and many more playwrights flourished. The comic writers Plautus and Terence and the tragedian Seneca are the best-known names.

Audiences in Roman times favored comedy more than did the Greeks, and before long, comedy came to dominate the Roman theatre. Satirical themes, witty characters and literary dialogue were introduced, then in time the comedies became coarse, immoral and unsavory.

The Roman playwrights, like the Athenian, generally used a chorus to enliven their plays with passages of singing and dancing.

At first, Rome had no such elegant stone theatres as did Athens. Roman audiences sat on the ground, or on wooden benches; the actors performed on temporary wooden platforms. As the theatre showed a lasting popularity, however, the Romans constructed large, permanent outdoor theatres of stone. The typical Roman stage was about sixty yards wide from side to side, and quite shallow from rear to front. Conventionally it represented a city street. The exit at the actors' right supposedly led out of town, to the harbor; that on the actors' left, to the center of the city. A few openings in the rear wall of the stage represented the doors of houses facing the street.

The characters wore Roman or Greek dress, whichever suited the story. Men played all the female roles, till about the time of Julius Caesar. Then actresses began to appear on stage.

The stage had a trap door, through which characters representing demons could pop up to street level. There was usually some kind of crane or hoist, also. A playwright might work his story up to a situation that could not be resolved by any normal human means. Then a god *(deus)* would be lowered from the top of the stagehouse. He would step out of his flying chariot *(ex machina),* and use his divine powers to accomplish what mortals could not. The term *deus ex machina* is still used for an improbable turn of events inserted by a playwright to resolve a crisis; it is yet one more dramatic device the Romans borrowed from Greece. I shall have more to say about this technique in Chapter 10.

> EXERCISE 2:3
> Take a present-day street as your setting. A billfold is lying on the ground. Write a draft of a comic scene, preferably with yourself as one of the characters. When the situation is as complicated as you care to make it, bring on a policeman—*deus ex machina*—to settle the dispute.

> EXERCISE 2:4
> For the next few weeks, compile a "street-observation notebook." Whenever you are outdoors, watch for characters, situations or actions, and listen for bits of dialogue that stir up some emotion in you—anger, fear, pity, curiosity, mirth, etc.
>
> Such observations produce raw material for playwriting. Take a little time to note them down. Later, enlarge on your notes and try to develop the ideas into complete scenes.

RELIGION AND THE THEATRE

As the Christian religion gained converts and power in Europe, the church understandably turned against the theatre. Much of dramatic repertory glorified pagan gods and heroes; much of it was vulgar and obscene. So, for several centuries, the Roman Catholic church suppressed playwriting and acting.

Around A.D. 975, however, there began to develop, with ecclesiastical approval, a type of drama called the "miracle play" or "mystery play." Scripts were developed from the Bible or from the lives of saints. To make the plays longer and more interesting, authors often created villainous or mock-villainous devils or demons, and sometimes comic characters, too. Few people in those days knew how to read, so the mystery plays were a potent means of teaching the illiterate masses.

These mysteries were at first performed by priests in, or on the front steps of, church buildings. Later they were acted by members of trade guilds on the flatbeds of wagons, mobile stages easily hauled to market or fair—any place where a crowd might gather to see the edifying show.

The fifteenth century saw the development of morality plays. In these, characters were not drawn from the books of the Bible, or from the calendar of saints. They were named after, and made to personify, human vices and virtues: Lust, Sloth, Hypocrisy, Pride, Avarice, Honor, Prudence, Temperance, Charity, and so on. The typical morality storyline depicted the conflict of good against evil for the main character's soul.

The next new form in the late fifteenth century was the "interlude," a short play with no religious plot and with characters, classical or contemporary, of little or no moral significance. It was straight entertainment, provided as part of the hospitality at a nobleman's or a monarch's banquet. The interlude might be performed in segments between courses of the meal, or all of a piece after the feasting was done.

There was no sudden disappearance of one type of drama with complete replacement by another. Yet, within one lifetime, the morality plays and interludes developed into the European non-religious theatre, which was heavily influenced by Renaissance study of Roman drama. Plays were supplied by writers whose names are well-known today: in England, John Lyly (1554-1606), Christopher Marlowe (1564-1606), and William Shakespeare (1564-1616); in France, Pierre Corneille (1600-1684), Jean Baptiste Poquelin, alias Molière (1622-1673) and Jean Baptiste Racine (1639-1699); in Spain, Lope de Vega, author of more than 1,800 plays! (1562-1635) and Calderon de la Barca (1600-1681).

Some religious and moral themes were still being used, but the overpowering influence of the church, even in Catholic countries such as France and Spain, was gone. Playwrights wrote, theatre managers chose, and actors performed plays that would tickle the tastes of the crowds who flocked to enjoy this new form of entertainment.

TRAGEDY AND COMEDY

From the very dawn of drama, plays have been classified into two groups: tragedies and comedies.

Roughly defined, tragedy deals with *serious* subjects. It often, though not necessarily, portrays lofty characters (gods, kings, queens, princes, presidents, generals) engaged in important affairs (wars, revolutions, treasons, murders, etc.). The primary function of tragedy is to arouse in an audience the emotions of fear and pity. A tragedy may also indirectly teach some ethical lesson, one that is considered significant for the time and place of its performance. The usual, though not inevitable, ending of a tragedy is an "unhappy" one for the main character(s) (murder, suicide, divorce, defeat, disgrace, or some other unpleasant event).

Comedy had its roots in the buffoonery and coarse jokes that used to enliven some of the old Dionysian festivals. Laughter has long been recognized for its therapeutic effect, and the early playwrights lost no time in harnessing its healing power. The main purpose of comedy, of course, is to make the audience laugh.

Comedy, as a rule, deals with subjects that, though supposedly serious to the characters on stage, seem less than momentous (even ridiculous) to the audience. Examples: an old man's infatuation with a young girl, a mistaken identity, a jealous husband's suspicion of his wife, a miser's fanatical pursuit of wealth, the exposure of a cowardly braggart, and so on.

Nevertheless, the purpose of comedy need not be entirely frivolous. Many writers of comedy have sought to expose and correct social evils, by making people laugh at them!

The typical comic ending is the converse of the tragic: engagement, marriage, reconciliation, honor, wealth, or some such "happy" event for the main characters.

EXERCISE 2:5
Think of three tragic events from your own life, or from the lives of people you know. For each one, make some brief notes on:
(a) The main characters involved: say a 50-word sketch of each, and two characteristic bits of dialogue.
(b) The force(s) (personal, social or other) that produced the tragedy. (Answering the question, *"Why* did this or that happen?" is the very basis of play construction.)
(c) The final outcome in each case.
(d) What you (or someone else involved) could have done, if you had had the benefit of later knowledge, to change the outcome. (The playwright, of course, does have the benefit of later knowledge in constructing the play.)
N.B. Don't worry, in this exercise and the next, about trying to write complete plays. For the present, you are just gathering material, tuning your mental radar, as it were, to pick up ideas that are potentially useful to you.

EXERCISE 2:6
Recall three comic events from your own life, or from the lives of people you know. For each one, make some brief notes on:

(a) The main characters involved: say a 50-word sketch of each, and two characteristic bits of dialogue.
(b) The force(s) that operated to produce the comedy.
(c) The final outcome in each case.
(d) What you—or someone else involved—could have done, if you had had the benefit of later knowledge, to make a funnier, more complete, more satisfying outcome.

Too Much of a Sad Thing

Some theorists and critics have said that the two forms should be kept separate, that every character, speech or action in a tragedy or comedy should contribute to the desired emotional effect. In practice, many playwrights have used some comic material in tragic scripts. The theory behind this is that the audience cannot comfortably endure *too much* pity, *too much* horror, for *too long*, without a break. (After all, the theatre is an entertainment!) The interjection of a small dose of comedy ("comic relief") will heighten the effect of a subsequent tragic scene, much as the visual effect of a picture may be heightened by enclosing it in a frame of some contrasting color.

A famous example: the comic Porter's scene in *Macbeth*, Act II, Scene 3. In Scene 2, Macbeth has murdered King Duncan—the deepest tragedy so far in the play. Now he needs time to wash his bloody hands and change into his night-clothes for his next appearance. So something has to fill that time, and Shakespeare uses the grotesque Porter, first alone and then, for a little variety, with Macduff and Lennox. Shortly after this comic interlude, Macduff's discovery of the murder returns the play to its predominant tragic tone.

PLAYERS AND PLAYHOUSES

In the late sixteenth century, some French and Italian towns had old Roman-style theatres still usable for performances of the new secular comedies and tragedies.

Elsewhere, in Britain and Spain, for instance, play producers had to improvise. The essential elements were: (a) a convenient stage area, preferably raised above ground-level; (b) space for the spectators to sit or stand; (c) some means of excluding people who had not paid to see the show.

That third point had not mattered when miracle plays were being performed by amateurs on church steps or wagon-beds. It became important when actors were acting, and playwrights writing, for money!

The enclosed courtyard of an inn was found to serve the purpose very well. The stage would be backed against one wall that had convenient doors and windows for entries and exits. Some spectators could stand or sit on the level center of the yard; others could sit at the open windows in the other three walls, with a good view over the heads of the groundlings. The cashier sat at the courtyard gate to control admissions.

The stage had no representational scenery. Printed placards were hung up to show the supposed site of the action: A ROOM OF STATE IN THE PALACE; THE GRECIAN CAMP; ELSINORE, THE CASTLE, etc.

Properties appropriate to the setting and action (chairs, tables, benches, beds, chests, cauldrons, barrels and such moveables) were freely used. They were carried on and off by attendants between scenes, in full view of the audience.

This shifting of properties, or leaving the stage briefly empty, indicated the end of a scene. Spectators simply used their imaginations to travel through space and time to the next scene. To help them, the playwright sometimes included a few lines descriptive of the place or conditions. For example, in *Macbeth*, Act I, Scene 4, BEFORE THE CASTLE: Duncan says,

> This castle hath a pleasant seat; the air
> Nimbly and sweetly recommends itself
> Unto our gentle senses.

Lanterns and torches might be carried by actors to add a little realism to scenes supposedly taking place at night, but there was no attempt at artificial illumination of the stage. The theatre-yard was open to the sky, and performances took place in the afternoons.

The actors at this time were all men and boys. A chronic scarcity of good female impersonators accounts for the relatively small number of important female roles in the plays of this period. A royal court or noble household might have a dozen "ladies in waiting," needed simply to fetch and carry, to dance perhaps, and to look ornamental. But the play would include only one or two female parts requiring any great amount of talking and acting. Playwrights often used the plot device of a female character disguising herself and living as a man through most of the play.

Built to Order

Obvious technical and commercial advantages eventually led play producers to erect special buildings, solely for their own use. Theatres of Shakespeare's time strongly resembled the inn-yards: the stage against one wall, facing the flat, unroofed center, and two or three levels of room-like enclosures (later called "boxes") around the perimeter.

By the late seventeenth century, thanks to the patronage of King Charles II, and to the emergence of several distinguished new British playwrights, playwriting, production and attendance all boomed.

Theatres came to be roofed structures, allowing more performances per annum. Artificial lighting allowed night performances, thus widening the potential audience to include people who worked all day and could come to the theatre only in the evenings. Perhaps most important, the theatre, as an art-form and as a business, became "respectable." Actresses took over the female roles, giving the playwrights a notably increased scope for characterization, dialogue and action.

As public support increased, producers began building bigger theatres.

That change required the stage to be made higher, and the auditorium floor to be sloped, so that people sitting in the rear could see over the heads of those in front.

Yet there was a limit to the enlargement. Spectators in the back row had to hear every word spoken on stage, even when characters were talking softly. Moreover, those back-row spectators expected, quite rightly, a clear view of characters' faces. Without visible facial expressions, a major element of the actor's art would be lost.

The maximum useful seating capacity for a theatre was found to be about 1,200. This limit has remained unchanged right up to the present. (N.B. This applies to live plays: halls for operas and orchestral concerts may well be much larger.) Many theatres, indeed, are much below this maximum; some companies flourish in theatres with 250 seats or fewer.

Two other important changes over the years were the increased use of representational scenery on stage, and the installation of the front curtain.

THE PLAYWRIGHT-AUDIENCE RELATIONSHIP

Samuel Taylor Coleridge wrote of a "willing suspension of disbelief" as contributing to the effect of poetry upon readers. Just the same emotional effort is required of every theatre audience.

The playwright is saying to the audience, "Please *pretend* that these people you see are *not* actors, but gods and goddesses, kings and queens, criminals and detectives, infatuated young lovers, or whomever my script requires. *Pretend* that they are not on stage, that they are living their lives in the city street, in the palace, in the courtroom, in heaven, in hell, or wherever else I tell you."

The audience, as a rule, co-operates. It *pretends* that those characters on stage don't know that spectators are present, overlooking and overhearing everything they (the characters) do and say.

These are the elements of that "suspension of disbelief" that make play-acting different from singing, dancing, oratory, instrumental music, and other arts where the performer addresses himself directly to the audience. These elements create the *magic* of a successful play performance.

The pretense is not always unbroken. Playwrights sometimes bring on a special narrator (or maybe a member of the cast) to address the audience directly, before and/or after the play, in a prologue or epilogue. In some plays, during the main action, characters use "asides" (remarks supposedly unheard by the other people on stage) to let the audience know what they are thinking.

But the players usually keep their imaginary distance from the audience. The spectators play their assigned roles of spies and eavesdroppers, so they experience whatever intellectual and emotional stimulation the playwright and producers have provided for them.

From their surviving scripts, we know how well the old-time playwrights understood this indirect relationship with their audiences. Nowadays, we too must remember that we are not writing for printers and readers, but for the eyes, ears and imaginations of a live audience.

THEATRE IN AMERICA

Theatrical production in North America began at Williamsburg, Virginia, in 1716. In the northern colonies, the Puritans and Quakers vigorously opposed theatres and actors, considering them to be influences for evil. Consequently, the educational and inspirational aspects of the theatre were stressed in script writing and advertising. Plays were often promoted as "lectures," "concerts" or "exhibitions." Theatre companies, often actors' co-operatives, were expected to donate much of their income to charities, and to worthy civic operations such as fire companies.

There were at first no theatre buildings, so performances had to be given in schools, public halls, barns, etc. It was not till the late 1760s that the first few buildings specifically designed as theatres were erected.

For several decades, scripts from Europe were used, but by the end of the eighteenth century, American playwrights were writing plays dealing with local subjects and portraying local characters. The first American professional playwright was William Dunlap (1766-1839), who wrote or adapted sixty-one plays.

The theatre-going public was small. In most places one-night or two-night stands were the rule. Even in New York, in the early 1800s, a run of a dozen performances of the same play was considered a fantastic success.

Lighting and Effects

In 1816, the first gaslights were installed in the Chestnut Theatre, Philadelphia.

Indoor theatrical performances had been, up till that time, illuminated like all other nighttime activities—by candles or oil-lamps. The new technique was such a great improvement (rapid, simultaneous brightening or lowering of all the lights, for example) that it was taken up everywhere, as soon as the gas became available.

It was only in the last quarter of the nineteenth century that electric lighting gradually ousted gas. That innovation substantially reduced the risk of theatre fires, an ever-present, ghastly feature of the older systems.

Present-day producers and playwrights have, with the electric light, an infinitely flexible system at their disposal. It is controllable, from moment to moment, in color, intensity and direction. Electric lights can suggest anything from moonlight on the blasted heath to midday in the Sahara Desert.

Though the lighting may have been primitive in those early days, scenic effects were often elaborate: waterfalls with real water, heroines riding horseback through forests, ships sailing and locomotives running, all on stage.

Here, for example, are the stage directions for the final scene of *The Glory of Columbia*, written in 1803 by William Dunlap:

Yorktown—at a distance is seen the town, with the British lines and the lines of the besiegers—nearer are the advanced batteries, one more distant from the audience than the other—cannonading commences from the besiegers on the town—explosion of a powder magazine—the French troops advance towards the most distant of the advanced batteries—the battery begins to cannonade—the troops advance and carry it at the bayonet's point—while this is yet doing, the nearest battery begins to cannonade, and the American infantry attacks and carries it with fixed bayonets, striking the English colors— shouts of victory. Enter on one side, General Washington, Melville, Bland, officers, soldiers, drums and colors—on the other, Williams, Paulding, Van Vert, Dennis O'Bogg, officers and soldiers.

(Remember, this is for *one* scene of *one* act of a five-act play!)

Casting

Casts of many nineteenth-century plays seem large, by present-day standards. *Across the Continent* (James J. McCloskey, 1870) has twenty-three named characters, plus numerous unnamed Men, Women, Indians and Soldiers. *Po-ca-hon-tas* or *The Gentle Savage* (John Broughton, 1855) has thirty named characters, plus numerous unnamed Soldiers, Sailors and Indians.

Many actors were poorly paid, and some producers used amateurs to supplement the efforts of the professionals. At one performance of *The Drunkard* in 1856, more than a thousand children were added to the cast in various crowd scenes, parades and dances!

In most plays, male characters still outnumbered the females by two or three to one.

The Railroad

For a long time, the typical city theatre operated a stock company, with visiting stars now and then as added attractions.

Rapidly increasing railroad development in the 1860s and 1870s, however, made it practicable and profitable to transport a whole company of actors, with all their sets and props, hither and thither across the continent, performing the same play, week after week, month after month.

These touring companies were important to actors, providing steady, if monotonous, work. They were an asset to playwrights too, making possible much longer runs than any single theatre could offer.

The Motion Picture

The theatre, in one form or another, survived for some 2,450 years as the principal medium of dramatic entertainment. That supremacy was rapidly destroyed by the invention of motion picture cameras and projectors.

The Great Train Robbery, in 1903, was the first notably successful presentation of a coherent drama on the screen.

Early motion picture showings were held in "nickelodeons." These were small halls or empty stores equipped with projector, chairs, screen and a piano. The piano player's job was to drown out the rattle of the projector, and to provide some suitable mood-making accompaniment to the story being portrayed silently on the screen.

By 1910, there were 9,000 nickelodeons in the U.S.A. The live stage rapidly lost much of its former audience to the movies, which by now were commonly offering "feature-length" films, running 90 minutes. Thousands of theatres shut down.

Movie operators, as their business boomed, moved out of the cramped, shabby nickelodeons and took over thousands of the now-dark theatres. It soon appeared that the movies, with their low admission prices, were attracting many people who could not have afforded, or who had not cared, to go to the theatre. The old theatres were not enough to house the huge movie audience. Many new large buildings were erected specifically for showing movies.

Broadway survived, of course, an island of big-scale theatrical activity tending to feature more musicals and fewer straight plays. The big productions served largely as tourist attractions. But the theatre in its nineteenth-century form, as a nationwide, popular form of mass entertainment, was dead.

Little Theatres and Off Broadway

Though motion pictures (particularly with the advent of the "talkies" in 1926) severely shrank the potential theatre audience, they did not destroy it. Theatre enthusiasts found new means of enjoying their favorite entertainment, through the "Little Theatre" movement.

During the 1910s and 1920s, thousands of little-theatre groups sprang up all over the country. Some were co-operatives, semi-professional or amateur; many were run by schools, colleges, universities, churches, scout troops, community centers and other organizations.

The little theatres had much lower production costs than did the old stock and touring companies. They never expected any mass response to their productions, so they felt free to put on plays that pleased and interested *themselves*. Thus they could offer stage-room to many plays, classical and modern, that the old-style theatres would have brusquely rejected.

The Little Theatre movement continues today, vigorously active. It seeks a wide range of subject matter. Some groups want light, noncontroversial entertainment—comedies or farces showing present-day characters in funny situations. Some groups want musical comedies or revues.

Some want thought-provoking plays on serious contemporary subjects (women's, ethnic, minority, gay, or senior citizens' rights, and various other political issues).

Some groups write their own scripts, maybe because they can't find any existing plays that meet their needs. Undoubtedly the best, most wide-open market for the beginning playwright is in Little Theatre.

What remained of the old-style professional theatre received another hard battering in the 1940s from the increasing competition of television. A result was the growth of "Off Broadway." This is a loose grouping of semi-professional and professional theatres in New York, producing classic dramas, translations of foreign plays, and controversial and experimental works by modern playwrights—mostly material that would never appeal to the typical Broadway audience.

During the 1950s, more and more professional playwrights turned their efforts toward Off Broadway productions. These plays were often presented in old warehouses, churches, closed-down movie houses and other low-rent facilities. Experimental script formats and production techniques were enthusiastically tried out.

The trend continued through the 1960s. Well-known playwrights such as Samuel Beckett, Harold Pinter, Bertolt Brecht, Edward Albee and Arthur Kopit had plays staged in this specialized, localized market.

Gradually, Off Broadway productions tended to become more elaborate, more conventional and more costly. So there was a reaction in favor of small, unconventional and cheap productions from which evolved a loose grouping of playwrights and producers that soon acquired the title of "Off-Off Broadway."

Another trend has been toward the trying-out of new plays in regional professional theatres. Those that succeed in the provinces may go to Off Broadway for further testing and polishing. Only the few that develop into smash hits there have any chance of reaching Broadway.

Future Trends

There is no current sign of any large or rapid change in the four-level stage production system described above: Broadway, Off Broadway (including Off-Off Broadway), Regional and Little Theatre.

There undoubtedly will be some continued experimentation: increased writing for, and use of, the old-style open stage, as opposed to the proscenium theatre; some new developments in lighting and sound equipment, projection techniques, etc. But the intelligent writer can easily keep up to date with such changes.

Read theatrical news in newspapers and magazines. (The *New York Times* and *Village Voice* are good, if you can get them.) Attend a variety of stage plays. Get actively involved with theatrical productions in your hometown. Make friends with some actors and directors. They will make you aware of what you should be doing at your typewriter.

SUMMARY

Greek and Roman religious festivals: the origins of drama.
Non-religious subjects gradually took over.
Actresses appeared in Rome, first century B.C.
Christianity at first suppressed the theatre; A.D. 975 on, mystery plays taught Christianity.
Fifteenth century: morality plays and interludes developed: sixteenth century, European non-religious theatre develops.
Tragedy: lofty characters (as a rule), serious themes, unhappy endings.
Comedy: ludicrous characters (as a rule), trivial themes, happy endings.
Comic relief: used to heighten overall tragic effect.
Sixteenth-century: inn yards used as outdoor theatres; theatres of the period modelled on inn yards.
Late seventeenth century: roofed theatres with artificial light.
Late seventeenth century: actresses take over female roles.
Audience contribution: the "willing suspension of disbelief."
Eighteenth-century American theatre: small-scale productions, short runs.
Early nineteenth century: gaslight in theatres; late nineteenth century: electricity replaces gas.
Nineteenth-century casts often very large; scenery and effects very elaborate.
Railroads facilitated touring companies.
Early twentieth century: development of motion pictures.
Little Theatres: the present-day nationwide play market.
Regional professional theatre: small market for skilled playwrights.
Off Broadway and Off-Off Broadway: small markets in New York.
Broadway: small, specialized market for experienced playwrights.

CHAPTER THREE

Dramatic Structure

"IF WE WANT TO learn the playwright's art," said Goethe, "Molière is the man we should study. Do you know his *Imaginary Invalid?* It contains a scene  which, in my opinion, displays his perfect stage technique. It is the scene where the Invalid asks his little daughter Louison whether she has seen a young man in her big sister's room. Now a less skillful playwright would have let little Louison answer plainly and promptly, and that would be that.

"But see what delays Molière introduces into the interrogation. First he makes little Louison pretend she does not understand her father; then she says she knows nothing; then, threatened with a whipping, she falls down and plays dead; then, when her father cries out in remorse, she jumps up laughing and at last, little by little, she tells everything.

"Study this scene. You will agree that there is more practical instruction in it than in all the theories in the world."

Here is the scene that Goethe recommends: *The Imaginary Invalid*, Act II, Scene 9:

LOUISON

What do you want, Papa? My stepmother said you were calling for me.

ARGAN

Yes. Come here. Nearer! Turn around. Look up, now. Look at me. Eh?

LOUISON

What is it, Papa?

ARGAN

Well?

LOUISON

What?

ARGAN

Have you nothing to tell me?

LOUISON

If you like, I'll tell you the tale of the Ass's Skin; that'll amuse you. Or else the fable of The Crow And The Fox that I learned the other day.

ARGAN

That's not what I want to hear.

LOUISON

What, then?

ARGAN

Ah, little slyboots, you know perfectly well what I mean.

LOUISON

I beg your pardon, Papa.

ARGAN

Is this the way you obey me?

LOUISON

I don't understand.

ARGAN

Haven't I told you to to come straight to me and tell me everything you see?

LOUISON

Yes, Papa.

ARGAN

And have you done it?

LOUISON

Yes, Papa. I've told you everything I see.

ARGAN

And haven't you seen anything today?

LOUISON

No, Papa.

ARGAN

No?

LOUISON

No, Papa.

ARGAN

Are you quite sure?

LOUISON

Quite sure, Papa.

ARGAN

Oh, then I'll have to teach you to keep your eyes open.
(He brings out a whip)

LOUISON

Oh, Papa!

ARGAN

Ah, you little story-teller, you didn't tell me you saw a man in your sister's room!

LOUISON

(Weeping) Oh, Papa!

ARGAN

(Seizing her arm) I'll teach you to lie to me.

LOUISON

(Kneeling) Oh, Papa, forgive me. It's just that my sister told me not to tell; but I'll tell you all about it.

ARGAN

First, you must be whipped for lying. Then, afterwards, we'll see about that.

LOUISON

Forgive me, Papa!

ARGAN

Oh, no!

LOUISON

Papa, darling Papa, don't whip me.

ARGAN

I will whip you.

LOUISON

For heaven's sake, Papa, don't whip me.

ARGAN

(Trying to whip her) Come on, come on!

LOUISON

Oh, Papa, you're hurting me. Stop: I'm dying! *(She plays dead)*

ARGAN

Hey, what's the matter? Louison! Louison! Oh, heavens! Louison! Oh, my little daughter! Oh, misery! My little girl is dead! What have I done, wretch that I am? Confound the whip! Devil take the whip! Oh, my poor daughter, my poor little Louison!

LOUISON

Come now, Papa, don't cry. I'm not quite dead.

ARGAN

Oh, what a little trickster! All right, I'll forgive you, just this once, on condition that you tell me every last detail.

LOUISON

Yes, yes, Papa.

ARGAN

But take care. Look, my little finger knows everything, and it will tell me if you lie.

LOUISON

All right, Papa, but don't tell my sister that I told you.

ARGAN

Certainly not.
(Louison looks around to see if anyone is listening.)

LOUISON

All right, then, Papa. It's like this. A man came to my sister's room while I was there.

ARGAN

Well?

LOUISON

I asked him what he wanted, and he said he was her singing teacher.

ARGAN

(Aside) Ah-hah! So that's the little game. *(To* LOUISON) Well, what then?

LOUISON

Then my sister came.

ARGAN

Yes?

LOUISON

She said to him, "Go away! Go away! For heaven's sake, go away. You'll get me into trouble."

ARGAN

Well?

LOUISON

He wouldn't go.

ARGAN

What did he say?

LOUISON

All kinds of things.

ARGAN

What kinds of things?

LOUISON

He said this, and that. . .that he loved her, and that she was the most beautiful girl in the world.

ARGAN

And then what?

LOUISON

And then he knelt down in front of her.

ARGAN

And then?

LOUISON

And then he kissed her hands.

ARGAN

And then?

LOUISON

And then my stepmother came to the door, and he ran away.

ARGAN

Is that all?

LOUISON

That's all, Papa.

ARGAN

Wait. My little finger is whispering something. *(He puts his finger in his ear)* Listen! Ah. . .oh. . .yes?. . .oh, oh! My little finger says that you saw something more, something you haven't told me.

LOUISON

Oh, Papa, your little finger is lying.

ARGAN

Be careful now!

LOUISON

No, Papa. Don't believe it. It's lying, I tell you.

ARGAN

Oh, all right. Run along now, and keep your eyes open. Off you go. *(She goes)* Ah, children aren't what they used to be. Oh, what a lot of bother! I simply haven't got time to worry about my health. I can't stand it any longer. *(He collapses into a chair)*

Johann Wolfgang von Goethe, in addition to being a great playwright, novelist and poet, had twenty-seven years' experience as a theatre manager—an undoubted genius. Molière was a playwright, star actor, play director, theatre manager—also a genius. Molière is widely acknowledged as the greatest of playwrights, the Mozart of playwrights, the playwright's playwright.

When one literary genius and man-of-the-theatre says of another, "Look, here is the key to his success," then ordinary writers should examine that key minutely.

THE SIX C's

What is there in the Molière excerpt that has "more practical instruction in it than in all the theories in the world?"

It contains all the elements of drama:
 Conflict
 Characters
 Complications
 Crisis
 Catastrophe
 Conclusion

The *conflict* is between a parent's authority and a child's defiance.

The *characters* are Argan, the imaginary invalid, and Louison, the vivacious, mischievous little girl.

The *complications* are the "delays" that Goethe mentions.

The *crisis* is Argan's last "And then?"

(*Catastrophe*, as we use the word in connection with dramatic structure, does not mean a convulsion or disaster, an earthquake or hurricane. *Catastrophe* comes from Greek roots meaning "downward turn.") The catastrophe of a scene or play is the point at which the action takes the turn that leads to the resolution of the conflict. So in this scene the catastrophe is Louison's "and then my stepmother came to the door and he ran away." This item of information is the "turn": it changes Argan's mental state— relieves his fear for his older daughter's chastity.

The *conclusion:* Argan is content to know that the older girl is safe.

So a play must have at least two characters in conflict. The conflict must develop by way of complications. An uncomplicated conflict might make a very short sketch, but it would not sustain a play of conventional length.

The complications lead to a crisis, when the emotional effect of action upon audience is as intense as the playwright cares or dares to make it.

The crisis must be solved by a catastrophe—nowadays a credible catastrophe. Present-day audiences do not believe in fairy godmothers, and don't feel satisfied with coincidences.

The play must reach a satisfactory conclusion: one that satisfies, not necessarily the characters, not exclusively the playwright, but that satisfies the audience.

ACTS AND SCENES

By long-established custom, an evening of theatre is divided into several sections, with intermissions between them. This is partly for the comfort of the audience, many of whom have come straight from dinner table to theatre. Then there is the technical point that intermissions are often necessary to allow for changes of scenery and costume. Moreover, for many theatres, the practice has an economic basis: the sale of refreshments is an important source of revenue.

Each major section of a long play is called an *act*. In Shakespeare's day, and for some time afterward, the customary length was five acts. Nowadays, a full-length play generally has two or three acts. The typical short play has one act.

In most old plays, and in some modern ones, too, the acts are broken down into *scenes*. Each scene represents a part of the story occurring *in one place, at one time.*

If it is necessary to show a lapse of time between two scenes, the stage lights may be dimmed, or the curtain lowered briefly.

French Scenes

In old French playscripts, the acts are broken down into still smaller divisions. The entrance of a main or secondary character marks the beginning, and the exit of a main or secondary character marks the end of each French "scene."

There is normally no curtain drop and no dimming of the lights to mark the transition from one French scene to the next, yet the divisions make convenient starting and stopping places in rehearsal and the French scene itself is the unit with which the writer builds his play.

So it is important for you, as a writer, to begin thinking in these terms. In ordinary life, people often wander from room to room, or from house to street, without any apparent purpose. That will not do on stage: the stage-world is more purposeful and orderly than life. The audience feels that each character who comes on stage must have some business there, and expects that he will quickly reveal it. Each character who leaves the stage must be going somewhere to do something: his destination and purpose must be revealed. Therefore, each entrance and exit on stage is a significant event, and makes a suitable division point for writing, rehearsal or analysis.

One, Two, Three. . .

For convenience in analyzing the structure of plays, we often talk of *one-scenes, two-scenes, three-scenes* and so on, referring to French scenes that have one, two, three or more characters playing significant parts in them.

The Teahouse of the August Moon (John Patrick, adapted from the novel by Vern Sneider) opens with a one-scene: Sakini, the interpreter, on stage alone, addressing the audience.

The Importance of Being Earnest (Oscar Wilde) opens with a two-scene between Algernon and Lane.

ACT I

(Midsummer, 1895. Morning room in Algernon's flat in London, England. The room is luxuriously and artistically furnished. The sound of a piano is heard from an adjoining room. LANE, a manservant, is arranging afternoon tea on the table. The music stops. Enter ALGERNON.)

ALGERNON

Did you hear what I was playing, Lane?

LANE

I didn't think it polite to listen, sir.

ALGERNON

I'm sorry for that, for your sake. I don't play accurately—any one can play accurately—but I play with wonderful expression. As far as the piano is concerned, sentiment is my forte. I keep science for life.

LANE

Yes, sir.

ALGERNON

And, speaking of the science of Life, have you got the cucumber sandwiches cut for Lady Bracknell?

LANE

Yes, sir. *(Hands them on a salver)*

ALGERNON

(Inspects them, takes two, and sits down on the sofa) Oh!. . .By the way, Lane, I see from your book that on Thursday night, when Lord Shoreman and Mr. Worthing were dining with me, eight bottles of champagne are entered as having been consumed.

LANE

Yes, sir: eight bottles and a pint.

ALGERNON

Why is it that at a bachelor's establishment the servants invariably drink the champagne? I ask merely for information.

LANE

I attribute it to the superior quality of the wine, sir. I have often observed that in married households the champagne is rarely of a first-rate brand.

ALGERNON

Good heavens! Is marriage so demoralizing as that?

LANE

I believe it *is* a very pleasant state, sir. I have had very little experience of it myself up to the present. I have only been married once. That was in consequence of a misunderstanding between myself and a young person.

ALGERNON

(Languidly) I don't know that I am much interested in your family life, Lane.

LANE

No, sir; it is not a very interesting subject. I never think of it myself.

ALGERNON

Very natural, I am sure. That will do, Lane, thank you.

LANE

Thank you, sir. *(Exit Lane)*

ALGERNON

Lane's views on marriage seem somewhat lax. Really, if the lower orders don't set us a good example, what on earth is the use of them? They seem, as a class, to have absolutely no sense of moral responsibility.

The two-scene ends with the exit of Lane. Then Wilde gives us the short one-scene—Algernon alone—before the next major character, Jack, is introduced. Jack and Algernon have a long two-scene that leads deeply into the complex plot of this great comedy.

I said that we label French scenes by the characters playing "significant parts" in them. For example, if a host, a hostess and one guest are eating, drinking and talking together, with one waiter unobtrusively serving the food and drink, that would count as a three-scene. But suppose the audience knows that the waiter is really a terrorist with a gun in his pocket, waiting an opportunity to murder the guest; then this becomes a four-scene.

Take another example. The second French scene of *King Lear* (Shakespeare) is a seven-scene: Lear, Cornwall, Albany, Kent, Regan, Goneril and Cordelia have the significant roles in it, although a number of Attendants stand looking on. In a small company, there might be four Attendants; a big company might have fourteen. All the same, for our analysis it would still be a seven-scene.

THE STRUCTURE OF THE FRENCH SCENE

Experience shows that the most satisfactory structure for a French scene is the same, on a smaller scale, as that of a play. The Molière scene, as I pointed out, contains all the elements of drama—conflict, characters, complications, crisis, catastrophe and conclusion.

The conclusion of a French scene, of course, is only an interim conclusion. It marks the end of one part of the action, but it must leave the way open to a further development of the conflict in the next French scene.

Analyze the structure of the Oscar Wilde scene.

Conflict: the employer-employee relationship.

Characters: Algernon and Lane.

Complications:

(a) Lane scores a point over the piano-playing.

(b) Algernon challenges the servants' wine-drinking; Lane scores again.

Crisis: the discussion about marriage. (Important, because this is a *romantic* comedy.)

Catastrophe: Lane's "It is not interesting. . .I never think of it. . ."

Conclusion: Algernon agrees. (At least, he agrees *to Lane's face*, although in the ensuing one-scene he seems to reverse himself.)

A FAMOUS EXAMPLE

Here is the opening French scene from *Ghosts*, by Henrik Ibsen, translated by Eva Le Gallienne.

Ghosts created a furor when it was published in 1881. "Bestial!" "A loathsome enterprise!" "A wicked nightmare!" "A revolting obscenity!" were typical comments by critics who had read the script.

Ibsen was described as "a gloomy sort of a ghoul"; his male characters were blasted as "all rascals or imbeciles," and his women as being "in a chronic state of rebellion against. . .the conditions which nature has imposed on their sex."

Why all the fuss?

1. The play deals with a young man who has congenital syphilis (in those days incurable); his father had been a rake.

2. The "villain" of the piece is a clergyman: mean, hypocritical—a thoroughly nasty character.

No theatre in Europe would stage the play; it was first performed in New York. However, *Ghosts* gradually won acceptance in Europe, too, and eventually came to be seen as the technical and artistic masterpiece that it is.

So here is the script; numbers at the end of certain lines refer to notes at the end of the excerpt.

SCENE

A spacious garden-room; in the left wall a door, and in the right wall two doors. In the center of the room a round table, with chairs about it. On the table lie books, periodicals and newspapers. In the foreground to the left a window, and by it a small sofa, with a work-table in front of it. In the background, the room is continued into a somewhat narrower conservatory, the walls of which are formed by large panes of glass. In the right-hand wall of the conservatory is a door leading down into the garden. Through the glass wall, a gloomy fiord landscape is faintly visible, veiled by steady rain.

ENGSTRAND, *the carpenter, stands by the garden door. His left leg is somewhat bent; he has a clump of wood under the sole of his boot.* REGINA, *with an empty garden syringe in her hand, hinders him from advancing.*

REGINA

Well—what is it you want? No!—stay where you are—you're dripping wet. (1)

ENGSTRAND

It's only God's rain, my child.

REGINA

It's the devil's rain, that's what it is! (2)

ENGSTRAND

Lord, how you talk, Regina! *(Limping a few steps into the room)* But here's what I want to tell you—

REGINA

Don't go clumping about with that foot of yours! The young master's upstairs asleep. (3)

ENGSTRAND

Asleep at this hour—in broad daylight?

REGINA

It's none of your business.

ENGSTRAND

Now—look at me—I was on a bit of a spree last night.

REGINA

That's nothing new. (4)

ENGSTRAND

Well—we're all frail creatures, my child—

REGINA

We are that!

ENGSTRAND

And temptations are manifold in this world, you see—but that didn't prevent me from going to work at half past five as usual!

REGINA

That's as it may be—and now, get out! I can't stand here having a rendezvous with you. (5)

ENGSTRAND

What's that?

REGINA

I don't want anyone to see you here—so get out!

ENGSTRAND

(Comes a few steps nearer) Damned if I go till I've had a talk with you.
Listen—I'll be through with my work at the school-house this
afternoon—then I'm going right back to town by the night boat—

REGINA

(Mutters) A pleasant journey to you!

ENGSTRAND

Thank you, my child! Tomorrow's the opening of the Orphanage;
they'll all be celebrating—sure to be a lot of drinking, too—I'll prove
to them that Jakob Engstrand can keep out of the way of temptation.
(6)

REGINA

Ha!

ENGSTRAND

Lots of grand people'll be here—Pastor Manders is expected from
town—

REGINA

He gets here today.

ENGSTRAND

There—you see! Damned if I give *him* a chance to say anything
against me!

REGINA

So that's it, is it?

ENGSTRAND

That's what?

REGINA

(Gives him a searching look) What are you going to try and put over
on him this time?

ENGSTRAND

Are you crazy? As if I'd try and put anything over on *him!* No—Pastor
Manders has been too good a friend to me—and that's just what I want

to talk to you about. As I was saying, I'm going back home tonight—(7)

REGINA
You can't go soon enough to please me!

ENGSTRAND
But I want you to come with me, Regina.

REGINA
(Open-mouthed) I, go with *you?*

ENGSTRAND
Yes—I want you to come home with me.

REGINA
(Scornfully) You'll never get me to do that!

ENGSTRAND
Well—we'll see.

REGINA
Yes! You'll see all right! After being brought up here by Mrs. Alving—treated almost like one of the family—do you suppose I'd go home with you—back to that kind of a house? You're crazy!

ENGSTRAND
What kind of talk's that! You'd defy your own father, would you? (8)

REGINA
(Mutters, without looking at him) You've said often enough that I'm no concern of yours—

ENGSTRAND
Never mind about that—

REGINA
Many's the time you've cursed me and called me a—*Fi donc!*

ENGSTRAND
When did I ever use a foul word like that?

REGINA
I know well enough what word you used!

ENGSTRAND

Well—maybe—when I wasn't feeling quite myself—hm. Temptations are manifold in this world, Regina!

REGINA

Pah!

ENGSTRAND

And then your mother used to drive me crazy—I had to find some way to get back at her. She put on so many airs: *(Mimicking her)* "Let me go, Engstrand! Leave me alone! Don't forget I spent three years in Chamberlain Alving's house at Rosenvold!" *(Laughs)* God Almighty! She never got over the Captain being made Chamberlain while she was working here! (9)

REGINA

Poor mother! You certainly hounded her into her grave! (10)

ENGSTRAND

(Shrugging his shoulders) Oh, of course! I'm to blame for everything!

REGINA

(Under her breath as she turns away) Ugh! And then that leg of yours!

ENGSTRAND

What did you say, my child?

REGINA

Pied de mouton! (11)

ENGSTRAND

What's that? German?

REGINA

Yes.

ENGSTRAND

Yes—well, you've certainly got educated here—and that may come in handy, too.

REGINA

(After a short silence) Why do you want me to go back with you?

ENGSTRAND

Why wouldn't a father want his only child with him? Aren't I a lonely, deserted widower?

REGINA

Oh, don't talk rubbish to me! Why do you want me with you?

ENGSTRAND

Well—I'll tell you—I'm thinking of setting up in a new line of business.

REGINA

(Whistles) What, again! What is it this time?

ENGSTRAND

You'll see—this time it'll be different. Christ almighty!

REGINA

Stop your swearing! *(She stamps her foot)*

ENGSTRAND

Sh! You're right, my child. Well—what I wanted to say was—I've managed to save quite a bit of money—from this work on the Orphanage—

REGINA

You have, have you? So much the better for you.

ENGSTRAND

There's nothing to spend your money on in this God-forsaken hole—

REGINA

Well?

ENGSTRAND

So I thought I'd invest it in a paying concern. I thought of starting a sort of tavern—for seamen—

REGINA

Ugh!

ENGSTRAND

A really high-class tavern, you know—none of your cheap dives. No—by God, I'd cater to Captains and First-mates—really high-class people.

REGINA

And I suppose I'd be expected to—

ENGSTRAND

Oh, you could be a great help, Regina. You wouldn't have to do anything—it wouldn't be hard on you, my child—you'd have everything your own way!

REGINA

Oh, yes, of course!

ENGSTRAND

After all, there must be some women in the house—that goes without saying. We'd have to have a bit of fun in the evenings, singing and dancing—and that sort of thing. You've got to remember—these poor fellows are sailors—wanderers on the seas of the world. *(Comes nearer to her)* Don't be a fool and stand in your own way. What future is there for you out here? What good's all this education the Mrs. has paid for? You're to look after the kids in the new Orphanage, I hear—is that a job for you? Do you want to wear yourself to the bone looking after a lot of dirty brats?

REGINA

If things turn out as I hope—well—it could be—it could be

ENGSTRAND

What "could be?"

REGINA

You keep your nose out of that! How much money did you save?

ENGSTRAND

I'd say—in all—close to two hundred dollars.

REGINA

Not so bad!

ENGSTRAND

Enough to get me started, my child.

REGINA

Do I get any of it?

ENGSTRAND

You do not!

REGINA

Not even enough to buy myself a new dress?

ENGSTRAND

You come with me—you'll get plenty of new dresses then.

REGINA

I can get them myself, if I set my mind to it.

ENGSTRAND

But a father's guiding hand is a good thing, Regina. There's a nice little house right on Harbor Street—not much money down, either—it'd be like a kind of Seamen's Home, you know.

REGINA

But I don't want to live with you! I don't want to have anything to do with you! So now—get out!

ENGSTRAND

You wouldn't be with me for long, my child—I know that well enough. All you've got to do is use your wits—you've turned into a handsome wench—do you know that?

REGINA

Well, what of it?

ENGSTRAND

Before you know it, some First-mate'll come along—maybe even a Captain.

REGINA

I don't intend to marry any such trash. Sailors have no "savoir vivre."

ENGSTRAND

Well, I couldn't say about that—

REGINA

I tell you I know all about sailors. I wouldn't think of marrying one of them!

ENGSTRAND

Who says you'd have to marry? You can make it pay just the same. *(More confidentially)* That Englishman—the one with the yacht—he gave three hundred dollars, he did—and she wasn't any better looking than you are. (12)

REGINA

(Goes towards him) Get out of here!

ENGSTRAND

(Retreating) Now, now! You wouldn't hit me, would you?

REGINA

You just say anything against Mother, and you'll see whether (13) I'd hit you or not! Get out, I say! *(She pushes him towards the garden door)* And don't bang the door; young Mister Alving . . .

ENGSTRAND

Is asleep—I know! Why should you be so worried about him? *(In a lower tone)* God—Almighty! You don't tell me that *he*—? (14)

REGINA

You must be out of your head—you fool! Go on now—get out this minute. No—not that way—here comes Pastor Manders; the back stairs for you!

ENGSTRAND

(Goes toward door right) All right—I'll go. But listen—you have a talk with him—he'll tell you what you owe your own father—for I am your father after all, you know; I can prove that by the Church Register. (15)
(He goes out through the other door that REGINA has opened for him and closes after him. She glances at herself quickly in the mirror, fans herself with her handkerchief and straightens her collar; then she sets about tending the flowers. . .)

Notes

1. A physical and verbal demonstration of conflict right at the outset. He wants to come in; she bars his way. This makes a far stronger opening than, for example:

FATHER

My daughter, I want to have a few words with you.

DAUGHTER

Certainly! Come in, Papa. I'm pleased to see you.

2. A wide difference between the two characters is shown by their comments on the rain. ENGSTRAND's line also makes prompt revelation of the father-daughter relationship.

3. Draws early attention to his deformity; otherwise some of the audi-

ence might not notice. The deformity is important later in the play. Preliminary mention of "the young master" who appears later.

4. A glimpse of his character; also, by the way she says it, shows what she thinks of him.

5. Her use of French, which she knows he does not understand, shows something of her character.

6. Tells his name; shows something of his character.

7. The imminent parting that motivates the scene. Note that an *early* parting: "going back home tonight"—is more dramatic than would be a distant one: "going back home in six weeks." "Tonight" implies, "Whatever we decide, we've got to do it *fast.*" Haste heightens the dramatic effect.

8. Father-daughter conflict is intensified.

9. Reveals bygone conflict in the Engstrand family. Also reveals the social status of the Alving family. "Chamberlain" is a non-hereditary Norwegian title of nobility, granted by the king to certain wealthy, distinguished men.

10. Reveals that Regina's mother is dead; again heightens father-daughter conflict.

11. Literally means "sheep's foot"—another snobbish use of French.

12. Hints at the real nature of Engstrand's proposed new business.

13. Conflict reaches the use of physical force.

14. Suggestion of a relationship between Regina and young Mr. Alving.

15. A mysterious emphasis on the father-daughter relationship. This, too, is preparation for a later plot development.

EXERCISE 3:1
Analyze the *Ghosts* scene as I analyzed the Wilde scene earlier.
(a) What is the conflict?
(b) What are the complications (or "delays")?
(c) What is the crisis?
(d) What is the catastrophe?
(e) What is the conclusion?
(f) What seems to be the scope for further development, after this interim conclusion?
(g) Can you find more clues as to the past of this pair, and what's to come later in the play?

EXERCISE 3:2
Write a present-day scene, in some location of your choice, using the same main elements: a parting; a parent-child quarrel.

Try planning the scene before you begin to write: define the characters (a 50-word description of each); choose the subject for the quarrel; list a few other characters that they will mention in the quarrel, but who will not appear in the scene; choose some physical actions that they will perform.

EXERCISE 3:3
Take a French scene from one of your Exemplary Dozen. Analyze it as you did the *Ghosts* scene in Exercise 3:1.

Then invent and write out one or two more complications of your own before letting the scene reach its crisis.

Try to create a different catastrophe to the scene—which will, of course, lead on to a different conclusion.

EXERCISE 3:4
Take some incident from your own life—something out of the ordinary with strong emotional content—and create a two-scene that would play from five to ten minutes.

Be sure to include all the elements that will make it a complete, satisfying French scene. Give it an interim conclusion: i.e., one that, sooner or later, has to lead on to some further development of the story.

THE THREE UNITIES

Some theoretical works on drama mention the "Three Unities" (*time, place* and *action*) as essential, or at least highly desirable elements of good playwriting.

Unity of Time
The oft-violated rule concerning unity of time, in its strict form, says that stage time and real time should be matched. In other words, a play lasting two hours should depict only such a series of events as would occupy two hours in real life.

In practice, the action time of each scene of a play is usually *less* than the time that comparable actions would take in real life. There are two reasons for this. Dramatic dialogue is more concise than real speech; every word is to the point. Dramatic action is directed solely to the purposes of the play: it is free from the irrelevancies that confuse and delay real-life events.

Audiences are accustomed to this time compression and accept it readily. A trial that might last a day in a real courtroom can very well be gotten over in thirty minutes on stage; a four-hour party can be played in fifteen minutes. A similar time compression applies to actions occuring offstage. A farmer can go out to milk half a dozen cows and come back in five minutes with the job finished.

But the audience will not accept too severe a compression of time. The trial could not be cut down to four minutes; the milking could not be done in fifteen seconds.

So, with a little care, you should have no trouble maintaining the unity of time in one-act plays, and within the individual acts of longer plays.

The chief erosion of unity comes with the assumption that long lapses of time take place during intermissions. Act II may occur weeks, months or years after Act I. (Sometimes, indeed, you see the acts of the long play or the single act of a short play divided into scenes, with substantial time lapses between them.)

Beginning playwrights should remember nonetheless that as a general rule, the shorter the imagined time lapse between the beginning and the end of a play, the more powerful will be its effect upon the audience.

Ill-contrived time lapses in a realistically staged play may badly shake the audience's involvement. For example, during a quick curtain drop a week or a month is supposed to pass. In the next scene the audience notices that the actresses are wearing the same clothes and jewelry as before, and that the same flowers are still in the same vase on the table!

If early drafts of your play show considerable time lapses between scenes or acts, think carefully whether there is not some way of shortening those lapses.

Suppose you have a tragedy that shows the disintegration of a marriage. Act I is the wedding day. Act II, on the tenth anniversary, shows the husband and wife quarreling. Act III, five years later still, shows the final breakup of the marriage.

To eliminate those long time lapses, you could *open* on the tenth anniversary. The wife is getting out her carefully stored wedding gown and headdress, and reminiscing about the wedding with a woman friend who had been her bridesmaid. Then suppose the husband comes home and raises Cain because the wife has spent all afternoon "gossiping" instead of getting his dinner ready. You could show without much difficulty this final quarrel and the breakup all on the same day.

In fact, to place the entire action of a play within the span of 24 hours is generally regarded as a handsome gesture toward the rule concerning unity of time.

The all-in-one-day scheme that I suggested for the "marriage breakup" play would have another advantage. "Dressing up" is an important element of theatre, and although it is a pretty sight to see a new bride in all her finery, it is even more dramatic—at least for the women in the audience—to see a wife of ten years' unhappy experience wistfully dressing up in her wedding gown.

A safe rule to follow is, "Begin the play as near in time to the main crisis as you can; end it as soon as possible after the main catastrophe."

With thought, it is generally possible to follow this rule. Audiences will never be aware of the technical point, but they will enjoy the heightened emotional effect that it usually provides.

Unity of time, then, is an ideal, seldom attained perhaps, but a highly recommended goal.

EXERCISE 3:5
Look through the Exemplary Dozen, and calculate the lapse of

time between the opening and conclusion of each.

EXERCISE 3:6
Take a couple of ideas from your own notes or experiences; plan how they could be shaped into plays, each occurring within a 24-hour lapse of time.

Unity of Place

In the old Roman theatre, all the action of a play occurred in one place, on that symbolic stretch of city street, in front of those same few symbolic houses.

The medieval morality plays knew no such unity of place. The church steps might, in the imagination of the audience, represent the Garden of Eden, Sodom, Gomorrah, Jerusalem, Nazareth, Rome, Heaven or Hell.

The playwrights of Shakespeare's time cared nothing for unity of place, as you can see by glancing through a few of their scripts.

In the late nineteenth century, the mechanical and artistic resources of the theatre could vividly depict a wide variety of locales for one play, and change sets rapidly behind closed curtains as the action demanded.

Unity of place, in fact, has been a mostly theoretical concept, expounded by book-writers, but often ignored by playwrights, actors and audiences.

Nowadays, if you use an elaborate representational set, considerations of cost will probably lead you to favor unity of place. But without such sets, or with cheap, nonrepresentational scenic devices, there seems no particular merit in striving to maintain unity of place.

With no sets, you can change the place of action in the Shakespearean manner, without a curtain drop or blackout, and therefore without losing the attention and the emotional involvement of the audience. Present-day audiences, thoroughly accustomed to the frequent changes of place in movies and TV, have no difficulty adjusting to changes of place on stage.

Unity of Action

Unity of action is observed pretty generally nowadays. The play follows one main character, or a small group of main characters, through one well-defined line of action, to one decisive conclusion. The trend toward shorter plays has eliminated the elaborate subplots that were the chief offenders against this rule.

FILM AND TV

I must say a few words about film and TV in this chapter, because so many people nowadays have gained all their ideas of dramatic structure from the movie screen and the picture tube.

The basic unit in film and TV is not the French scene, but the *shot*—something radically different! The duration of a French scene is usually measured in minutes; each contains, in miniature, all the elements of drama, the six C's.

But the shot usually has no dramatic structure; it is simply a glimpse of action, setting or property from one viewpoint. For example: hero's lips press heroine's lips = one shot; swinging pendulum and turning second-hand of a clock = one shot; snowflakes falling past windowpane = one shot; cat rousing from sleep and stretching itself = one shot.

The dramatic effect is produced, not so much by what is shown in any particular shot, as by the skilled editorial assemblage of hundreds, even thousands of shots. The individual shot might be compared to a mosaic tile: the individual tile has little meaning, but the arrangement of many tiles makes a picture.

Also, the mechanical/electronic media are capable of actions and effects that are impossible on stage. To mention one obvious example: the stage offers no closeups. Movie and TV cameras can enlarge the boy's snapshot of his girlfriend, or the mother's slow-moving tear of grief, for everyone to see. No such magnification is available on stage. Your story must be portrayed by life-sized actors to spectators twenty or thirty yards away, some of them near-sighted, some with hearing defects.

EXERCISE 3:7
Watch a 30-minute TV show and, with a notebook and pen, or with some kind of hand-held counter, keep score of the number of shots it contains. At the same time, mentally note which elements of the picture you see could not be presented by actors on the stage of a theatre.

What to Do

If you are determined to write for the stage, you must begin to cultivate the playwright's eye and ear. I suggest that you sharply cut down your watching of the screen media. If you must watch TV, concentrate on public-affairs shows—interviews, debates, panel discussions, etc. These have at least some resemblance to the stage format. So does radio drama.

Some of the salvaged time should be spent in reading playscripts, and books about the theatre.

Take every opportunity of seeing and taking part in live theatre. No matter if the performances are good, bad or indifferent. You are not an ordinary member of the audience, passively waiting to be entertained. You are watching *with the playwright's eye.* You are *learning,* so for you, every performance will be interesting.

SUMMARY

The rule of the Six C's:
Conflict between opposing wills or forces of some kind.
Characters portray the conflict in some form suitable for the stage.

Complications: "delays" in the working out of the conflict create suspense and heighten interest.

Crisis: the high point of the conflict in any particular scene.

Catastrophe: the action, or turn of events, which resolves the crisis.

Conclusion: the final state of affairs; the reasonable result of the catastrophe.

Long plays are divided into acts; acts (and short plays) are sometimes divided into scenes separated by curtain-drops or blackouts.

"French scene": a part of the action beginning with the entrance, and ending with the exit, of a main or secondary character. A satisfactory French scene has the same structure, in miniature, as the whole play.

"Two-scene," "three-scene," etc: the term shows the number of significant characters.

Unity of time: beware excessive time-compression within acts, or excessive time-lapses between acts.

Unity of place: enforced by representational sets; otherwise not essential.

Unity of action: follow one main character, or just a few, through a clear course of action. Avoid strings of loosely connected events; avoid elaborate sub-plots.

Film and TV: the basic unit is the shot—usually with no dramatic structure of its own. Don't try transferring movie/TV techniques to the stage. Cut down movie/TV viewing; cultivate the playwright's eye and ear.

CHAPTER FOUR

Conflict

A PLAY MUST BE interesting, or no one will sit through it. The sure-fire way to arouse the interest of an audience is to present a conflict.

"Football player goes to old school and receives silver cup" might attract half a dozen of the player's relatives and friends. "Two football teams compete for silver cup" can attract 60,000 people to a stadium and twenty or thirty million more to watch on TV. They want to see a conflict!

"Boy proposes to girl; girl accepts first time." That is the way things often happen; but the situation has no conflict, so it will not make a successful play. "Boy wants girl; girl's (and/or boy's) parents oppose the match." There is conflict, so there is the beginning of a play.

How could you develop the idea? "Boy overcomes parents' opposition and eventually gets girl" gives you a happy ending.

"Despite all efforts, boy loses girl" might make *Romeo and Juliet* or *The Cassilis Engagement* (St. John Hankin).

"Boy wants girl; boy loses that girl, but gets a different girl" makes *Mary, Mary* (Jean Kerr).

"Widow marries second husband and lives happily ever after." There is no conflict, therefore no play. Add conflict: "Widow's son bitterly resents her second marriage." Now you have the makings of a play. Then, for a happy ending: "Stepfather gradually wins respect of son."

But "Son's resentment increases till he kills his stepfather" gives the tragic ending of *Hamlet*.

There are five kinds of conflict.

MAN AGAINST NATURE

This kind of conflict used to be portrayed on the big, elaborately-equipped stages of some nineteenth-century playhouses: earthquakes, landslides and such natural phenomena were effectively done.

The famous "Cakes of Ice" scene in *Uncle Tom's Cabin* (George L. Aiken) follows.

ACT I: Scene 6

The entire depth of stage, representing the Ohio River, is filled with
Floating Ice. Bank on right hand.
Eliza appears with Harry on a cake of ice, and floats slowly across.
Haley, Loker and Marks, on bank, right hand, observing. Phineas on
opposite shore.

Those were the author's stage directions; the scene includes no dialogue. Most productions used exciting orchestral music to cover the creaks
and groans of the moving ice-floe machinery, and also to heighten the emotional effect of the scene. This was the curtain-scene of Act I, so it *had* to be
strong!

This was one of the most effective moments in a popular play that held
the boards well on into this century. Maybe it's worth pointing out why
such a scene would not work nowadays.

(a) Few theatres have the equipment to do it.

(b) Modern audiences have been spoiled by movies and TV for large-scale,
realistic depiction of natural phenomena (typhoons, volcanoes, tidal
waves, ice jams and the like). Any attempt to portray such disasters on
stage today would seem technically unprofessional and unconvincing.
Shipwrecked sailors dying of thirst on a raft, or the citizens of Pompeii being overwhelmed by Vesuvius, would likely fail.

A man-against-nature conflict is used in *Riders to the Sea*, but Synge
keeps nature offstage.

There is a strong man-against-nature element in *Desire Under the*
Elms (Eugene O'Neill). It is the grinding struggle of Ephraim Cabot and his
three sons to wring a living from the poor, stony soil of the farm. Here too,
the playwright keeps nature offstage; but we vividly see the conflict reflected in the men's dirty hands, boots and clothes, and in their physical
and emotional exhaustion.

EXERCISE 4:1

Describe some situation where you have experienced conflict
against natural forces. Describe:

(a) how it actually ended;

(b) another way that it might have ended.

If the conflict has not yet ended, describe two possible ways
that it might end—one favorable, and the other unfavorable to
yourself.

For each of the above situations, jot down a few notes on
how you think it might be depicted on stage: e.g., What setting?
What other characters besides yourself?

Refer back to what I said about unity of time in Chapter 3.
Consider the best starting and finishing points for your proposed situations.

Try writing one or two of these ideas in regular play format,
with character names, dialogue, and stage directions.

EXERCISE 4:2
Look Through your Exemplary Dozen for examples of man-against-nature conflict.

EXERCISE 4:3
Study a copy of *Desire Under the Elms*. Copy out what you think are the key lines of dialogue and stage directions that emphasize the man-against-nature conflict.

What can you learn from O'Neill for depicting your man-against-nature motif?

MAN AGAINST MAN

Most "triangle" plays use this kind of conflict: two men compete for one woman, or two women for one man. The conflict of *Romeo and Juliet* is man-against-man; Romeo Montague against the Capulet family. *The Father* (August Strindberg) is man-against-man: the Captain against his wife.

This may be a useful place to mention that you can very well have two or more types of conflict in a full-length play, all combining to heighten the dramatic effect. I already mentioned the man-against-nature element in *Desire Under the Elms*, but the more important line of conflict is man-against-man. Old Ephraim grimly desires to hang on to the farm as long as he lives and by deputy of his young third wife even after he is dead. In opposition is the young son Eben with his manic determination to get possession of the farm, by fair means or foul. Note, too, that since the Cabot farm has been developed and maintained with such excruciating difficulty, it becomes a more important prize for the contestants.

But plot carefully! If you want to use more than one type of conflict, decide which is the most important, and see that it is kept predominant in the minds of the audience. You do that by giving it the biggest share of the dialogue and action, and by attaching to it the strongest emotions of your characters.

EXERCISE 4:4
Describe some situation where you have experienced a conflict with another person. Describe:
(a) how it actually ended;
(b) another way that it might have ended.

If the conflict has not yet ended, describe two possible ways that it might end—one favorable, and the other unfavorable to yourself.

For each of the above situations, jot down a few notes on how you think it might be depicted on stage: e.g., What setting? What other characters besides yourself and the main opponent?

Consider the best starting and finishing points for the proposed situations.

EXERCISE 4:5
Look through your Exemplary Dozen for examples of man-against-man conflict.

EXERCISE 4:6
Note down some other examples of man-against-man conflict that you have known, or read of. Make some notes on how each might be used as basis for a play: what characters, costumes, settings, effects, etc., would be needed?

EXERCISE 4:7
Here is an interesting story I read in the paper a few days ago.

A married woman, mother of three teenagers, felt that they were abusing her with their rudeness, disobedience and sloppy habits. Their rooms where always in a mess, they often violated curfew, and they expected her to wait on them hand and foot at home, and act as their chauffeur for school and social activities.

One day she took action: she prepared no dinner, threw the eldest daughter's dirty laundry out on the porch, and settled herself in a deck chair on the front lawn beneath a big sign, "Mother on Strike."

Plan how you would dramatize this. What setting? (The lawn is obvious; but could there be a *better* site?)

What characters? Consider adding one or two other people besides the family: who should they be?

Plan two different ways of ending the conflict.

MAN AGAINST SOCIETY

All societies have codes of conduct to define the rights and responsibilities of their members. Constitutions, charters, laws and regulations are formal expressions of society's will. States, cities, schools, sports clubs, social clubs and drama groups all have their "thou shalt's" and "thou shalt not's." Moreover, custom, tradition and fashion may be no less powerful in shaping people's conduct.

A lot of people conform readily enough to all these pressures, maybe never even realizing how their lives are being shaped for them. Other people will not, or cannot, conform. Many crime plays set the criminal in conflict with society, the latter being personified by a detective. In *Pillars of Society* (Ibsen), Doctor Stockman is presented as being in the right, and society as being wrong.

The Cassilis Engagement (Hankin), produced in 1907, is a good example of what was then a new trend—using an element of sharp social commentary in popular plays. Geoffrey Cassilis, a young, upper-class Englishman, has lately become engaged. Now he sees signs that Ethel, his fiancée may not fit into his social circle.

GEOFFREY

Ethel, be reasonable. You must know that you can't go on doing that sort of thing here. You must conform to the ideas of the people around you. They may seem to you narrow and ridiculous, but you can't alter them.

ETHEL

You don't think them narrow and ridiculous, I suppose?

GEOFFREY

No. In this case I think they are right. In many cases.

You probably would not need to spell out the man-against-society conflict so plainly in a modern play. What was a new and daring theme in 1907 is well-known and well understood nowadays.

Edward Albee's *Everything in the Garden* opens with a dispute between Richard and Jenny over her proposal to find a job. Richard's objection is based upon fear of "what the neighbors would think" if they knew that his wife was working. That was in the 1960s. In most social circles, there would be less prejudice against the working wife nowadays. In fact, in many circles a non-working childless wife would be regarded as a drone. (Times do change!)

Here is a story that I read in the newspaper on the morning that I am writing this paragraph. A country, suffering from severe overpopulation, passed a law that no couple could have more than one child. One woman's first child was a girl; her husband had badly wanted a son. Now, because of the new law, he could never have one. So he began to abuse and beat his wife for—as he thought—letting him down. The husband's mother and brother joined in the abuse. Eventually the wife drank disinfectant and killed herself.

That tragedy took place in China, but man-against-society conflicts occur everywhere. A man in my home town had a bitter struggle with the civic authorities because he wanted to name his chain of restaurants after himself, using his own well-known nickname with racial connotations, a nickname that the authorities did not approve of. The restaurateur nearly lost his business.

EXERCISE 4:8

Describe three incidents where you have been in conflict with society (school, the law, church, public opinion, etc.). For each incident give:

(a) the way it actually ended;
(b) another way that it might have ended.

For each of these situations, jot down a few notes on how you think it might be depicted on stage: e.g., What setting? What characters?

What would be the best starting and finishing points?

EXERCISE 4:9
Look through your Exemplary Dozen for examples of man-against-society conflict.

EXERCISE 4:10
A small-town school principal (male or female, as you prefer) is accused of sexual "indiscretion" with a student. The student is old enough that no criminal charges are involved, but is twenty years or more younger than the principal. Make some notes on how this might be used as basis for a play.

What setting? What characters? (Try to figure out who, and how many, will be required to serve as representatives of society.)

Work out two different endings (more, if you can).

MAN AGAINST HIMSELF

This type of conflict requires some depth of characterization. Many stage characters can be presented simply with one predominant motive or style of behavior: the coward, the bully, the glutton, the lecher, the hero, the innocent, etc. But to show a character as being in conflict with himself, you have to give him some degree of complexity.

Macbeth is presented as being in conflict with himself. Lady Macbeth says:

> . . . .Art thou afraid
> To be the same in thine own act and valor
> As thou art in desire?

We see him as a great military hero, the Douglas MacArthur of his day and place, before we ever suspect that he may be a rebel and a traitor. It is this duality in the main character that gives *Macbeth* much of its dramatic power.

Liubov Andryevena in *The Cherry Orchard* (Anton Chekhov) is in conflict with herself, and in severe financial difficulties. (N.B. Money troubles are a useful and widely used occasion for bringing different kinds of conflict to a head.) It has come to the point where Liubov Andryevena's estate is going to be sold out from under her. She has the chance to fell the cherry trees, subdivide the orchard, and sell it for building lots but she can't make herself take the step. So she loses the estate, and finally sees the purchaser do what she herself could not decide to do.

I will cite Chekhov again, to show that the man-against-himself theme works just as well in humorous as in serious situations. Chekhov's delightful one-act farce, *The Proposal*, is based upon the internal conflict of the main character, Lomov. His desire to be married is frustrated by his extreme bashfulness. Early in the play, we see him in the house of Choobukov, a neighboring landowner. Lomov has arrived, in full evening dress and white gloves (the period is around 1900), to make his formal proposal to

Choobukov's daughter, Natalya. Lomov is alone, waiting for Natalya to be ushered in.

LOMOV

I'm so cold! . . . I'm shaking all over, head to foot, as if I were just going to write an examinaton. The essential thing is to make up one's mind . . . be decisive. If a man procrastinates, keeps hesitating, waiting for the perfect woman, or for unmistakable, true love, he'll never get married. Brrr! I'm so cold!

Natalya Stepanovna is a first-class housekeeper, well-educated, not at all bad looking. What more could a man want? But I'm so worked up, I'm starting to hear noises in my head. (*He drinks water from a carafe and glass on the table.*)

Yet I daren't stay single. In the first place, I'm already thirty-five . . . a critical point in life, so to speak. Secondly, I must have a regular, well-ordered life. I have heart trouble, with continual palpitations . . . I lose my temper so easily . . . I simply can't keep calm and cool.

Right now, my lips are quivering; my right eyelid is twitching. And at night, I'm worse . . . worst of all. I get into bed, then, just as I think I'm falling asleep, something stabs me in the left side. Jab! Right on through the shoulder, and up into the head! I spring out of bed like a madman, walk around for a few minutes, and lie down again . . . but the moment I start slipping off to sleep . . . Stab! There it goes again . . . left side, shoulder and head! And so it goes on, five, ten, twenty times or more . . .

(*Enter* NATALYA)

A good actor finds ample scope here for action that will set the audience laughing as they grasp the character of this wretched hypochondriac.

It's worth mentioning here, to show something more of what goes into good play writing, that his speech serves other purposes besides depicting Lomov's character. It contains several "plants," as we call them—bits of information that serve to prepare the audience for surprising events later in the play.

Natalya Stepanovna arrives, but instead of proceeding with his marriage proposal, Lomov promptly flies into a quarrel with her, disputing the ownership of some meadows that lie between their estates. Seem absurd? Audiences accept it, because Lomov's hot temper has been "planted."

Near the end of the play, it becomes dramatically useful for Lomov to faint and remain unconscious for a minute or so. Here, too, the idea has been planted earlier, by Lomov's own description of his symptoms.

I shall have more to say about planting in Chapter 8: Complications.

EXERCISE 4:11
Write a speech (serious or comic, as you prefer) describing some

internal conflict in your own life. Make it at least 150 words,
longer if you can.

EXERCISE 4:12
If the above-mentioned conflict has been resolved, describe
some other way it might have ended.

   If the conflict has not been resolved, describe two possible
ways that it might end, one favorable and the other unfavorable
to yourself.

   For each of these outlines, make some notes on how it
should be depicted on stage. What setting? What other characters besides yourself?

EXERCISE 4:13
Study your Exemplary Dozen for examples of man-against-himself conflict.

EXERCISE 4:14
The pupils of a school were challenged to abstain for one week
from watching television. Most of them agreed. In some homes,
the parents went along with the experiment.

   Imagine yourself trying to cut out TV for a week. Would this
produce a strong internal conflict?

   Consider how this situation could be handled, presumably
as a comedy. Where would you set the action: What characters
would you use? What would be the opening situation? What
complications could you introduce to make it more difficult?

MAN AGAINST FATE

Fate: a mysterious force, uncontrollable, that determines the destiny of
each human being. A fated event may sometimes be foreseen by those few
people who have special visionary powers (like the three witches in Macbeth), but it cannot be prevented.

   The doctrine of fatalism has been prevalent in various periods and cul-
tures: among the ancient Greeks, Hebrews and Romans, for example. You
can see the man-against-fate theme in various portrayals of the Oedipus
story by Sophocles, Corneille and Voltaire, and of the Prometheus story by
Aeschylus, Shelley and other writers.

   The book of Job, in the Bible, is in essence a man-against-fate drama.

   Fatalism is not the dominant doctrine in our society and time. Many
religious, philosophical and artistic theorists prefer the idea that each person is largely responsible for his or her own life. They believe that we can
learn from our pasts, make choices by the exercise of free will, and thus
shape our own futures.

   There are limits, of course: children do not choose their own parents, and many people find after marriage that they did not really know their wives or husbands and so could not be said to have made free choices.

The "heredity-is-fate" theme is at the heart of Eugene O'Neill's *Strange Interlude*: Nina's belief that her husband, Sam Evans, carries his family's taint of insanity shapes two thirds of the play. *Bad Seed* (Maxwell Anderson) and *The Elephant Man* (Bernard Pomerance) also use this "heredity-is-fate" conflict.

Fate struck at little Helen Keller in the form of non-hereditary disabilities—blindness and deafness. The conflict between that fate and Helen's teacher, Annie Sullivan, is the basis of *The Miracle Worker* (William Gibson).

I said that fatalism is not the dominant doctrine in present-day society, yet it still is influential. The vast popularity of astrology, which implies that each person's fate is largely determined by the date and time of birth, shows that fatalism still has a strong following.

Fatalism finds expression, under thin disguise, in such conversational turns as:

"We were made for each other."

"She had it coming to her."

"You can't keep a good man down."

"We could have won, with a little bit of luck."

Fatalism shows itself in the fact that tall buildings have no thirteenth floors; some people on those floors would fear being overtaken by some malicious fate. The flourishing business of fortune-telling, by cards, palmistry, crystal gazing, tea leaves, and umpteen other methods, implies belief in a fated future.

So don't assume that the man-against-fate conflict went out with the horse, buggy and bustle. There is ample scope for use of this motif with present-day characters and circumstances.

EXERCISE 4:15
Write down two of the man-against-fate encounters that you have personally experienced. Make some notes on how each of them could be used as the basis for a play. What characters, costumes, setting, effects, etc., would it need? What would be the most suitable times for starting and finishing the action?

EXERCISE 4:16
Search your daily newspaper for three up-to-date examples of man-against-fate conflict. Similarly consider how each of them might be used in a play.

(Be realistic and practical here. In my paper yesterday, the "Personal" column carried an ad by a woman 5 feet 10 inches tall, seeking a manfriend taller than herself. Undoubtedly a good man-against-fate conflict! But impractical for the stage because it would be too hard to cast.)

EXERCISE 4:17
Search your Exemplary Dozen for examples of the man-against-fate conflict. Particularly note the words and actions by which the playwright depicts the force of fate. Now look back at the previous two exercises; does this study give you ideas for improving your treatment of those themes?

FINDING IDEAS

Where can you find ideas for plays?

1. Personal experience. Don't underestimate your own life as a source of material. What if it seems dull to you? The struggle to transform a dull life, to seek excitement or adventure, could make a good play. Parent-child conflicts, boy-girl conflicts, husband-wife conflicts, employer-employee conflicts, conflicts with friends and neighbors, clashes with the law, struggles with ill health, strokes of good or bad fortune—you must have experienced some of them, and perhaps they can be turned into plays.

Recall in particular whatever has gone wrong in your life. Jot down these calamities and analyze them. What or who prevented you from doing or getting what you wanted? Who are your enemies? Why are they persecuting you? How have you defended yourself in the past? How do you propose to defend yourself in the future.

What's wrong with your society? Where does it grate on you? (What grates on me, at this moment, is excessive traffic noise outside my window.) How would you change society if you had the power? (In my case, what prevents me from attaining such power is that I prefer to spend my time writing, instead of campaigning, and then sitting in a legislature. Man-against-self conflict!)

Has a character analyst, or a drunken friend, ever told you what other people don't like about you? Do you know how you hurt yourself, how you make your passage needlessly rocky, how you prevent yourself from attaining your own goals? Has anyone ever told you that you are your own worst enemy?

How much freedom do you feel you have had in your life? Just why are you a writer? Has anyone ever told you you have a "gift for words?" Then who gave you that gift? Why are you reading this page? Can you imagine why I am writing it? Do you feel you've had good luck in life, or bad? Have you ever tried, or would you like to learn, ways to improve that luck?

Look at your life with the same curiosity you would feel if you were reading someone else's diary; you will find usable material there.

2. Newspapers are an inexhaustible source of material. I often tell writers: "Spend less time watching TV, and more time reading the printed page. As you read, you are getting a non-stop lesson in *writing*."

Yes, I know that newspapers contain some errors of fact and style, but that is largely because they are produced in great haste. (By detecting such errors, you are giving yourself still more instruction in writing.) Moreover, newspapers contain a lot of good writing. As you discern the good from the inferior, try to analyze exactly what makes good writing "good."

Most important: newspapers print volumes of up-to-date information about people, places and things. You will find many ideas on a wide variety of topics that you won't find anywhere else.

Here are three stories from just one page of the newspaper I read over breakfast this morning.

Man-against-fate: a boy genius graduates from university at the age of twelve, having completed the course with honors in just two and a half years, making the Guinness Book of World Records. Think of the problems such a prodigy might experience with parents, fellow students, employers, fellow workers, lovers and spouses.

Man-against-society: a multi-million-dollar evangelical TV show runs deeply into the red, so has to shorten its program, fire some of its staff, and cut the wages of others.

Man-against-man: a young man is convicted of rape; his mother develops a personal grudge against the judge who handled the case, and tries to have him murdered.

Don't read only the front-page stories of your newspaper—the wars, revolutions and monstrous crimes. Read the small items in obscure corners: the return of an amnesiac husband after twenty years' absence; the marriage of an elderly couple after a fifty-year courtship; a religious dispute over the treatment of a sick child. Read the personal advertisments; guess what motives drive the advertisers to spend money and seek publicity. Puzzle out, if you can, the stories behind the coded messages that sometimes appear in those columns.

3. Your friends, when they begin to think of you as a writer, will offer you ideas, some of which may be serviceable. But don't accept the offer of "a wonderful idea for fifty percent of what you make on it." You need not pay such a high price as that! Beware of the nonliterary friend who offers you the complete plot of a play: he may have plagiarized it, knowlingly or unknowingly.

Whenever a friend suggests some useful idea, it's good strategy to whip out a notebook and write it down immediately. That makes sure that you won't forget it, and the friend will be pleased.

4. Adaptation should not be overlooked. One advantage of adapting existing work is that you know it has interested people before, and so it stands at least some chance of interesting them again, now.

The Bible, history books, biographies, legends, fables and old plays in the public domain all offer useful material. Shakespeare reworked old stories and plays; so did Aeschylus, Plautus, Molière, Corneille, Dryden, Shaw, Anouilh, Odets and many more, including myself. Jean Giraudoux's *Amphitryon 38* is so titled because it is the thirty-eighth known dramatization of the Amphitryon story.

But make sure that any works you wish to adapt are not copyrighted; failing to do so may put you in trouble. The general rule is that an author's works are in the public domain after he has been dead fifty years. But you may run into complications with works originally written in foreign languages, and since translated. The translation becomes copyrighted, and you cannot use it without securing permission from the translator or publisher.

The Idea File

It is essential that, when you come across a good idea, you get it down on paper. Have some kind of filing system for these potential play subjects. Failure to do that tends to produce the "one-script playwright." He has written one play (likely based fairly closely on his own life), and keeps hawking that one script around, while failing ever to produce another.

With a well-filled idea file, you can keep turning out new plays. You will be ready when someone says, "Could you write a play for our group?" You will have an assortment of subjects to offer.

DEPICTING CONFLICT

You have the germinal idea for a play. How are you going to develop it?

For a satifying play structure, use the fomula M + G + O = C: Main character(s) + Goal + Opposition = Conflict.

Suppose your original situation is: "Citizen feels angry because government proposes to confiscate his house." This sentence simply describes a state of mind; it is not yet the basis for a play. You will need to personify the main character and the opposition.

Who do you want for your main character(s): man, woman, or man *and* woman? Are you going to make them old, middle-aged or young? Rich, middle-income or poor? Clever, average or stupid? Aggressive or timid?

As for goals, why does the main character want to defy the government? Is it because of a sentimental attachment to his old home and his precious, well-tended garden? Or does he simply feel that the compensation being offered is inadequate?

Now, for the government's goal: Why do they want the property? Is it for a new school or for a new courthouse and city jail? Will it provide the site for a depot on a new interurban line? Are there plans to widen a freeway or to build a new stadium? Or is it for some vague scheme of civic beautification, drawn up by a planner who lives hundreds of miles away? You'll agree that these different purposes and many other possible ones that I haven't mentioned could have widely different emotional values for an audience.

Now choose the opposition. Who is to represent society here? A policeman? A judge? The mayor?

What about the neighbors? What about other members of the main character's family? Each of these groups, too, could include widely varied characters—some who support, and some who oppose the main character and his goal.

Thus, by speculating about, and making notes about, the three elements, *M*, *G* and *O*, you begin to transform your original idea into a plot that can be portrayed on stage.

Consider a different situation. Your *main character* is a detective whose *goal* is to solve a murder; the *opposition* is the murderer's plan to throw the blame on an innocent party: the result equals *conflict*.

A mother has a burning desire to get her daughter married: *M* and *G*. The *opposition* is the daughter's painful shyness. This is the *conflict* of *The Glass Menagerie* (Tennessee Williams).

Remember that the strength of the conflict (and the success of the play) depends not so much upon the strength of the main character, as upon the intensity and interest of his goal, and upon the strength of the opposition. This explains the old saying: "A play is as strong as its villain."

In the Bible story, the boy David fights and defeats the giant Goliath. David is fighting for his country and for his life—strong goals! Strong opposition! Strong conflict! But if the hero were a giant, and the opposition a boy, the story would simply seem ridiculous.

> EXERCISE 4:18
> For over a hundred years, a city has been electing and crowning a May Day Queen from among the local school girls. A group of teachers, parents and politicians now says the custom is sexist, and that all activities—even this—should be equally open to boys and girls.
>
> Here is an interesting idea. Develop it by way of the formula M + G + 0 =C.

> EXERCISE 4:19
> Choose one of the play ideas drawn from your own experience that you have noted in earlier exercises. Develop it by way of the formula M + G + 0 =C.
>
> Then narrate the whole plot of that play in 250 words or less. Adhere strictly to the limit! If you can't tell the story in 250 words, it needs to be simplified.

> EXERCISE 4:20
> Analyze the story lines of your Exemplary Dozen. Try to discover where the authors found their original ideas. Narrate one of the plots in 250 words or less.

EXPOSITION

Exposition is the part of the play that gives spectators the information they need in order to understand the opening situation. They must be told the location and period of the action, the names, stations and relationships of the characters (at least, those who are on stage), and the nature of the conflict. This must be done in such a way as to capture their interest.

The set (if any is used) and costumes will give some information as soon as the curtain rises, but the chief means of exposition are dialogue and action. Don't rely on putting exposition into the printed programs: not all of the audience will read it there. (Some are long-sighted and can't read it; others will be talking with their companions until the curtain rises.)

Exposition must be adequate, or the audience will be puzzled by the play; it must not be too prolonged, or the audience will be bored. There are two ways of giving exposition: direct or indirect.

Direct Exposition

A special character, who has no ordinary role in the play, comes in alone and addresses the audience directly, explaining what the play is going to be about. This character is called a "prologue" (derived from the Latin, meaning *preliminary speech*) or chorus.

In *Henry IV, Part II*, Rumour is the prologue.

RUMOUR

Open your ears; for which of you will stop
The vent of hearing when loud Rumour speaks?
. . . . Why is Rumour here?
I run before King Harry's victory;
Who in a bloody field by Shrewsbury
Hath beaten down young Hotspur and his troups
Quenching the flame of bold rebellion
Even with the rebels' blood. But what mean I
To speak so true at first? My office is
To noise abroad that Harry Monmouth fell
Under the wrath of noble Hotspur's sword,
And that the king before the Douglas' rage
Stooped his anointed head as low as death.
Thus have I rumor'd through the peasant towns
Between that royal field of Shrewsbury
And this worm-eaten hold of ragged stone
Where Hotspur's father, old Northumberland
Lies crafty-sick . . . .

Henry IV is a famous historical figure, the first constitutional monarch of England. The battle of Shrewsbury was fought only 195 years before Shakespeare wrote the play. So the prologue, which sounds obscure to us, would have been as clear to English audiences in 1598 as would be a similar mention of the Revolution and George Washington to an American audience today.

The prologue establishes the time of the action (July, 1403) and the place (Northumberland castle). (Remember, there would be no scenery on that stage to represent the castle.)

I wanted to give you a well-known modern example of direct exposition—the opening of Thornton Wilder's *Our Town*—but Wilder did not permit excerpting from his works, and his publishers are continuing that policy. So I suggest you get the play and study it for yourself. The prologue there is delivered by the "Stage Manager."

Alternatively, direct exposition can be given by one of the regular characters of a play who, for a little while, steps out of his role and serves as prologue.

At the beginning of *Talley's Folly* (Lanford Wilson), one of the two characters comes out and addresses the audience. He tells them the play they are about to see will be a waltz, a valentine. He asks for the sound and light effects and the lights soften and crickets chirp. In short, he makes it very clear that this is *theatre*, not reality. Then the lights black out and the play proper begins.

Here is another piece of direct exposition, from my play *Roast Pig*, a stage adaptation of *A Dissertation Upon Roast Pig*, by Charles Lamb.

Here, the "special character," as in *Our Town*, is the Stage Manager. He delivers the opening exposition; in addition, each of the major characters delivers a bit of direct exposition when he or she enters.

All characters wear Chinese costumes. The sets are small, light, symbolic flats; each can be carried by one stage hand, and each stands in place by itself. Set changes are made without lowering the curtain.

> *The stage is empty as* Stage Manager *enters L, bows, and addresses the audience.*

STAGE MANAGER

Ladies and gentlemen, I am the Stage Manager. We are going to enact for you a great event in the history of mankind: the discovery of roast pig. Roast pig, of all delicacies the most delicate. (*Smacks lips*) One of your Western authors, the late Mr. Charles Lamb, mentions this incident. Unfortunately, Mr. Lamb knew only part of the story, but here, tonight, we shall portray it in full. Pray travel back, in imagination, through many centuries, back to an ignorant and barbaric age when the art of cookery was unknown and men ate their meat raw, cutting or tearing it from the live animal. Now, the play begins.

(Stage Manager *bows and goes off* R *as* STAGE HAND ONE *enters* L *with the house and places it* UC. *As* STAGE HAND ONE *exits* R, HO-TI *enters* L, *bows and addresses the audience. Exits and entrances throughout the play must be timed so that the stage is never left empty.*)

HO-TI

I am a poor swineherd named Ho-Ti. Here, close by the forest, I live with my son and raise pigs. Unfortunately my son is lazy and stupid. (*Sigh*) Still, Heaven has spared me the supreme disaster of having a daughter. Undoubtedly Heaven knows best. (*He calls off* L.) Bo-Bo! (*Pause: no reply.*) Bo-Bo!
(BO-BO *enters* R, *bows and addresses the audience.*)

BO-BO

I am Bo-Bo, son of this old man. When I forget to feed the pigs, he beats me. When I play with fire, he beats me. (*Sigh*) Still, Heaven created fathers, and undoubtedly Heaven knows best. Yes, father?

HO-TI

Bo-Bo, have you fed the pigs today?

BO-BO

Not today, Father, I . . . .

HO-TI

Wretch! The pigs could die for all you care.

BO-BO

Father, you see, I . . . .

HO-TI

Shut up, you booby! Come here!
(HO-TI *seizes* BO-BO *by the ear and begins to thrash him.*)

Later in the play, Ho-Ti and Bo-Bo are brought to trial. The magistrate's first speech is a piece of direct exposition.

MAGISTRATE

I am a magistrate, struggling year in, year out, to eliminate vice and encourage virtue among the wretched people of my district. What a discouraging task! Heaven has created a never-ending supply of criminals. (Sigh) But undoubtedly Heaven knows best. I'm now dealing with a tiresome case of witchcraft. For six months the preliminaries have dragged on, but this is the day of the trial. All morning the jury listened to the evidence. Then I sent them out for lunch. Now they are returning to the courtroom.
. . . . and the trial goes on.

EXERCISE 4:21
Write some direct exposition for one of the play ideas you noted in EXERCISE 4:15. Have a "special character" speaking first, and two of the main characters directly introducing themselves to the audience when they enter.

Indirect Exposition

Indirect exposition uses no direct address to the audience. It begins with the action of the play, and spectators are allowed to deduce the necessary information from what they see and hear on stage. Indirect exposition used to be handled in a style that would not be acceptable nowadays. For example, in *The Miser*, Act I, Scene 1, Elise is talking to Valere, her lover.

ELISE

I should have nothing to fear if everybody saw you through my eyes, for I see in you good reasons for all that I do for you. My heart pleads, in its own defense, your great worth. In addition to the strong feeling that Heaven meant us to be united, I recollect hourly the frightful peril which first brought us together; the supreme generosity with which you risked your life to save mine from the fury of the waves; the tender care which you lavished on me when you had drawn me from the water; your assiduous attentions to me: your ardent love, which neither time nor difficulties has diminished and for which, neglecting family and fatherland, you linger here, conceal your real condition and, in order to be able to see me, work, dressed as a servant, in my father's employment.

These lines sound incredible because Elise is telling Valere what he already knows perfectly well. This may be called "you-remember" exposition. Here is a modern example, the kind of exposition often written by beginners.

MARY

How long have you been working for the firm now, dear? All of ten years, isn't it?

TOM

Yes, just over ten years. When I started, the boss told me I'd get ahead if I stuck with him. It's certainly worked out that way, hasn't it?

MARY

Yes. After two years you rose to regional sales manager, and in four more years to general sales manager.

TOM

And then don't forget that eighteen months ago I got the vice-presidency . . . . etc.

You're likely to be trapped into you-remember exposition if you make the mistake of opening your play with characters who are well-known to each other, in an everyday situation, talking about familiar subjects. The harder you try to make such exposition informative, the more unrealistic it becomes.

(Notice, too, in that example, that although the names of the characters are written in the script, *the dialogue does not reveal them to the audience*. Neither does it reveal the name or business of Tom's firm.)

To give natural-sounding exposition, some ingenious playwright invented the gossiping-servant technique. A couple of servants, or other minor characters, open the play by gossiping about the major characters and the setting, and dropping hints about the nature of the coming action.

SERVANT A

I think I know who's going to wear the pants when Master Edward marries that Miss Priscilla Ludwig.

SERVANT B

Heh-heh! Yes, and it won't be Master Edward, eh?

The gossiping-servant technique is outmoded now. It belonged to a theatrical era when stars refused to come on stage until their entrance had been prepared by twenty minutes' talk about them and their affairs. Nowadays, the trend is to get the main characters on stage right at the start, or at least without much delay.

Exposition by Special Occasion

Exposition is easier if the play opens on a special occasion, when something out of the ordinary is happening, or is about to happen. Obviously this gives the characters something significant and informative to talk about.

Here are the opening lines of my melodrama, *Wedded to a Villain*. The language is old-fashioned to suit the appearance of the characters; they are wearing costumes of the year 1850.

Script	Expository Function
(As the curtain rises BONNIE, *a girl of 18, sits polishing an old guitar. There is a knock at the door.)*	Costume, set and action begin to establish BONNIE's character and financial status.
BONNIE: Come in!	
(JACK enters, dressed as a milkman, carrying a milk-pail.)	Costume and props begin to establish JACK's character.
JACK: Good morning, Miss Hartwell.	Tells BONNIE's surname. Tells time of day.
BONNIE: Good morning, Mr. Manley.	Tells JACK's surname.
JACK: *(Embarrassed)* Lovely weather we are having.	Embarrassed conversation about weather between young man and woman suggests romantic interest.
BONNIE: Yes, it is lovely for the time of year.	

JACK: The village wiseacres predict a hot, dry spell.

They live in a village.

BONNIE: Oh, indeed!

JACK: Er . . . yes. A very long, hot, dry spell of drought.

Season is summer.

BONNIE: Ahem! Half a pint of milk today, please, Mr. Manley.

Confirms JACK's occupation. The small quantity suggests the size of the Hartwell household.

JACK: Yes, certainly, Miss Hartwell. Half a pint it is.

(JACK *ladles milk into the jug which* BONNIE *holds out for him.*)

BONNIE: And can you please bring us half a pound of butter tomorrow? Fresh butter. My stepmother cannot bear to eat salted butter.

Prepares for entry of next character, the stepmother. Hints at stepmother's fussy temperament.

JACK: I shall not be calling tomorrow, Miss Hartwell.

BONNIE: (*Anxious*) Oh!

BONNIE is concerned. The "special occasion":

JACK: I shall never call here again, Miss Hartwell.

BONNIE: Never again?

JACK: No. I have sold the dairy and am leaving the village.

JACK is selling his dairy business.

BONNIE: (*Distressed*) Leaving!

BONNIE seems fond of JACK.

JACK: (*Sitting beside her*) Oh, Miss Hartwell . . . Bonnie . . . can you, do you feel more than a casual interest in my departure?

Tells BONNIE's first name. Obviously the first time JACK has used it. He reveals a romantic interest in BONNIE. The "special occasion" drives him to speak.

BONNIE: Perhaps . . . perhaps I do.

She reciprocates the feeling.

The exposition here is easy and natural because the play opens at a dramatic moment—*right on* the special occasion. This is more interesting than if Jack said he might sell the business in six months' time.

Note two technical points about this sample of exposition:

1. The characters' names are promptly revealed. Remember, the audience doesn't see your script; they can't know the characters' names unless the names are spoken!

2. The opening is not *too* fast. To have Jack's first line tell about leaving the village would be too soon. It was once customary to put no speech or action of any consequence in the first ten minutes of a full-length play because latecomers would be moving about finding their seats, rustling programs, whispering, and otherwise disturbing the audience.

Modern audiences are more punctual. The play, however, still cannot rush ahead too fast. The audience needs a little time to withdraw its thoughts and emotions from real life, from the world of the lobby and the street, and to enter the imaginary world of the stage. So, crucial information must not be given too early. If it is given early, it should be repeated later on.

Choosing a special occasion, then, simplifies your task in creating credible, interesting exposition. *The Three Sisters* (Chekhov) opens on the first anniversary of the father's death, a special occasion when it's natural for characters to talk about the past. In so talking, they can give information to the audience.

A birthday, a graduation day, a holiday, a festival, a wedding day, a battle (e.g., *Arms and The Man* by George Bernard Shaw) are special occasions that can well be used to facilitate exposition. *Christmas* has limitations, though: a Christmas play can be performed only at one season of the year.

EXERCISE 4:22
Choose one of your self-against-society situations from Exercise 4:8. Plan and write an opening for it, using some special occasion that would be relevant to that particular subject.

Exposition by Introduction

The introduction of a stranger is another natural occasion for the giving and receiving of information. Suppose a girl brings her boyfriend home to meet her family for the first time. It's an occasion interesting in itself, and useful to the playwright because, as the girl introduces her family to the boyfriend, she is introducing them to the audience.

Here is a modern example of exposition by introduction: the opening of *The Madwoman of Chaillot*, by Jean Giraudoux, in the adaptation by Maurice Valency.

SCENE: *The café terrace at* Chez Francis, *on the Place de l'Alma in Paris. The Alma is in the stately quarter known as Chaillot, between the Champs Elysées and the Seine, across the river from the Eiffel Tower.*

Chez Francis *has several rows of tables set out under its awning, and, as it is lunch time, a good many of them are occupied. At a table, downstage, a somewhat obvious Blonde with ravishing legs is sipping a vermouth-cassis and trying hard to engage the attention of the* Prospector, *who sits at an adjoining table taking little sips of water and rolling them over his tongue with the air of a connoisseur. Downstage right, in front of the tables on the sidewalk, is the usual Paris bench, a stout and uncomfortable affair provided by the municipality for the benefit of those who prefer to sit without drinking. A* Policeman *lounges about, keeping the peace without unnecessary exertion.*

TIME: *It is a little before noon in the Spring of next year.*
AT RISE: *The* President *and the* Baron *enter with importance, and are ushered to a front table by the waiter.* (1)

THE PRESIDENT

Baron, sit down. This is an historic occasion. It must be (2) properly celebrated. The waiter is going to bring out my special port. (3)

THE BARON

Splendid.

THE PRESIDENT

(Offers his cigar case) Cigar? My private brand. (4)

THE BARON

Thank you. You know, this gives me the feeling of one of those enchanted mornings in the *Arabian Nights* when thieves foregather in the market place. Thieves—pashas . . . (5)
(He sniffs the cigar judiciously, and begins lighting it.)

THE PRESIDENT

(Chuckles) Tell me about yourself.

THE BARON

Well, where shall I begin?
(The Street Singer *enters. He takes off a battered black felt hat with a flourish and begins singing an ancient mazurka.)*

STREET SINGER

(Sings) Do you hear, mademoiselle,
Those musicians of hell?

THE PRESIDENT

Waiter! Get rid of that man. (6)

WAITER

He is singing *La Belle Polonaise.*

THE PRESIDENT

I didn't ask for the program. I asked you to get rid of him. *(The* Waiter *doesn't budge. The* Singer *goes by himself.)* As you were saying, Baron . . . ?

THE BARON

Well, until I was fifty . . . *(The* Flower Girl *enters through the cafe door, center)* my life was relatively uncomplicated. It consisted of selling off, one by one, the various estates left me by my father. Three years ago, I parted with my last farm. Two years ago, I lost my last mistress. And now—all that is left me is . . . (7)

THE FLOWER GIRL
(*To the* Baron) Violets, sir?

THE PRESIDENT
Run along.
(*The* Flower Girl *moves on.*)

THE BARON
(*Staring after her*) So that, in short, all I have left now is my name. (8)

THE PRESIDENT
Your name is precisely the name we need on our board of directors. (9)

THE BARON
(*With an inclination of his head*) Very flattering.

THE PRESIDENT
You will understand me when I tell you that mine has been a very different experience. I came up from the bottom. My mother spent most of her life bent over a washtub in order to send me to school. I'm eternally grateful to her, of course, but I must confess that I no longer remember her face. It was no doubt beautiful—but when I try to recall it, I see only the part she invariably showed me—her rear. (10)

THE BARON
Very touching.

THE PRESIDENT
When I was thrown out of school for the fifth and last time, (11) I decided to find out for myself what makes the world go round. I ran errands for an editor, a movie star, a financier . . . I began to understand a little of what life is. Then, one day in the subway, I saw a face . . . My rise in life dates from that day.

THE BARON
Really?

THE PRESIDENT
One look at that face, and I knew. One look at mine, and he knew. And so I made my first thousand—passing a boxful of counterfeit notes. A year later, I saw another such face. It got me a nice berth in the narcotics business. Since then, all I have to do is to look out for

such faces. And now here I am—president of eleven corporations, director of fifty-two companies, and beginning today, chairman of the board of the international combine in which you have been so good as to accept a post. (*The* Ragpicker *passes, sees something under the* President's *table, and stoops to pick it up*) Looking for something?

THE RAGPICKER

Did you drop this?

THE PRESIDENT

I never drop anything. (12)

THE RAGPICKER

Then this hundred-franc note isn't yours?

THE PRESIDENT

Give it here.
(*The* Ragpicker *gives him the note, and goes out.*)

THE BARON

Are you sure it's yours?

THE PRESIDENT

All hundred-franc notes, Baron, are mine. (13)

THE BARON

Mr. President, there's something I've been wanting to ask you. What exactly is the purpose of our new company? Or is that an indiscreet question . . . ?

THE PRESIDENT

Indiscreet? Not a bit. Merely unusual. As far as I know, you're the first member of a board of directors ever to ask such a question.

THE BARON

Do we propose to exploit a commodity? A utility?

THE PRESIDENT

My dear sir, I haven't the faintest idea.

THE BARON

But if you don't know—who does?

THE PRESIDENT

Nobody. And at the moment, it's becoming just a trifle embarrassing. Yes, my dear Baron, since we are now close business associates, I must confess that for the time being we're in a little trouble.

THE BARON
I was afraid of that. The stock issue isn't going well?

THE PRESIDENT
No, no—on the contrary. The stock issue is going beautifully. Yesterday morning at ten o'clock we offered 500,000 shares to the general public. By 10:05 they were all snapped up at par. By 10:20, when the police finally arrived, our offices were a shambles . . . windows smashed—doors torn off their hinges—you never saw anything so beautiful in your life! And this morning our stock is being quoted over the counter at 124 with no sellers, and the orders are still pouring in.

THE BARON
But in that case—what is the trouble?

THE PRESIDENT
The trouble is we have a tremendous capital, and not the slightest idea of what to do with it.

EXERCISE 4:23
Analyze the *Madwoman of Chaillot* excerpt as follows:
(a) What is the audience supposed to discover about the characters and the situation from each of the numbered passages of dialogue?
(b) Where would you expect the performance to bring laughs?
(c) After you have read Chapter 6, come back to this piece, and locate all the little internal conflicts that make the dialogue sparkle.
(d) Again, after you have read Chapter 6, come back to this piece and locate five applications of the three-times rule.

EXERCISE 4:24
Write a similar scene between two women. One is the head of some charitable or artistic organization; the other is some distinguished social, political or show business personality who is to be used as a figurehead.

EXERCISE 4:25
Write an opening scene for the play-idea that you outlined in Exercise 4:19. Use the technique of exposition by introduction.

Exposition by Parting or Reunion
When people are about to part—I don't mean just going out for an after-

noon's shopping, but parting for a long time—it's natural for them to review what they've done together. They may assess the present state of their relationship; they might realistically discuss plans for the future. All this will reveal useful information about them. *Ghosts* opens with a parting scene—Engstrand and Regina.

Similarly, when people meet *after* a long separation, it's natural for them to ask questions and exchange information about themselves and their affairs. *The Cherry Orchard* employs exposition by reunion; so do *A Streetcar Named Desire* (Williams) and *Hedda Gabler* (Ibsen).

Exposition by Irritation
    When people quarrel they often talk about themselves and their affairs more freely and specifically than they would at other times.

TOM

Eight years we've been married, and never a day passes without you dragging up your first husband. "Philip used to buy this!" "Philip used to give me that!" I'm sick of Philip!

MARY

And I'm sick of you! Mother warned me against you. "Never marry a man who doesn't smoke or drink or gamble," she said. "A man like that is bound to be a cheapskate." And that's just what you are—a cheapskate.

TOM

Cheapskate? Me? Who bought you this house, because the one on Cherry Street was too small for you—your afternoon tea-parties and your evening receptions?

And so on. Angry people can credibly be made to repeat facts that the listening character already knows quite well. (Of course, a character who is a *bore* can do this credibly too, but it might be dangerous to open your play with a bore.)

Ghosts, as we have seen, opens on a parting. Ibsen rapidly develops the parting into a quarrel, combining two methods to make his exposition still more vivid and informative.

EXERCISE 4:26
Study the openings of your Exemplary Dozen to find what methods the playwrights used for exposition.

EXERCISE 4:27
Write the opening scene for a play, using yourself as one of the characters, and providing exposition by irritation.

SUMMARY

The essential factor for arousing interest: conflict.
Five kinds of conflict:
1. Man against nature. (But don't ask for grandiose, big-scale scenic effects.)
2. Man against man: the more valuable the prize, the more interesting the conflict.
3. Man against society: as represented by tradition, custom, law, regulations, the neighbors, etc.
4. Man against himself: fear, indecision, procrastination, hypochondria, temper, etc.
5. Man against fate: heredity, sickness, bad luck, chance, fortune, etc.
    If you use several kinds of conflict in one play, keep one predominant.
Many sources of ideas for plays:
1. Personal experience: search your life for conflicts.
2. Systematically study newspapers for ideas.
3. Get ideas from friends.
4. Adapt old stories, books, plays.
The conflict formula: $M + G + O = C$. Main character(s) + Goal + Opposition = Conflict.
    Main characters must be clearly defined, capable of holding audience's sympathetic attention.
    Goal must be credible and interesting.
    Opposition must be strong: "a play is as strong as its villain."
    Exposition gives audience the information needed to understand what's going on.
Sets, costumes, give some information: most must come from dialogue and action.
Direct exposition: an explanatory address to the audience—
(a) By a special character—prologue.
(b) By one or more of the regular characters in the play.
Indirect exposition: with no direct address, the audience can deduce necessary data from what they see and hear on stage.
    Beware of "you remember" and "gossiping servant" techniques.
    Some situations make for easy, effective exposition:
1. **Special occasion:** something out of the ordinary is happening.
2. **Introduction:** (of one character to another by a third character) naturally leads to giving information about the character being introduced.
3. **Parting or reunion:** natural occasions to review relationships.
4. **Irritation:** quarrelling naturally leads people to speak out about hidden facts and feelings.
    Good exposition provides time, place, characters' names, ages, relative positions, economic conditions, plus other "atmospheric" details.

CHAPTER FIVE

Characters

SHORT STORIES and novels are built around characters, but those literary characters seldom make such a quick, powerful appeal to readers as do the characters of a good play to their audience.

The fiction characters are presented only by a code of black marks on white paper; an author depends on the reader's imagination to bring them to life. But the characters in your play are live human beings, with real skin, hair and clothes. They have the ability—you hope—to establish a strong, emotional relationship with the audience.

Consider yourself: you are a character yourself, now, and throughout your life, you are acting upon, and reacting to other characters. Probably much of that interaction is taken for granted and never analyzed. But as a playwright, you should conscientiously study those real-life interactions to help you create credible, interesting interactions on stage.

EXERCISE 5:1
Draw an up-to-date character sketch of yourself. What qualities set you apart from the other people you know? Besides the obvious individualities (name, age, sex, height, weight, marital status, education, occupation, hobbies) describe at least ten more characteristics that are particularly distinctive. Include some that you especially like about yourself, and also some that you dislike. Take your time with this character sketch; write at least 500 words.

Some beginning playwrights, unfamiliar with exotic characters (criminal bosses, international financiers, rock stars, queens, presidents, etc.), nevertheless try to use them. For a while, at least, you will get the best results by portraying characters like yourself and the people you know.

EXERCISE 5:2
Write a similar character sketch of a person with whom you have an important congenial relationship (work, friendship, family, love, hobbies, politics, or whatever). Give some space to

general description; also give details of what it is about the person that makes your relationship a good one. Try to identify a few faults also.

EXERCISE 5:3
Write a similar character sketch of a person with whom you have, or have had, some important conflict. Give some general description; also give details of the characteristics that produced the conflict. Try to describe a few good points also.

HOW MANY CHARACTERS?

A two-character play tends to be monotonous. It is perforce built mainly of two-scenes (i.e., scenes between two characters) relieved only by passages of monologue, or bits of silent business performed by one character on stage alone.

The spectators, after the first two-scene, know that they cannot expect any more characters to appear; therefore an important stimulant to their curiosity is missing. Some of them feel cheated.

Mind you, there is nothing wrong, artistically or technically, with two-character plays. Many of them have been produced on and off Broadway in recent years; some have achieved popular success and critical awards—the aforementioned *Talley's Folly* and *'night, Mother* (Marsha Norman) are two-character plays that won the Pulitzer Prize. It's also worth mentioning that such plays are economical to produce—an important factor in professional theatre.

But most such successes have been achieved with scripts by experienced playwrights, performed by professional actors. The two-character form is difficult for the inexperienced playwright: I will give some of the reasons later in this chapter. So I would advise that you avoid it, at least until you have more experience.

By adding one character to make a cast of three, you immediately give your play variety. With only two characters, A and B, you have (apart from soliloquies) only one possible grouping of characters: call it AB.

Add character C, and you have (again not counting soliloquies) *four* possible groupings: AB, AC, BC and ABC.

Three-scenes can be visually more varied and interesting than two-scenes. The director will be glad of that, and so will the audience, without thinking of it in technical terms.

Another advantage of a three-scene is that you can have an exit—and any experienced actor will tell you the dramatic value of a good exit—without having the play collapse on stage behind the character who has just left.

The three-character play seems varied, however, only by contrast with the extreme limitations of the two-character play. If one character is off and two are on, the audience can never be surprised at an entrance; when the doorbell rings, they know who it must be.

By using four characters you overcome this difficulty. With characters A, B, C, and D, you have three types of scenes—two-scenes, three-scenes and four-scenes—and a total of eleven possible groupings: AB, AC, AD, BC, BD, CD, ABC, ABD, ACD, BCD and ABCD.

If any two characters, say A and B, are on stage, you have three possible entrances: C alone, D alone, or C and D together.

Five characters give four types of scenes (two-scenes, three-scenes, four-scenes and five-scenes) and a total of twenty-four possible groupings. With two characters (A and B) on stage, you have seven possible entrances: C alone, D alone, E alone, CD, CE, DE or CDE. With five characters there should be little difficulty in maintaining variety right through a full-length play.

The five-character play, then, is a good one for you to begin with. It gives you ample scope for variety, yet does not overly tax your planning powers.

Most amateur drama groups can cast the five-character play. Amateurs, as a rule, don't like two-character or three-character plays, in which all the roles are equally important. The few leading members, who get the best parts all the time, will perform them, and the less experienced people will be left out. The typical five-character play probably contains one or two minor roles suitable for inexperienced actors. (Bear that in mind when planning and writing your plays.)

After writing a few successful five-character plays, you may want to work with a larger cast. But remember that most amateur groups are fairly small. Some of them cannot cast a ten-character play; few could scrape together twenty actors at a time.

One useful compromise lies in the writing of multiple roles in which some cast members play two or more secondary characters each. For example, in a play that I'm writing as I finish this book, one woman has a few lines as a prim, prudish housewife (the period is the late nineteenth century). In the next act, she appears as a brash, tough, wisecracking singer. The actress will enjoy this double characterization. (I must be sure to allow her ample time offstage to change costume and makeup.)

In the professional theatre there is no shortage of actors and actresses. Indeed, for every one performing, there are probably twenty out of work. The problem is money: every member of the cast means an extra salary to pay and perhaps an extra costume to buy.

Plays with very big casts, then, probably won't be produced by either amateurs or professionals. Tennyson, in *Queen Mary* brought all the members of both houses of the English Parliament on stage for one short scene! This is one play that never gets a performance.

Keep the number of characters proportional to the scale of the work. I once read a script that called for seventeen characters and a costly set. So much trouble and expense might have been justified perhaps for a three-act play; but this was a ten-minute sketch! That's another script doomed to the "Rejected" basket by its author's unrealistic attitude.

To sum up, then: for a start, you'll do well to work with five characters, in one-act and in full-length plays. As your experience grows, you can try handling more characters. But as the cast list grows beyond ten names, the play's chances of production tend to dwindle.

WHAT KIND OF CHARACTERS?

Real life, in the school, street, home, hospital, factory, legislature, barroom or wherever you may be, presents a fantastic assortment of characters: fools, sages, whiners, blowhards, heroes, bullies, victims, saints and devils.

Study them, in the flesh, on television (not too much TV, though!), in movies, newspapers and magazines, via other people's memories and commentaries. Try to become a connoisseur of character.

There's a very snooty-looking woman who often eats breakfast in the restaurant where I go. Every time, before sitting down, she grabs a bundle of paper napkins and vigorously wipes every square inch of the seats and tabletop in the booth where she plans to sit. (The place is, in fact, kept quite clean by the staff.) What does this show about her character?

> EXERCISE 5:4
> Open a character collection file. List characters that you meet, or hear of, that might be useful in plays. Allot a sheet to each one. Note name, occupation, age, a few words of physical description, and write a brief character summary.

But bear in mind that some kinds of characters are more useful than others. Let's look at a few of the qualities that make characters more or less serviceable to us, the playwrights.

Articulate

Most stage characters are articulate, rather more articulate than people in real life. They talk readily, concisely and clearly. You might be able to use one dumb character in a play, or one who has little to say for himself, but such characters tend to create difficulties for the playwright. It's better to use characters who can reasonably be expected to keep talking, because, except for the occasional moment of dramatic silence, a successful play needs a continuous flow of dialogue.

> EXERCISE 5:5
> Add to your character collection file some characters who are notable for what they say, or the way they say it. For each of these, not a few bits of dialogue that reveal something of the personality, the prejudices, the emotions, etc., of the person who is speaking.

Simplified

Stage characters must be simpler than real-life people. Some playwrights will not face this requirement, and try to transfer characters, unchanged, from life to the stage. That won't do. Most real-life characters are
not dramatic, because they are too vague, too ill-defined, too complex.
Most real-life situations, therefore, are too obscure for the stage.

When you are first introduced to a family or to a social group, you do
not know who is who. Much of their conversation is mysterious to you. It
may take you years to discover that old Aunt Louisa, who has such a razor-
edged tongue, really has a heart of gold, and that kindly-looking Cousin Arthur has abandoned a wife and three children, defrauded his creditors, and
is now living with a seventeen-year-old imbecile mistress.

A theatre audience cannot wait months or years. They have half an
hour or so in a one-act play, two-and-a-half hours in a full-length play, to
understand a group of unfamiliar characters, to identify to some extent
with one or more of them, and to go through a satisfying emotional experience with these characters.

So, stage characters must be fairly simple, obvious. Over-subtle characterization is not only wasted, it is harmful, because it will confuse at
least some in the audience.

Exaggerated

Stage characters must be exaggerated, larger than life. Emile Augier
says, in his "Essay on Comedy," "The spectators . . . did not come, they
did not pay, to see the same characters that they see every day. They want
something better, something bigger, than the miser, the grumbler, the
trickster or the pedant whom they know in their own families, as next-
door neighbors or as fellow townsmen. So the comic dramatist presents on
stage the *ideal* of intellectual deformity, of vice, folly and stupidity." The
same principle of exaggeration applies—though perhaps not always so
strongly—in other, more serious play forms.

> EXERCISE 5:6
> From three of your Exemplary Dozen, select six important char-
> acters. Imagine that, for someone who has not read or seen the
> plays, you are trying to sum up each character in ten words or
> less: i.e., begin to think about these characters, not as a specta-
> tor, but as a playwright. Write down the simplified character de-
> scriptions.

> EXERCISE 5:7
> For six of your own collected characters, provide similar concise
> descriptions, simplifying and exaggerating where necessary.

The Telephone as a Character

The telephone, of course, has its uses on stage. But there's a problem
with outgoing calls. *Dialing* an outgoing call and waiting for two or three

rings at the other end takes 17 to 20 seconds. That seems a long time on stage; it slows the action of a play. Getting the number is faster with a push-button phone; and talking to the operator on the old-fashioned, pre-dial phone helps fill in the time.

So, if you want to make an outgoing call, have the character say something to someone on stage while he is going through the mechanics of dialing and *then* wait for a few seconds to see if there's an answer.

Another problem with the phone: it's hard to write one end of the conversation so that it is: (1) credible—sounds enough like a phone conversation to pass for the real thing; (2) interesting; (3) informative.

There is a way of letting the audience hear both ends of a phone conversation—by the use of an offstage actor, microphone and loudspeaker. But that system produces a hybrid performance, a cross between a stage play and a radio play. By forcing an audience to switch rapidly from one set of conventions to another, it tends to inhibit their acceptance of either.

Incoming calls tend to be more effective than out-going ones. The sound of the bell interrupting the action at a well-chosen spot, but coming as a surprise to the audience can be used to heighten the excitement of a scene. Moreover, it is credible for the person taking the call to cover the mouthpiece from time to time, and tell the other characters what the caller wants.

Examine the phone call in the *Mary, Mary* excerpt, Chapter 7. Notice that it is kept very short. And it is supplemented and explained by dialogue between the characters on stage.

To sum up: the telephone is less interesting and less versatile than a live character. I would recommend against depending too heavily upon it.

Beware!

Don't write big parts for young children. They (and their mothers) can be absolute pests in adult plays. In the main show-business centers, there are some trained, dependable infant actors, elsewhere they are hard to find.

Avoid using animals on stage. They are a great nuisance, and they are sure to misbehave. Cats will scratch furniture or run up the curtains; dogs will bark; monkeys will bite; rabbits will copulate. Any animal, before the run of a play is over, will urinate on stage.

Moreover—and this is important—adult actors hate performing with infants or animals. They know that any animal or child can, by malice or accident, steal any scene from an adult. This is not simply a wound to the adult's pride, it is an injury to the play. It means that the audience's attention has been diverted from the author's lines and from the course of the plot to the irrelevant antics of the animal or child.

Don't call for deformed characters (people with fingers missing, legs amputated, etc.). Don't ask for exceedingly tall, short, fat or thin people.

One more warning: don't write scripts that require actors with unusual skills (acrobats, jugglers, conjurers, fire-eaters, etc.). There was a day when many actors could play the violin or flute, when most actresses could play the piano and sing. Every actor could fence, every actress dance. But no longer!

Here's an interesting example. Act III of *The Cassilis Engagement* includes a posh party scene that typifies Geoffrey Cassilis's man-against-society conflict. Mabel, a girl from Geoffrey's own upper-crust section of society, sings two verses of Schubert's "Adieu" in German, accompanying herself on the piano. Immediately afterward, Ethel, his middle-class fiancée, takes over the piano and accompanies herself in a music-hall ditty, "Just you stop that ticklin' or I'll slap yer." Most of the company is horrified! Nowadays you could not bank on finding two such singer-pianists to perform the scene! Maybe that's why we never see the play produced any more.

EXERCISE 5:8
Plan a scene in which, *without* music or singing, a present-day young woman conspicuously shows that she does not fit in with her sweetheart's family and friends.

NAMING THE CHARACTERS

Playwrights used to give their characters descriptive names: *Croaker* for the chronic grumbler, *Lofty* for a snob, *Miss Richland* for an heiress, *Filch* for a thief, *Betty Doxy* for a prostitute, *Lockit* for a jailer, and so on. Such names were common up to the mid-nineteenth century; you seldom see them in modern plays.

This is as good a place as any to say something about literary fashions. Like fashions in clothes and automobiles, they come and go. The writer must accept them. There's no more use in trying to go against the fashion in play writing than there is in setting up a dress shop stocked with outdated clothes.

A graceful yielding to fashion does not necessarily mean a prostitution of your literary talents. Within the limits of what's fashionable, you can produce craftsmanlike, honest, worthwhile work.

The writer who insists on writing plays five acts and four hours long is being not noble, but stupid. He is showing not genius, but stubbornness. Genius has seldom scorned to work within the limits of the fashionable and the practical.

The wise writer, then, will not set him- or herself out of fashion by giving characters descriptive names. Type names, such as "The Little Guy" and "The Big Boss" are also out of fashion, and it's just as well that they are.

You should still take the trouble, however, to choose names that are appropriate to the characters who bear them. *Oscar* and *Jack*, for example, have no commonly known meanings, but they have acquired connotative stereotypes. There is an important difference between a Veronica and a Trixie.

The man who is well-suited by *Henry* might seem misnamed as *Har-*

ry, Hank, Henri, Heinrich or *Hal. Bess, Beth, Betty, Libby, Lise, Lizzie, Ilse, Bettina,* and *Elizabeth* all imply nuances of personality.

The choice of surnames, too, calls for care. There are differences between *Forrestall* and *Fotheringham, Wharton* and *Warkentin, Laplante* and *Lipsky.*

Each character's name, then, must not be descriptive, but appropriate. It sometimes takes much thought to select the right names. What I do is to begin with names that seem somewhere near right, and use them for the first draft or two. Inspiration for selection of better names often comes in the process of revision.

Famous Names

Avoid names that have acquired strong connotations from famous people (first names such as Elvis, Groucho, Dashiell and Thurgood; surnames such as Gandhi, Strindberg, Toulouse-Lautrec, or Daimler). A famous name can only hinder at each repetition the process of character building that should be going on in the spectator's mind. The famous name hinders that process by constantly distracting the spectator from the play.

Variety of Names

Names of characters must not sound too much alike. Don't have a Pete and a Pat in the same play, a Norma and Noreen, an Albert and Alfred, or an Andrea and Amanda. Some actors don't articulate very clearly; indeed some characters require that the actor *not* articulate clearly. If names that are too much alike are pronounced indistinctly on stage, they will not be distinguished easily by a deaf lady in the back row of an echoing high school gymnasium/auditorium. Write for that deaf lady in the back row; if she understands, everyone will understand.

> EXERCISE 5:9
> Review Exercises 5:1, 5:2 and 5:3. Suppose you are going to include those three characters (yourself included) in a play, but don't want to use real names. Choose three new names—first name, surname and nickname for each—that will nicely suit the characters.

> EXERCISE 5:10
> Review three of your Exemplary Dozen to pick out three character names that seem to you especially fitting. Analyze *why* each of them is well-suited in its context.
>
>   Similarly choose three names that don't seem to ring true; analyze *why* each of them is defective in its context.

> EXERCISE 5:11
> Suppose you want to write a play about an amateur drama group whose treasurer loses all the group's funds in playing the stock

market or some other form of gambling.

Choose your characters (not more than six). Who will you need to provide strong, well-balanced conflict (i.e., so that you don't have all the rest of them against the defaulter)? Give good *variety* to your cast. Give a physical description of each; choose a suitable name for each.

Plan your first two or three French scenes. Which characters will you bring on first? Which will you reserve for later?

THE CAST LIST

The first page of the playscript contains a list of characters. In this list it is sufficient to enter for each character:

1. Name.

2. Brief statement of the character's occupation or station in life ("a lawyer," "a schoolteacher," "a housewife," "a high-school student," etc.).

3. Age, if relevant. Usually an approximation will do ("late teens," "mid-forties," "very old," etc.). If you are writing a play about an historical personality it may be necessary to specify the character's *exact* age at the time of the action.

4. Peculiarities of physical appearance, speech, or manner ("shabby looking," "Irish accent," "vivacious manner," "timid manner," etc.).

5. Costume, if this needs any special description. If a character is dressed in the ordinary way for his position in society at the period and place of the action, no description of costume is necessary.

Don't clutter up the cast list with detailed descriptions, precise measurements, or potted biographies of the characters. The audience will never see them. The director will probably ignore them, because he has to use the actors he has available, whether or not they fit the playwright's preconceived picture. Directors will seldom go outside the general limits of an age bracket; but they will probably not feel bound by the playwright's specification of blue eyes, golden hair, and a tip-tilted nose, or by his exact figures for height and weight.

Here are some examples of what would be adequate descriptions for the cast of a modern play:

JAMES HARDWICK: a prosperous businessman of fifty.
MARY: his wife.
PHYLLIS: their daughter, age twenty-four, a schoolteacher.
UNCLE ARTHUR: Mary's younger brother, a real estate salesman in his late thirties.

Don't use the cast list to summarize the story of the play, e.g., "Janice Czolovsky, a young girl of eighteen, in love with Rinaldo Bianchin, but who will later see that Rinaldo is unworthy of her, and will give her heart to

Artur Martinez, the man who has truly loved her all along." That is by no means an exaggeration of what some playwrights do in this line.

CHARACTER LISTS IN PROGRAMS

You cannot depend on the program to set the scene, to tell any part of the story, or to describe the characters of your play. Many in the audience will not read the program; they are too busy talking to friends or looking at other people's clothes. Some of them cannot read it: they have not brought their reading glasses. Others arrive late, after the house lights are down.

For those who do read the program, try to have it laid out so as not to impair their pleasure in the show. Do not include the note, "Characters listed in order of appearance." It robs every program reader of the pleasure he might have obtained from a surprise entrance because he always knows which character is due to appear next.

Beware too, of letting the program give away the plot, as when in a crime play the program reader sees that a late-appearing character is named EXECUTIONER.

The principal purpose of a program should be to identify the actors and actresses with the roles they are playing. You, as a playwright, should not depend on it to assist you in any way. You will do a more craftsmanlike job if you imagine the play to be given without the use of programs.

DEPICTING THE CHARACTERS

You have many elements at your disposal for depicting your characters, giving them individuality, making them interesting and credible:

1. *Appearance.*

Physique: tall, short, fat, thin, sturdy, frail.

Complexion: pale, ruddy, tanned, black, brown, yellow, smooth, wrinkled, hairless, hairy (moustached, bearded).

Hair: abundant, scanty, or absent; tidy or untidy; long, medium or short; fashionably or unfashionably dressed; red, blond, brunette, black or white.

Deformities: (It is best not to use these, although such things as a clubfoot or a limp can be portrayed without much difficulty.)

Age: usually need not be specified too narrowly.

Sex: may need to be specified in the cast list if the character has a name common to both sexes.

2. *Speech:* this is fully dealt with in Chapter 6.

3. *Actions:* this is fully dealt with in Chapter 7.

4. *Attire.*

Are a character's clothes expensive or cheap, fashionable or unfashionable, well-fitting or ill-fitting, dirty or clean, new or worn, bright or somber? Costume can show the period and place in which the character lives, his or her occupation, rank or social status, and temperament.

5. *Special habits.*

Does a character smoke, drink, chew tobacco, spit or cough? Or crack knuckles, tap fingers on tables, suck his teeth, pick his nose, twiddle his thumbs, or play with his handkerchief? There are many such mannerisms, some of which are deeply revelatory, that can help to give depth, individuality and conviction to characters. (Study Freud's *Psychopathology of Everyday Life* for some illuminating information on this point.)

6. *Occupation.*

A character becomes incredible if he or she has no apparent source of income to support his or her standard of living. The kind of job that a character holds may be significant. The same job may have different meanings at different times. Robin Hood, the gangster, was a hero in his day; the present-day gangster is probably a villain.

7. *Reputation.*

What do other people say about a character behind his or her back? You know quite well how this process operates. It is useful, before a major character enters the stage, and after he exits, to have other characters talk about him, truthfully or untruthfully, as the plot requires.

8. *Judgment.*

What does he say about other people? When we meet a man who says that everyone is against him, that the whole world is full of liars, cheats, swindlers and whores, we realize that he is not really describing other people, but is saying something important about himself. The man who generally speaks well of others similarly reveals himself.

9. *Friends.*

Who are the character's friends? A man is known by the company he keeps!

10. *Temperament.*

Is the character contented or discontented, modest or boastful, aggressive or submissive? There are scores of possible temperaments. Carlo Goldoni gives a useful hint: "To bring out a character, I place it in direct contrast with another whose nature is the opposite."

Skillful playwrights regularly follow that practice. Gullible Othello is opposed to scheming Iago. In *Don Juan*, the blustering Don is shown off to perfection by the timorous Sganarelle. In *The Glass Menagerie*, Amanda's rosy romanticism contrasts sharply with Tom's stolid, down-to-earth practicality.

Not *all* these questions need to be answered for *every* character; but the more important a character is, the more detailed, the more vivid, should be the portrayal. Don't try to give such character description all in a lump on a character's first appearance. Give the audience the pleasure of playing detective, getting to know and judge your characters step by step as the play proceeds.

TO SKETCH OR NOT TO SKETCH

Some playwrights like to create a biographical sketch of each character before beginning to write the script—parentage, date and place of birth, temperament, education—all the distinctives that differentiate this character from others. An alternative method is to let the characters come gradually to life as you write the script, beginning with only name and sex, and building from there.

I think that the labor involved in the two methods is about equal. What you save by not writing biographies is lost in the extra rewriting required to keep the developing characters consistent and credible.

For example, suppose that by the middle of Act II, Horatio, your leading man, establishes himself as a wit. You may then have to rewrite some of his lines in Act I to make him witty, and probably some of the lines of the other characters—particularly his fiancée Louise will have to be revised to contrive opportunities for Horatio's wit to sparkle.

Each method can produce perfectly good results. Experiment to find which best suits your style.

MAIN CHARACTERS

Every play needs one or more *main* characters. The main characters perform the important actions in a play; they are deeply involved in the conflict; the conclusion affects *them* and changes *their* situation, for better or worse, from what it was at the beginning of the play.

It is with the main characters that the spectators become emotionally involved. They are usually not satisfied to know *what* a play is about; they want to know *who* it is about. (I shall describe the process of audience identification in Chapter 13.)

In many plays the title names one or more of the main characters (e.g., *Hamlet, Romeo and Juliet, Abraham Lincoln, Victoria Regina, Miss Julie*), or describes one or more of the main characters (*The Miser, The Doctor Despite Himself, The Man Who Came to Dinner, Three Sisters*).

Whether or not the title identifies your main characters, the dialogue and action must. It is best to bring them on without delay, or have other characters talk about them early in the play. Once entered, the main character(s) should dominate the play, be on stage most of the time, have the biggest share of the lines, and the most interesting actions.

This domination must be continuous. I saw a play in which the main character hanged herself at the end of Act I. My attention flagged throughout Act II. I thought I had picked the wrong main character. I was trying to find, among half a dozen others of equal importance, which one was really the main character. Five minutes before the end of Act II the woman came on again, her throat bandaged; she had been found and cut down in time! But we in the audience did not know that; we had written her off as dead and had lost interest in her, and consequently lost interest in the play. If the main character is off stage, the attention of the audience must be kept on him or her (a) by the knowledge that whatever is being said and done on stage somehow concerns the main character or (b) by the expectation that he or she will soon return.

Julius Caesar is among the less successful of Shakespeare's plays; one reason is that the title character (whom we naturally assume to be the main character) is murdered less than half-way through. Obviously, nothing of the remaining action concerns him, and we know that he won't return.

When you have several main characters, they should not be of precisely equal importance; moreover, they should be differentiated by age, sex, temperament, etc., etc. Hamlet, the King, and the Queen make a well-differentiated group of main characters; so do Tartuffe, Elmire and Orgon in *Tartuffe* (Molière); so do Jo, Helen and Geof in *A Taste of Honey* (Shelagh Delany); so do Julie, the neurotic young noblewoman, and Jean, the cunning manservant, in *Miss Julie* (Strindberg).

SECONDARY CHARACTERS

Secondary characters may have a good many entrances and lines, but they are not of central importance in the story. There is little, if any, audience identification with secondary characters. They are useful only as they act upon the main characters and react to them. Their fate does not concern the audience: no one worries about Polonius when Hamlet kills him.

The conclusion of the play need not conclude anything for the secondary characters; their fate may be left unresolved. Peter and the Sailor in *A Taste of Honey* simply leave the stage and disappear; they have served their purpose, and we do not wonder about their futures. In *Miss Julie*, Kristin the cook simply walks off to church, and we forget about her. Our thoughts and feelings are centered on Miss Julie and Jean the valet, who remain on stage for the final French scene.

MINOR CHARACTERS

Minor characters are in the play only for technical reasons—to bring messages, to listen to more important characters saying things that the audience is intended to hear, to ask questions that will draw out necessary statements, or simply to dress up the stage by their presence. They are the servants, the spear-carriers, attendants and distant relatives. They are the troupe of singers and dancers in *Miss Julie*.

Minor characters are not fully developed; time does not allow that. Yet it is not amiss for some of them to be given little characteristic touches of costume, speech or action. An old man can smoke a battered pipe, an old lady can be deaf, a maidservant can be saucy, a butler haughty, a youngster untidy.

EVERYONE IN HIS PLACE

Keep your characters in their places all through the play. They should neither slip downward nor climb upward in importance. I saw one play where the main character faded out toward the end, given less and less to say and do. A minor character, who had sat mute through two-and-a-half acts, took over and dominated the end of the play. Such shifts of emphasis tend to leave spectators dissatisfied. It is as if, at dinner, when you are partway through a succulent steak, the waiter snatches it away and gives you dry bread instead.

(This is not to say that you can't have surprising developments of the plot, or surprising turns of character. Surprise is one of the most important ingredients of the successful play. But every surprise must be well-prepared. I shall describe that process in Chapter 8.)

EXERCISE 5:12
Review your Exemplary Dozen. Identify the main, secondary and minor characters in each.

EXERCISE 5:13
Draft the outline of a play, using the six characters you described in Exercise 5:7. Choose which of them will best serve as main, secondary and minor characters for the story line you have chosen.

Choose a suitable time and place for the action. Consider what the main characters are likely to desire or to oppose: X seeks something; Y doesn't want him to get it—there's the basis for a story line.

From your characters, decide what is to be the tone of your play (sad, funny, thrilling, inspirational, etc.). Decide how the story is going to end: what will be the feeling of each character toward your concluding situation (joy, rage, relief, mirth, etc.).

Work all this out fully enough to make what you think would be a half-hour, one-act play. We shall deal in detail later with various aspects of this planning and construction, but you'll enjoy making a stab at the procedure here and now.

SUMMARY

Characters create emotional relationship with the audience.
Long two-character and three-character plays tend toward monotony; four or five characters give more variety.
Plays with excessively big casts are unlikely to be produced.
Make yourself a habitual student of character.
Useful stage characters must be articulate, simplified and exaggerated, by comparison with real-life people.
There are technical difficulties in depending on the telephone as a major character.
Don't write big parts for young children; don't use animals on stage.

Don't call for exceptional physical characteristics; don't demand unusual performing skills.

Avoid descriptive names for characters; yet take care that names are appropriate.

Avoid famous names; avoid names that sound too much alike.

Don't clutter the cast-list with needless descriptive details; see that the program doesn't give away the plot.

The main elements for depicting character: appearance, speech, actions, attire, special habits, occupation, reputation, judgment, friends and temperament.

Show characters who are in strong contrast.

Main characters: deeply involved in the conflict; the main objects of audience interest.

Secondary characters: interact with main characters, but create little or no audience identification.

Minor characters: the messengers, servants, spear-carriers, etc.

Keep characters in their places throughout.

CHAPTER SIX

Characters ~II
Dialogue

FOR SOME 2,400 YEARS, playwrights customarily wrote, and audiences seemed happy to hear from the stage, a style of language more formal, more elaborate, than anything ever used in real life. Umpteen thousand plays were written and performed in verse, despite the fact that real people don't buy and sell, quarrel and make love, in meter and rhyme! Even in prose, most playwrights, till fairly recently, gave their characters a stately, oratorical, unrealistic turn of speech.

For example, *The Drunkard* (W.H. Smith, 1844) opened with Mrs. Wilson and her daughter, Mary, sitting in their pretty rural cottage.

MRS. WILSON

It was in that corner, Mary, where your poor father breathed his last. This chair is indeed dear to me for it was in this he sat the very day before he died. Oh, how he loved this calm retreat, and often in his last illness he rejoiced that the companion of his youth would close his eyes in these rural shades, and be laid in yon little nook beside him; but now. . . .

MARY

Dear mother, it is true that this sweet cottage is most dear to us. But we are not the proprietors. Old Mr. Middleton never troubled us much. But as our late worthy landlord is no more, it is generally believed that our dear cottage will be sold. We cannot censure his son for that.

MRS. WILSON

No; the young must be provided for, and willingly would I bow with resignation to that great power that loveth while it chasteneth; but when I think that you, my beloved child, will be left exposed to the thousand temptations of life, a penniless orphan. . . *(A knock on the door)* Hark! Who knocks? Dry your tears, my darling. Come in.

No real American mother and daughter ever conversed like that, of course. Such language derives from the pulpit or lecture platform, not from the family living room. Nowadays we think such dialogue is funny; but audiences of the 1840s definitely did not! *The Drunkard* enjoyed a tremendous success as a serious play about a terrible social problem. Indeed, it was the first play on the American stage ever to achieve a run of one hundred consecutive performances. That was at Barnum's Museum, New York City, in the summer and fall of 1850.

EXERCISE 6:1
Write a short scene, in realistic modern speach, based upon a present-day situation: mother recently widowed; daughter in her late teens; they are about to be turned out of their rented house or apartment.

EXERCISE 6:2
Use your imagination to continue the scene. Who would you choose to have knocking at the door? What will he or she have to say after entering? How will the mother and daughter respond?

Dialogue like that in *The Drunkard* was quite acceptable when it was written. But already, in the mid-nineteenth century, signs of change were noticeable. See, for example, Anna Cora Mowatt's enormously successful comedy *Fashion* (first produced in 1845). Mr. Tiffany, a rich New York merchant, is arguing with his wife.

TIFFANY
Your extravagance will ruin me, Mrs. Tiffany.

MRS. TIFFANY
And your stinginess will ruin me, Mr. Tiffany! It is totally and *toot a fate* impossible to convince you of the necessity of *keeping up appearances*. There is a certain display which every woman of fashion is forced to make!

TIFFANY
And pray who made *you* a woman of fashion?

MRS. TIFFANY
What a vulgar question! All women of fashion, Mr. Tiffany . . .

TIFFANY
In this land are *self-constituted*, like you, Madam—and *fashion* is the cloak for more sins than charity ever covered! It was for *fashion's* sake that you insisted upon my purchasing this expensive house—it was for *fashion's* sake that you ran me into debt at every exorbitant upholsterer's and extravagant furniture warehouse in the city . . .

MRS. TIFFANY

Mr. Tiffany, such vulgar remarks are only suitable to the countinghouse; in my drawing room you should . . .

TIFFANY

Vary my sentiments with my locality, as you change your *manners* with your dress!

MRS. TIFFANY

Mr. Tiffany, I desire that you will purchase Count d'Orsay's *Science of Etiquette,* and learn how to conduct yourself—especially before you appear at the grand ball which I shall give on Friday!

TIFFANY

Confound your balls, Madam; they make *footballs* of my money, while you dance away all that I am worth! A pretty time to give a ball when you know that I am on the very brink of bankruptcy!

This dialogue contains much of the vocabulary, structure and rhythm of real conversation.

EXERCISE 6:3
Analyze in detail the differences between *The Drunkard* and *Fashion* dialogue samples.

EXERCISE 6:4
Rewrite the *Fashion* episode in language that might be used by a present-day husband and wife in a similar situation.

EXERCISE 6:5
Write a scene depicting a dispute about money between yourself and some other person.

DIALOGUE DISTINGUISHED FROM CONVERSATION

Alexandre Dumas said that dialogue is "the backbone of drama."

You must learn to write good dialogue! Clumsy dialogue will make the best plot seem dull; with keen dialogue, even a flimsy plot can be made to sound interesting.

Dramatic dialogue is not ordinary speech: it is speech concentrated and directed.

Here is a passage of ordinary conversation overheard on a bus.

"Oh, Dorothy, there was something I simply must tell you. You'll die when hear this. I simply died when I heard it myself. I was talking to Kathie the other day, down in Leffler's Coffee Shop and Delicatessen. Oh, and that reminds me, next time I'm down near Leffler's I must drop into that new garden shop next door—what's it called?"

"The Garden of Eden Floral Supply."

"Yes, I must buy some of that stuff—I don't know what they call it, but I know it when I see it, in the plastic bag with the purple picture on it—for my new African violets. The last lot died on me again, you know. Judd's always on at me about my flowers, and the fuss I make over them. But then, Dorothy, you know you simply have to fuss over flowers, particularly with the water supply we're getting nowadays."

"You're one hundred percent right, Marie. I just don't know what it is, whether it's the copper water pipes, or whether it's that awful acid rain . . . but I never will believe that my philodendrons grow so well as the philodendrons we used to have back at home, where we got our water out of the well."

"Yes, I said to Judd the other day that I simply must have . . . Oh, look at that cute corner table in that store window; it's just like the one I was trying to tell you about yesterday, the one that Marie got for her living room. But what I was going to say, Dorothy—here's my stop, I must go— Judd doesn't want to spend the money, but I keep telling him that a greenhouse is the only thing, if you want to grow good flowers."

This, not in the least exaggerated, is the way that some people talk. You cannot use it in a play. It is not concentrated; it is cluttered up with irrelevant information. It is not directed; it is not getting anywhere, not making the plot progress.

Here is the other extreme of realistic dialogue.

"Dorothy, you know that . . . er . . . what I was talking about?"
"Uh-huh!"
"Well! You know what I said!"
"You mean . . .?"
"Yeah!"
"Is that right?"
"Sure is."
"You don't say!"
"I said so, didn't I?"
"Well! What d'you know about that?"

This, too, is unexaggerated. It is useless for the stage. It contains too little information. The speakers know what they are talking about, but the listener does not.

THE FUNCTIONS OF DIALOGUE

Every speech in a play should serve at least one of three functions:
1. Create atmosphere;

2. Reveal character;
3. Advance the plot.
Let's look at some examples of how this is done.

Create Atmosphere

The speech tells something about the social, economic or natural environment in which the action is taking place. For example, a present-day character in a big-city suburb might enter with the speech: "Terrible smashup on Number Three tonight. Truck loaded with some explosive stuff blew up at the Five-Way Corner. Ambulances and fire trucks all over!"

In William Vaughn Moody's *The Great Divide*, first produced in 1906, the scene is inside Philip Jordan's roughly-built cabin in southern Arizona. The time, a spring evening. Philip has to go on an emergency trip, leaving his sister temporarily alone on the ranch. He says: "Mind you put out the light early. It can be seen from the Goodwater trail. There's no telling what riffraff will be straggling back that way after the dance."

Here are a few lines from *Secret Service* (William Gillette). During the Civil War, Richmond, Virginia, as capital of the Confederacy, is being besieged by the Federal forces. The scene: a well-finished living room in the city. The characters on stage: Mrs. Varney and her sixteen-year-old son, Wilfred.

MRS. VARNEY

I'm thankful there's a lull in the cannonading. Do they know why it stopped?
(Boom of cannon—a low distant rumble.)

WILFRED

It hasn't stopped altogether—don't you hear?

MRS. VARNEY

Yes, but compared to what it was yesterday—you know it shook the house. Howard suffered dreadfully.

WILFRED

So did I, Mother!
(Low boom of cannon.)

EXERCISE 6:6
Write a passage of dialogue, using two or three people, that will create the atmosphere of the place where you live.

EXERCISE 6:7
Write a passage of dialogue, using two or three people, that will create the atmosphere of some other place of your choice, preferably some place notably different from Exercise 6:6

EXERCISE 6:8
Identify and analyze three passages of atmospheric dialogue from your Exemplary Dozen.

Reveal Character

A speech often reveals the character of the person speaking. Here is another excerpt from *Fashion*. The characters are the fashionably dressed Mrs. Tiffany, and her French lady's maid.

MRS. TIFFANY

Is everything in order, Millinette? Ah! Very elegant indeed! There is a certain *jenny-says-quoi* look about this furniture—an air of fashion and gentility perfectly bewitching. Is there not, Millinette?

MILLINETTE

Oh, *oui Madame!*

MRS. TIFFANY

But where is Miss Seraphina? It is twelve o'clock; our visitors will be pouring in, and she has not yet made her appearance. But I hear that nothing is more fashionable than to keep people waiting. None but vulgar persons pay any attention to punctuality. Is it not so, Millinette?

MILLINETTE

Quite *comme il faut.* Great personnes always do make little personnes wait, Madame.

MRS. TIFFANY

This mode of receiving visitors only upon one specified day of the week is a most convenient custom! It saves the trouble of keeping the house continually in order and of being always dressed. I flatter myself that *I* was the first to introduce it among the New York *ee-light.* You are quite sure that it is strictly a Parisian mode, Millinette?

MILLINETTE

Oh, *oui*, Madame; entirely *mode de Paris.*

MRS. TIFFANY

This girl is worth her weight in gold . . .

EXERCISE 6:9
Write 25-word descriptions of the characters in this scene.

The speaker reveals his character: (a) by what he says; (b) by the way he says it.

What does he know? What's his education? What are his interests? What are his prejudices? What part of the country, or of the world, does he come from? Is he self-confident or timid? Does he think before he speaks, or speak before he thinks? How does he feel towards the person he's talking to? How does he feel about other people in the play? Is he rich or poor, sick or healthy, religious or atheistic, optimistic or pessimistic, witty or somber? These, and umpteen other questions—every question that one would want to ask about character—can be resolved by careful construction of the speeches that you give to a character.

There are a couple of special points with regard to this character-revelation by speech: *dialects* and *slang*.

Dialect parts are less common than they used to be. Some grotesquely rendered ethnic dialect (Jewish, Black, Hispanic, Welsh, English, Irish) was once a sure-fire source of comedy. Nowadays this kind of humor is coming to be seen as cruel and insensitive.

If you do want to write dialect parts, here are a few points to remember:

1. In amateur drama groups there are not likely to be many experienced dialect speakers, so if you write a play that depends on dialect for success, you reduce your chances of getting it performed.

2. If you write dialect, be moderate. Don't try to express the full strength of a broad dialect with all its peculiarity of accent and its wealth of uncommon words. If an actor renders such broad speeches faithfully, he will be unintelligible to many people in the typical audience.

It is better to provide only a *suggestion* of the dialect: a moderate accent and a few dialect words. Look at the plays of Sean O'Casey for examples of successful dialect writing.

3. Be sure that you know the dialect you are writing. I read a play set in London, England; a Cockney character talks about eating "candy," and about a girl being "homely" in the American sense of being unhandsome. But the real Cockney eats "sweets" or "suckers," not candy. *Homely* on the Englishman's lips is complimentary; it means "capable of making a good home; sweet-tempered."

For a listener who does know a dialect, such errors weaken the credibility of the character who commits them. So unless you are sure you can write a dialect accurately, don't write it at all.

4. If your play is set in a foreign country, don't make the characters talk like foreigners. If we establish the convention that German or French or Roman characters speak English, then let it be correct, normal, unaccented English.

5. Some slang expressions, temporarily trendy, soon fall out of use. Such things serve well in short-lived works such as TV and movie scripts, and revues. Before long, however, they will be incomprehensible to a big part of the general public, and so will tend to shorten the life of a play. How to tell which words and expressions are going to die, and which will become permanent parts of the language? I know of no general rule; I can only say, be careful.

Another important point: speech by Character A can often be used to reveal something about Character B, maybe about several others, too. Returning to *Fashion:* Mrs. Tiffany, a little later in the same scene, is speaking to her daughter, Seraphina.

MRS. TIFFANY

How bewitchingly you look, my dear! Does Millinette say that that head-dress is strictly Parisian?

SERAPHINA

Oh, yes, Mamma, all the rage! They call it a *lady's tarpaulin*, and it is the exact pattern of one worn by the Princess Clementina at the last court ball.

MRS. TIFFANY

Now, Seraphina, my dear, don't be too particular in your attentions to gentlemen not eligible. There is Count Jolimaitre—decidedly the most eligible foreigner in town—and so refined—so much accustomed to associate with the first nobility in his own country that he can hardly tolerate the vulgarity of Americans in general. You may devote yourself to him. Mrs. Proudacre is dying to become acquainted with him. By the way, if she or her daughters should happen to drop in, be sure you don't introduce them to the Count. It is not the fashion in Paris to introduce—Millinette told me so.

EXERCISE 6:10
Write a mother-daughter scene similar to this, set in the present day. Snobbish mother is coaching daughter about how to treat various guests. A "Grade A" guest arrives; they talk to him for a while. Then bring on the "Grade C" guest or guests. Create a comic scene with these characters.

Preparing for Entrances

A very useful method of preparing for the entrance of a new character is to have others talk about him or her before he arrives. The audience is not aware of what you are doing; nevertheless, that preparation helps them to grasp the new character more easily, more accurately, when he or she does appear.

Try to be subtle with this technique. For example, it's a bit obvious to have a woman look at her watch and say, "I'm expecting that lazy, no-good worthless husband of mine home any second. One thing about him, he's punctual for meals." The clock strikes, the door opens, and in comes the husband.

Alternatively, have something like this, a couple of minutes earlier in the script.

GUEST:

What's Jack doing nowadays?

WIFE:

(Scornful snort) He's eating three square meals a day.

Then the wife diverts the conversation to something else; but the preparation has been made.

Local References

Beware of putting into a character's mouth words or expressions that have only a local significance, words that are meaningful to you, but would not be understood by people elsewhere. Here's an example. Suppose I am writing a modern comedy. One character says, "I wonder what's happened to Millicent. I haven't seen her in months."

Another character replies, "I hear she's on Davie Street nowadays."

That would likely get a laugh here, in my home town, because Davie Street is where a lot of prostitutes hang out. But it would be meaningless anywhere else.

You may notice some apparent exceptions to this rule in certain successful published plays. The New York market is so huge that a play written and produced there may have several local touches (social, political, geographical, etc.) and run for years. That's one reason why some such plays don't seem to do as well out of town as they did on Broadway.

CONFLICT IN DRAMATIC DIALOGUE

Dialogue means "talking across," that is "cross-talk," talking at cross-purposes. A character must not be allowed, for any length of time, to accept or agree with everything another character is saying: he must question or oppose it. This sustains a sparkle of conflict within the framework of the greater plot. Such lively dialogue will keep the audience alert and entertained.

Look at another example from Molière. In *Le Mèdecin Malgrè Lui* (The Doctor Despite Himself), Sganarelle, the pseudo-physician, has been brought to the home of Gèronte, a rich old man. Now, before Sganarelle comes on to begin his "treatments," the audience must be told the state of affairs in Sganarelle's household. A less-skilled playwright would use two gossiping servants, like this:

JEANETTE

It will take a skilled doctor indeed to cure our master's daughter.

JACQUELINE

Yes, and heaven knows that a cure is urgently needed. You remember that Miss Lucinda has lost her voice.

JEANETTE

Dumbness is a serious disease.

JACQUELINE

Yes, indeed! How can she get married while she's in this state? No man would have her.

JEANETTE

And, talking of men, what's happened to that nice young Mr. Leander who used to come visiting Miss Lucinda so often?

JACQUELINE

Mr. Leander? Oh, he'll never have the chance to marry Miss Lucinda. He got his marching orders.

JEANETTE

What for?

JACQUELINE

He has no fortune.

JEANETTE

Oh! One of that sort, eh? Hoping to live off his father-in-law!

JACQUELINE

Yes, that's what he would have to do. True, he has a rich uncle who's going to leave him well-off some day. But that doesn't pay his bills now.

JEANETTE

That's true. One must be practical.

This dialogue does contain all the necessary information; but the information is handled dully, with no conflict! Such dialogue flows uselessly, like water down a pipe. Good dialogue bounces to and fro, like the ball in a game of tennis.

See how Molière does it. He has Jacqueline, a nurse, talking to the master, Gèronte.

JACQUELINE

You can do what you like, but for all the good she'll get of these doctors, you might as well give her a drink of plain water. She doesn't need rhubarb and senna pods. With a young girl, there's one cure for all ailments—a husband.

GERONTE

How can she possibly get married, the state that she's in? Even before she fell sick, I talked of marrying her off, and she simply defied me.

JACQUELINE
Oh, yes! You wanted to give her to a man she didn't like. Why don't you take this Mr. Leander now? She's fond of him. You'll see, she'll obey you quickly enough then. And I bet that, if you'd let him have her, he'd take her as she is, voice or no voice.

GERONTE
Leander? This Leander is a nobody, a scrounger with no fortune.

JACQUELINE
But he has a rich uncle, who's going to leave him well-off some day.

GERONTE
Some day! Some day! All this talk about legacies is so much waste of breath. A bird in the hand is worth two in the bush.

JACQUELINE
Well, love before money, that's what I say.

GERONTE
A man's taking a great risk when he counts on the good will of a rich uncle.

JACQUELINE
Oh, fathers and mothers always ask the same blessed question. "What's he got?" "What's she got?"

GERONTE
We have to be practical. Death doesn't stand listening to the prayers of people who are waiting for legacies.

JACQUELINE
Well, you know Pierre down in the village, how he married his Simonette to that fat old Thomas, just because he had a quarter-acre of vineyard more than young Robin, that Simonette was in love with. And what happened? Why, the poor girl turned yellow as a lemon and she's never been a bit of good to her husband since. There's a lesson for you, Master.

GERONTE
Nonsense! Why, waiting for a rich uncle to die, a man can grow old and gray himself.

JACQUELINE
Well, you only live once, that's what I say.

GERONTE

Confound it, nurse! How you chatter on and on! For goodness' sake, keep quiet . . .

Study this dialogue. See how it contains a series of small conversational conflicts, and all the while, it is conveying necessary information to the audience, creating atmosphere, revealing character and advancing the plot.

Atmosphere: it emphasizes that, in this segment of society, marriages are arranged by parents, and husbands are chosen primarily for their wealth.

Character: it reveals the characters of the two participants, Jacqueline and Gèronte; it also gives some clues as to the character of the daughter, who has not yet appeared on stage.

Plot: it advances the plot by clarifying the emotional relationship between the daughter and Leander, and also by emphasizing Gèronte's objections to Leander. (The stronger the opposition, the more interesting the conflict!)

And, of course, this scene also prepares for the entrance of Leander, later on.

EXERCISE 6:11

Write a present-day scene between a father and some adult female adviser (not his wife), discussing rebellious behavior by his teenage daughter. Work for a sparkle of internal conflict in the dialogue; create atmosphere; reveal character; advance the plot; and prepare for the appearance of some other important character(s).

When you are writing dialogue, bear in mind the tennis analogy. Make each speaker repel or deflect the idea that the opponent has just shot at him or her; let one character stumble and miss the chance to reply; let a player (suppose it is a doubles game) spring forward and make the stroke that by rights should have been left to the partner; let a spectator distract a player at an important moment; let someone steal the ball, or suddenly raise the net, or shout "Fire!"

To sum up: enliven your dialogue with conflict, with the unexpected. You will keep your audience hanging on every line.

ONE SPEECH, ONE IDEA

A general rule is that each speech must convey only one idea. This is not a stylistic quibble; it is a practical necessity. Audiences cannot grasp complicated speeches. You must feed them information as a bird feeds its young, piece by piece, and you must allow time for the digestion of each piece.

Consider, for example, this short scene between a man and a woman.

FRED

So it's all off: is that it?

MARY-LOU

We can be friends.

FRED

I don't want to be friends. I want to marry you. It's your mother, I can tell, with her high-society ambitions. She thinks I'm just not good enough for you. But for heaven's sake, can't you make your own mind up once in a while?

An audience will not grasp Fred's second speech; it contains too many ideas. It should be broken up like this, into one-idea units.

FRED

So it's all off: is that it?

MARY-LOU

We can be friends.

FRED

I don't want to be friends. I want to marry you.

MARY-LOU

I've already said "No" to that.

FRED

But you didn't give me a reason.

MARY-LOU

I don't have to give out reasons for what I say or do.

FRED

You don't need to. It's your mother, I can tell.

MARY-LOU

Forget my mother!

FRED

I wish I could! But can *you* forget her, and her high-flying social ambitions?

MARY-LOU

Social ambitions? What d'you mean?

FRED

You know what I mean. She thinks I'm not good enough for you.

MARY-LOU

Mother never said any such thing.

FRED

Maybe not in so many words; but she put the idea across clearly enough.

MARY-LOU

Are you suggesting I should utterly ignore my mother's advice in every little thing?

FRED

Of course not. But for heaven's sake, can't you make up your own mind, once in a while?

Although "one speech, one idea" is the general rule, that does not mean that every speech must be short.

The one appropriate idea may be expressed in a single word: "Yes" or "No."

It may take four words: "We can be friends."

It may take two lines: "Are you suggesting I should utterly ignore my mother's advice in every little thing?"

It may take eighteen lines, as in the Duke's speech from *As You Like It*, Act II, Scene 1.

> Now, my co-mates and brothers in exile,
> Hath not old custom made this life more sweet
> Than that of painted pomp? Are not these woods
> More free from peril than the envious court?
> Here feel we but the penalty of Adam,
> The season's difference, as the icy fang
> And churlish chiding of the winter's wind,
> Which, when it bites and blows upon my body,
> Even till I shrink with cold, I smile and say,
> "This is no flattery: these are counsellors
> That feelingly persuade me what I am."
> Sweet are the uses of adversity,
> Which, like the toad, ugly and venomous,
> Wears yet a precious jewel in his head;
> And this our life, exempt from public haunt,
> Finds tongues in trees, books in the running brooks,
> Sermons in stones, and good in every thing.
> I would not change it.

You will find apparent exceptions to the rule. These occur because the same character makes two or more speeches in succession. These "multiple speeches" naturally occur in scenes where several characters are present. The speaker addresses two or more of them in succession.

Here is an example from *Hamlet*, Act V, Scene 2. Laertes has just died with the words, "Mine and my father's death come not upon thee, nor thine on me."

HAMLET

Heaven make thee free of it! I follow thee.
I am dead, Horatio. Wretched queen, adieu!
You that look pale and tremble at this chance,
That are but mutes or audience to this act,
Had I but time—as this fell sergeant, death,
Is strict in his arrest—O, I could tell you—
But let it be. Horatio, I am dead;
Thou livest; report me and my cause aright
To the unsatisfied.

Here are five speeches:
1. A reply to Laertes
2. To Horatio
3. Adieu to the queen
4. An unfinished comment to the bystanders
5. To Horatio again

each of which obeys the one-idea rule.

So, in applying the rule "one speech, one idea," we define "speech" as an uninterrupted address to one person or party.

Understood in this way, and consistently applied, the rule will help you to write clear, comprehensible dialogue.

THE THREE-TIMES RULE

Every important piece of new information must be given to the audience *three times*. If you neglect this three-times rule, some of the audience will not grasp the information.

I remember seeing a performance of C.H. Hazlewood's *Lady Audley's Secret*. In the first act, the wicked Lady Audley pushed young George Talboys down a well, to prevent him from exposing her as a bigamist.

A few minutes before the final curtain, Talboys unexpectedly walked on and in loud, clear tones explained how he had escaped death. But he explained it only once!

I did not understand it myself; I questioned other members of the audience and could not find a single person who had grasped it. I had to read the script to find out what had happened.

The three-times rule is constantly applied by public speakers; their art has much in common with the playwright's. The speaker's rule is: "Tell the audience what you're going to tell them; then tell them; then tell them what you've told them."

Don't be obvious in your use of the three-times rule: don't force the audience to see that you are repeating. For example, suppose that a ship has run aground in the fog. Four passengers, while waiting for rescue, are playing cards in a cabin. You want to inform the audience that the ship is going to sink. It would be absurd to have a character rush in and shout, "The ship is sinking! The ship is sinking! The ship is sinking!"

Yet, if the character just sticks his head in the door, shouts, "The ship is sinking" and withdraws, most of the audience won't understand what he said.

Here's one way you could proceed.

(ALEC *is dealing the cards when* BOB *hurries in*)	
BOB: Everybody get out! The ship is sinking.	This is the first time.
ALEC: Bob, you have an infantile sense of humor.	Opposition: makes the audience attend more closely to what Bob says.
BOB: It's no joke. I just heard the first officer say the tide's lifting her, any minute she'll slide off the reef into deep water.	This is the second time.
ALEC: *(Sarcastic)* How come *you're* the only one who knows about this . . . er . . . crisis, Bob?	
BOB: I tell you . . .	
(*He is interrupted by short, repeated blasts of the ship's whistle*)	
VOICE OFF: Abandon ship! Abandon ship!	For the third time, we use a sound effect and an offstage voice.

Here's another example, showing the wrong way and the right way of conveying information. It is the opening of a one-act play. A man is sitting alone in a business office, writing at the desk.

(Phone rings. He answers it.)

FRANK

Yes. Who? All right. Ask her to come in. And, Maureen, when my wife comes, ask her to wait there, please.

(*He puts down the phone.* PAULA *enters, obviously distraught.*)

PAULA

Frank . . .

FRANK

Close the door, Paula. I thought I told you not to come here. I'm expecting Laura. I've asked her to meet me for lunch. What do you want?

PAULA

I had to come. I've been out of my mind. I haven't seen you in two weeks. You haven't even phoned.

FRANK

I thought you understood: I have to be careful. I've got a position to think about, and two kids.

PAULA

And what about me? Do you think I'm having an easy time? You said. . .

FRANK

I know what I said . . . (etc.)

This opening is too rapid: it gives too much information too quickly. Frank's name is mentioned only once, and so is Paula's. (And, speaking of names, Paula, Laura, and Maureen are too much alike in sound and structure. It would be better to use three names radically different in sound and structure; e.g., *Paula, Claire* and *Dorothy*.)

Other faults of this piece of dialogue: important items of exposition are skipped over hurriedly—the furtive nature of the relationship, and the immediate reason for Paula's visit.

The one-speech-one-idea rule is repeatedly violated. Frank's second speech, for example, contains four separate ideas:
1. Close the door.
2. I told you not to come here.
3. I'm expecting Laura for lunch.
4. What does Paula want?

An audience simply cannot grasp all these ideas at once. In fact, very little of this opening would be understood by an audience.

This sort of "galloping dialogue" has yet another weakness: it carries you too rapidly through your available plot material; it produces an outline instead of a play. Bear in mind that you are supposed to play upon, to play with, your material, so as to give the audience a *prolonged* emotional experience.

Let's see how this material might be rewritten to avoid those defects.

(The phone rings. FRANK answers it.)

FRANK: Yes. Who? All right. Ask her to come in. And, Dorothy, when my wife comes, ask her to wait there, please. — First mention of wife.

(He puts down the phone. PAULA enters, obviously distraught, leaving the door open.)

PAULA: Frank . . . — First mention of Frank's name.

(He silences her with a gesture, hurries across and shuts the door.) — Gesture and action show the need for caution.

FRANK: For heaven's sake, Paula, be careful! — First mention of Paula's name. Second mention of the need for caution.

PAULA: I'm sorry, Frank.
(PAULA *goes to* FRANK. *They embrace briefly. He quickly breaks away and moves to put the desk between them*)
FRANK: Paula, I thought I'd told you not to come here.

Second mention of Frank's name. Indication that Frank is not responsive.

Second mention of Paula's name. Third mention of the need for caution.
Third mention of Frank's name.

PAULA: I know you did, Frank, but . . .
FRANK: And today of all days! I'm expecting Claire.

Second mention of wife.

PAULA: But Frank, I had to see you, just for ten minutes.
FRANK: I haven't even got five minutes. Claire will be here any time now. I'm taking her to lunch.
(FRANK *sits in his chair.* PAULA *sits on the arm of it.*)
PAULA: Darling, I know you're awfully busy, but . . .

Third mention of wife.

(FRANK *pushes her away and glances anxiously at the door.*)
FRANK: Paula! What's the matter with you? Sit down. Behave yourself!
(PAULA *grudgingly sits on the chair opposite* FRANK.)
PAULA: Is that better, dear?
FRANK: Yes. Now, what do you want?

Second demonstration of Frank's unresponsiveness.
Third mention of Paula's name.

PAULA: You know what I want.
FRANK: I don't know what you're talking about. I'm not a mind-reader.

Third demonstration of Frank's unresponsiveness.

PAULA: You know perfectly well what I'm talking about. I haven't seen you in over two weeks. You haven't even phoned, and . . .
FRANK: Paula, I thought you understood: I have to be careful.

First mention of the cause for Paula's visit: Frank's neglect of her.

PAULA: So you have to be careful! That doesn't mean you have to completely ignore me!
FRANK: *(Anxious)* Paula, for

Second mention of Frank's neglect.

goodness' sake, keep your voice down!

PAULA: All right, then; I'm keeping my voice down. I'm waiting to hear what you have to say. Why this two weeks' silence?

FRANK: Paula, you know I have . . . I . . . er . . . I have my position to think about, and then we've been having trouble with the kids.

PAULA: You've been having trouble! What about me? Do you think I've been having an easy time? You said . . . (etc.).

Third mention of Frank's neglect.

This is about four times as long as the original version. It gives the audience time to take in what is happening. It uses the three-times rule for important bits of information.

Notice particularly how actions are used to tell part of the story. Frank's hasty closing of the door tells a great deal. His dodging away from Paula, his pushing her away from him, are even more revealing than the lines being spoken. When dialogue and action work vigorously together, we convey information rapidly and unmistakably.

One last example of the three-times rule—from *Uncle Tom's Cabin*.

For his trouble in adapting this play from Harriet Beecher Stowe's novel (1851), George Aiken received $40 and a gold watch. The play became prodigiously successful: by the end of the century there were about 500 companies permanently playing it. Many actors spent their entire professional lives as "Tommers."

Here is an excerpt from ACT I, Scene 3. The set is a well-furnished dining room. Shelby has just agreed to sell Uncle Tom, and is now discussing the sale of other slaves to Haley. Eliza, a beautiful young slave girl, and Harry, her little son, make a brief appearance, then leave. The scene continues:

HALEY

By Jupiter! There's an article, now. You might make your fortune of that ar gal in New Orleans any day. I've seen a thousand in my day, paid down for gals not a bit handsomer.

SHELBY

I don't want to make my fortune on her. Another glass of wine. *(Fills the glasses)*

HALEY

(Drinks and smacks his lips) Capital wine—first chop! Come, how

will you trade about the gal? What shall I say for her? What'll you take?

SHELBY

Mr. Haley, she is not to be sold. My wife wouldn't part with her for her weight in gold.

HALEY

Ay, ay! Women always say such things, 'cause they hain't no sort of calculation. Just show 'em how many watches, feathers and trinkets one's weight in gold would buy, and that alters the case, I reckon.

SHELBY

I tell you, Haley, this must not be spoken of—I say no, and I mean no.

HALEY

Well, you'll let me have the boy, tho'; you must own that I have come down pretty handsomely for him.

SHELBY

What on earth can you want with the child?

HALEY

Why, I've a friend that's going into this yer branch of the business—wants to buy up handsome boys to raise for the market. Well, what do you say?

SHELBY

I'll think the matter over and talk with my wife.

HALEY

Oh, certainly, by all means; but I'm in a devil of a hurry, and shall want to know as soon as possible what I may depend on. *(Rises and puts on his overcoat, which hangs on a chair. Takes hat and whip)*

SHELBY

Well, call up this evening, between six and seven, and you shall have my answer.

HALEY

All right. Take care of yourself, old boy. *(Exit)*

SHELBY

If anybody had ever told me that I should sell Tom to those rascally traders, I should never have believed it. Now it must come for aught I see, and Eliza's child, too. So much for being in debt, heigho! The fellow sees his advantage and means to push it. *(Exit)*

Note how Haley's suggestion that Shelby sell Eliza is made *four times;* Shelby refuses *four times.*

Use the three-times rule with discretion; don't apply it to every trifling bit of information, or to any fact that is already known to the audience. Used for *important, new* facts, it will ensure that the audience understands the play. Without understanding there can be no emotional response.

Each line must be characteristic of the person who delivers it. Common offenses against this rule are *interchangeable lines* and *author intrusion.*

Suppose that the second and third acts of a play were printed with no character names on the speeches. With uncharacteristic dialogue, the reader would have trouble deducing who said what. The ideas, the way of expressing them, could have come equally well from Tom, Dick, Betty or Jean. These are interchangeable lines.

Avoid this weakness! Let each character's lines fit as well as his costume, be as distinctive as his features.

You may break the rule, of course, if you particularly want to portray characters who have little individuality. The party scene of *The Adding Machine,* for example, is full of interchangeable lines. But this is a special case. Elmer Rice is satirizing what he sees as the puppet-like uniformity of twentieth-century industrialized man: the product, rather than the master of his machinery. Understandably, on this thesis, each "puppet" will talk much like all the others.

Author intrusion occurs when you put into a character's lines opinions that he would not be likely to hold, or facts that he could not be expected to know. Such dialogue destroys the credibility of the character. This error is most likely to be committed by the playwright who is burning to preach a sermon or to teach a lesson.

EXERCISE 6:12
Imagine yourself paying a visit to me, in my apartment. There is the usual furniture: sofas, a big arm chair, bookcases, a desk cluttered with papers, a typewriter table and a four-drawer file cabinet in gray steel. The picture windows overlook a mile-wide harbor, with ships frequently coming and going; on the other side is a backdrop of snow-covered mountains.

Construct a dialogue between yourself and me. Conflict: you want me to collaborate with you in writing a play; I don't want to do it. Use the three-times rule where it is appropriate for important points. Make the lines strongly characteristic: you know yourself and, after reading this book, you know me pretty well.

EXERCISE 6:13
The same setting as 6:12. This time you and one other person

(let's call him or her "Friend") are visiting me.

You are trying to persuade me to write Friend's life story, which contains some unusual incidents (invent them). I'm not showing any interest.

Try this exercise two ways:

(a) Friend is extremely shy; so you have to keep on trying to make him or her speak up.

(b) Friend is self-confident and talkative.

Again, use the three-times rule where it's appropriate; and create the three characteristic styles of speech.

NAMES IN DIALOGUE

A name placed at the beginning of a speech tends to make a strong line. A name at the end tends to make a weak line.

"Henry, please pick up that book" is a stronger command than *"Please pick up that book, Henry."*

"Muriel, I think I should tell you how I feel about that subject" is strong.

"I think I should tell you how I feel about that subject, Muriel" is weaker.

One reason for the difference is that the name at the beginning says, in effect, "Muriel, you listen to what I'm going to say." The name at the end is, in effect, a plea: "Muriel, were you listening to what I said?"

Name placement, then, helps to indicate the relationship between characters in a play. The audience will not be conscious of the device. Yet this, like other technical devices (the three-times rule, for example) will produce its effect.

STRONG DIALOGUE AND WEAK DIALOGUE

There are two strong positions in a line of dialogue: the beginning and the end. Of these, the end is by far the stronger. This is another reason why a name at the end of a line usually weakens that line: the name drives the point or subject of the sentence farther away from the end.

"I'm afraid the case is past human skill. Prayer is our only resource now, John." This is a weakly constructed line. The point of the sentence—the important word, *Prayer*—is buried in the middle. It should be rewritten: "I am afraid the case is beyond human skill, John. Our only resource now is in prayer."

By placing the important word at the end, you create suspense within the line. A line that thus creates suspense and sustains it to the last word will obviously hold a listener's interest.

Look back at the *The Madwoman of Chaillot* excerpt in Chapter 4:

"And so I made my first thousand—passing a boxful of counterfeit notes." This is a strong sentence: *counterfeit notes* are the key words—at the end. Notice how it is weakened with those key words in the middle: "And so I made my first thousand with counterfeit notes—passing a box-ful."

Similarly, "A year later, I saw another such face" is strong. "I saw another such face a year later" would be weak.

> EXERCISE 6:14
> Revise Exercise 6:13 for improved placement of names, and for use of strong and weak sentences where appropriate.

Another example: "The boss gave me a bonus of two thousand dollars this quarter instead of the usual fifteen hundred. I hadn't asked for that increase."

That's a dull line. Compare this expression of the same material: "This quarter, without my asking for it, the boss increased my bonus: instead of the usual fifteen hundred dollars, he gave me two thousand."

Internal suspense makes dialogue interesting. You cannot create internal suspense in lines like "I don't know" or "What did you say?" but you can in any line that extends beyond a few words.

Work unremittingly on this point. Weak, dull dialogue can spoil a clever plot; but with strong, suspenseful dialogue, even a trifling plot can hold an audience's attention.

COMIC DIALOGUE

Placing the Punch

The point or punch of a comic line should be placed at the end, because if you want it to produce the strongest possible effect (a good laugh), you must put it in the strongest position.

For example, consider this weak arrangement of the old chestnut:

> JACK
> Who was that lady I saw you with last night?

> JIM
> That was my wife; that was no lady.

This probably would not get a laugh. *My wife* is the punch, and must be placed at the end: "That was no lady: that was my wife."

Another reason for placing the punch at the end is a practical one: if, despite its weak position at the beginning or in the middle of a line, the punch gets a laugh, that laugh will drown out the remainder of the line.

Many comic effects depend upon an abrupt reversal to obtain a laugh: a sudden switch from the sublime to the ridiculous, from the grandiose to the trifling.

For example, the hero of a play has been offered a bribe. He replies,

"Madam, do not try to bribe me! *(Pause)* What have you to offer?" This never fails to get a laugh. The audience sees *suddenly* that despite his show of incorruptibility, the hero has his price.

"Madam, name the amount of your bribe. But I warn you, I won't accept it!" is so weak that it probably would not even produce a smile.

Note the importance of the *sudden* illumination, the *sudden* understanding, in the raising of laughter. Laughter is an *explosive* release of feeling. The best way to detonate it is by a *sharp* stimulus. Since the laugh follows immediately on the stimulus, any necessary explanations must be given before the punch.

Chapter 3 contains a quotation from *The Importance of Being Earnest*. Lane, the butler, is discussing marriage. Suppose he said, "I have only been married once, so I have had very little experience of it myself up to the present." That would produce no laugh: the punch *married once* is smothered by the following explanation. The line as it stands in Wilde's script—"I have had very little experience of it myself up to the present. I have only been married once"—is a sure-fire laugh.

Another example of comic dialogue, from Molière's *The Doctor Despite Himself*: the hero, Sganarelle, disguised as a physician, is examining the daughter of Gèronte, a wealthy old landowner.

SGANARELLE

I tell you, sir, that your daughter is dumb.

GERONTE

Yes. But what I'd really like to know is, what's the cause?

SGANARELLE

That's obvious! The cause is that she's lost the power of speech.

GERONTE

Yes, yes, yes! But *how* does she happen to have lost the power of speech?

SGANARELLE

The best authorities would agree that it's due to immobility of the tongue.

GERONTE

But how do you account for this immobility of the tongue?

SGANARELLE

Aristotle, on this subject, says . . . some very interesting things.

Examine Sganarelle's lines here. See how the laughs depend on the placing of the point or punch at the end. Rewrite the lines with the punch at the beginning, and see how the comedy is destroyed. For example: "She has lost the power of speech: that's the cause, obviously."

Repetition

Repetition is a powerful means of heightening comic effects in dialogue. The last example shows how Molière picks up and repeats or echoes words and phrases from line to line.

SGANARELLE

I tell you, sir, that your daughter is dumb.

GERONTE

Yes. But what I'd really like to know is, what's *the cause?*

SGANARELLE

That's obvious! *The cause* is that she's *lost the power of speech.*

GERONTE

Yes, yes, yes! But *how* does she happen to have *lost the power of speech?*

SGANARELLE

The best authorities would agree that it's due to *immobility of the tongue.*

GERONTE

But how do you account for this *immobility of the tongue?*

The lines would be far less effective if they conveyed the same sense, but omitted the repetitions.

SGANARELLE

I tell you, sir, that your daughter is dumb.

GERONTE

I realize that, but what I really want to know is the cause.

SGANARELLE

That's plain enough. She has lost the power of speech.

GERONTE

How?

SGANARELLE

The best authorities would agree that it's due to immobility of the tongue.

GERONTE

How do you account for that?

Here is a before-and-after example from my own comic sketch, *A Favorable Balance*. The first draft: two old men are sitting on a park bench, arguing about foreign trade.

FRED

You mean to say, Harry, you don't understand the foreign trade situation?

HARRY

No, and don't want to, neither. Takes me all my time to keep up with the racing results.

The basic humorous idea is here: the descent from the grandiose (foreign trade situation) to the trivial (racing results), but in this form it will not get a laugh. We must make the second speech echo some part of the first.

FRED

You mean to say, Harry, that you've never *taken time to study* the foreign trade situation?

HARRY

No. It *takes* me all my *time to study* my racing form.

The laugh line, by the way, has been shortened from 18 words to 12, and for that reason, as well as for the echo, it is more likely to succeed.

EXERCISE 6:15
Write a five-minute comic scene between yourself and someone—say a customs officer, hotel desk clerk, cleaner, etc.—over the loss of some item of your property.

DIALOGUE FOR ACTORS

Bear in mind that your dialogue is written not only for readers and for audiences; it is written *for actors*. It must be understood by actors (how else can they perform it effectively?), memorized by actors, and spoken by actors. Indeed, in the amateur theatre, unless your dialogue pleases the actors, your plays will stand very little chance of being performed at all. Look at some of the qualities that make dialogue acceptable to actors:

Comprehensibility

While writing your play, you have thought deeply about your characters. You know them almost as well as you know your own friends and family. You know exactly what each character means when he speaks each line. For example, suppose you wrote:

MARIE

Dorothy, you know that . . . er . . . what I was talking about?

DOROTHY

Uh-huh!

You know whether "Uh-huh!" means "Yes" or "No." But on first reading, the actor may not understand which meaning is implied. A wrong interpretation given on the first reading may persist throughout rehearsals and performances.

"But," you protest, "surely the director will correct an obvious misinterpretation like that!"

The director may, or may not. He or she is no more a mind-reader than are the actors, and too may misunderstand, unless you take pains to clarify the meaning.

"You have my full sympathy" can be a consolation or a sneer, depending on the way it is spoken.

Write so clearly that the directors and actors cannot go wrong. This does not mean that you have to load your script with detailed technical instructions to the actors.

BETTY

Oh, Tom! *(Her eyes open wide, she clutches at her throat, her voice becomes hoarse with emotion.)* You don't mean it! *(She sinks slowly to the chair)* It can't be true!

TOM

(Harshly) I said it. *(He turns away from her)* I mean it. *(A grim smile curls his lips)* You should know by now that I'm not in the habit of telling lies.

All you need do is to indicate the *effect* you want the actor to convey; let him work out the means to produce it.

FRED

(Sarcastically) That's great news, my dear! Wonderful!

Normally, such indications are needed only if the manner of delivery is not what would be expected from the sense of the words, or if the meaning of a line, as it stands in print, is obscure.

It is difficult, at best, for the actor to interpret what is in the playwright's mind. So don't add unnecessary difficulties: make certain that the meaning of each line is as clear as possible.

EXERCISE 6:16
Look through your Exemplary Dozen for some lines that might
have been obscure; see in each case what the playwright did to
clarify the meaning.

Memorizability

Obviously, if it cannot be memorized, dialogue will never be performed. The more *easily* memorable the dialogue (other dramatic elements being equal) the better will be the performance. Actors who are struggling to recall difficult dialogue cannot give their best efforts to acting their parts. They may feel that they had scored a triumph simply by speaking it. Therefore, dialogue that springs easily to an actor's mind allows him or her to concentrate on acting.

One of the best arguments for verse plays is that verse (*real* verse, not chopped-up prose) is easier to memorize than prose. But good verse plays are difficult to write, and they are not popular with modern audiences. The art of speaking verse is nearly forgotten: most contemporary actors make verse sound exactly like prose, so the enormous labor of the study often comes to nothing in the theatre.

Still, apart from writing verse, there are other means of making dialogue easy to remember. Make it coherent. Not only must each speech be comprehensible in itself, but the speeches must all hang together.

The playwright Samuel Foote gave this memory test to Charles Macklin, the actor. "So she went into the garden to cut a cabbage leaf to make an apple pie, and at the same time a great she-bear came running up the street and popped its head into the shop. 'What, no soap?' So he died, and she— very imprudently—married the barber. And there were present the Picninnies, the Joblillies, and Garyulies and the Grand Pandjandrum himself, with the little red button a-top, and they all fell to playing the game of catch-as-catch-can till the gunpowder ran out at the heels of their boots."

It's difficult because it's incoherent.

In coherent dialogue the lines follow one another in some orderly way: the connections between them help the actors to remember. The beginning of one speech should follow naturally from the previous speech; its conclusion should lead smoothly into the following speech.

The links between speeches can take several forms: question and answer; assertion and contradiction; statement and comment. But, for the actors' sake, there should be some connection. Consider for example, this piece of disconnected dialogue (three people talking; living-room set):

MABEL

I bought a new hat today, Fred.

LUCILLE

I hear that Susan is engaged.

FRED

This wet weather certainly makes the grass grow.

MABEL

Now that I see my new curtains in place, I don't really like them, you know.

LUCILLE

Nice to see the lilacs so lovely this year.

FRED

Our new furnace is a lot less trouble than the old coalburner used to be.

Actors would have trouble memorizing and performing this sort of dialgoue, yet some playwrights have no compunction in inflicting it on them. Here is how the piece might be rewritten to give the actors a chance.

MABEL

I bought a new hat today, Fred.

LUCILLE

So did I. What a coincidence! And while I was in the hat store I ran into Susan. She's just got engaged!

FRED

Hats! Hats! That's all you women think about. You won't get the chance to wear them, if this wet weather keeps up.

LUCILLE

Look on the bright side, Fred. The lilacs are lovely this spring. And, Mabel, talking of lilacs, I think your new window curtains are simply lovely!

MABEL

Now that I see them in place, I'm not so sure whether I really like them, you know . . .

And so on. This is not brilliant dialogue, but at least actors could remember it. The lines lead one into another. Recalling such connected dialogue is like hauling a chain out of a well: you pull the end, and link after link comes automatically to the surface.

Avoid duplicate cues: two speeches delivered by Actor A to Actor B that end with the same cue words. For example, suppose that at one point in your play you have:

TOM

So, Dick, that's what I would do if I were you.

DICK

You really think that would work, Tom?
And later on comes:

TOM

So, Dick, that's what I would do if I were you.

DICK
I don't need your advice. Keep it for your kid brother!

Dick is likely to confuse the two cues. He may skip from the first cue to the second response, thereby leaving out the intervening material; or he may go back from the second cue to the first response, repeating a section of the play. I have seen it happen both ways.

Duplicate cues are a special pitfall in writing for characters who use stock phrases over and over again. Such repetition can be an effective device; but because of the duplicate-cue danger, you must use it carefully.

Ease of Speaking

Remember that actors have to speak their lines under emotional and physical difficulties. There is always a certain amount of nervous tension in performing in front of an audience. Playwrights should not add unnecessary difficulties. Don't write tongue-twisters: "She says she's sure she'll be shocked if she sees them so suddenly."

I once wrote: "You can run the agency single-handed for a week, can't you?" At the first rehearsal, the actor faltered twice over "Agency single-handed" and over "week can't." I heard him mutter, "That's a bad line." I changed it to, "You can run the agency alone for a week."

Keep "s" sounds to a minimum. Many actors fear them. You can often replace "if necessary" with "if need be," or "if you have to," and so on.

Don't write sentences so long that actors cannot say them in one breath. Don't use obscure words that the actors can't pronounce. (Perhaps the director can't pronounce them, either.)

Don't expect actors to make long, complicated speeches audible from offstage. In many theatres, offstage speech can be heard only if it is shouted. The actor feels like a fool shouting, "Darling, I love you. Will you marry me?" or "Hush, sweetheart! Father will hear you." To be safe with offstage speech:

1. Write only short, simple speeches for offstage delivery.
2. Write only such material as can credibly be delivered in a loud voice.
3. Take care to direct the attention of the audience to the quarter from which the offstage speech is to come. (See "The Attention of the Audience," Chapter 13.)

Have friends, preferably actors, read your dialogue aloud and comment frankly on its ease of delivery and effectiveness. They can teach you a great deal about this aspect of your craft. You can teach yourself a lot, too, if you form the habit of reading all your dialogue aloud, perhaps into a tape recorder, right from the rough draft, through the revisions.

WRITE *ALL* THE DIALOGUE

When bringing a character on, don't write some such direction as: "They all greet him." It is not the actors' responsibility to create such bits of dialogue. Even if they are willing to do it, they will probably not express in their improvised greetings all the shades of characterization that are desirable.

"Harry, my dear boy, it's so good to see you again."

"Harry, what on earth brings you back so soon?"

"Morning, Harry!"

"Harry, you old bum! How are you?"

"Hi, Harry! Long time no see."

"Harry, you old bastard! You have a nerve, coming back here."

"Harry! Talk of angels!"

Each such speech reveals the character of the speaker, and something of his relationship to Harry. You know what each character should say in any situation. So write all the dialogue that you want to have spoken.

Similarly, if a group of people are required to shout, you write lines for them to shout. Failing that, they will either invent their own lines, which may be inappropriate, or they will shout, "Rhubarb!"

Poor crowd drill may leave one character shouting "Rhubarb!" by himself: this will hardly create the desired effect. But if each character has an appropriate line to shout, there is little danger in straggling starts or finishes of the crowd noises.

Don't leave actors standing on stage too long with nothing to say. Most of them don't like it. An inexperienced actor may become embarrassed and unduly conscious of the audience; an unscrupulous actor may do something—scratch his head or his backside—to steal the audience's attention from the actors who do have lines. (I knew one actor who would open and close his fly!)

So, give each actor (apart from nonspeaking parts, spear-carriers and such) enough to say to keep him interested. When you have nothing more for him to say, get him off.

Write Good Exit Lines

When a character makes an important exit, give him or her a good exit line. By an important exit, we mean one that has some dramatic significance. When the butler goes out to answer the doorbell, it is not an important exit; nor would it usually be important when someone goes to the kitchen to fetch a pot of coffee. But suppose we know that the coffee a woman is going to fetch is poisoned, and will be used to murder a guest who remains on stage. That exit *is* important, and deserves a good exit line.

Likewise, it is an important exit when the hero leaves his cell to face the firing squad, or when the heroine, dressed in her second-best, leaves to meet the man who answered her lonely-hearts advertisement.

A good exit line should be something more than, "Well, I have to go now," or "So long, fellows."

The Ghost has a good exit line in *Hamlet,* Act I, Scene 5:

Fare thee well at once!

>The glow-worm shows the matin to be near
>And 'gins to pale his ineffectual fire:
>Adieu, adieu! Hamlet, remember me!

Another good exit line appears in Act I of *The Importance of Being Earnest.*

LADY BRACKNELL

Me, sir! What has it to do with me? You can hardly imagine that I and Lord Bracknell would dream of allowing our only daughter—a girl brought up with the utmost care—to marry into a cloakroom and form an alliance with a parcel. Good morning, Mr. Worthing!

Here are a couple of exit lines at the end of Act I, Scene 2 of my melodrama, *The Drunkard.* Edward, the young hero, has just been lured into a spell of drinking by Cribbs, the villain. Cribbs now invites Edward to dine with him.

EDWARD

I shall accept with pleasure, sir. Ha-ha-ha! Really, I feel most unusually cheerful. Ha-ha-ha! *(CRIBBS takes EDWARD's arm and ushers him out.)*

A few moments later Cribbs' assistant gathers up the bottle and glasses and leaves also.

STICKLER

Heh-heh-heh! Liquor licks love! I believe he's right. There's no flies on Mr. Cribbs. *(He goes out with the tray, still laughing.)*

Screams or laughter make good exit lines. A good exit line allows the actor who delivers it effectively to win a round of applause as he or she leaves the stage. Few things please actors more than getting this kind of individual recognition. They will bless the playwright who gives them the chance to do it.

Be Concise

Some writers, trying to make their stage dialogue sound realistic, pad the lines with the kind of hesitant, irrelevant material that people use in everyday life. For example:

FRED

Now, Harry, don't get me wrong. I'm not trying to stick my nose in—and if you tell me it's none of my business, I'll understand—but just exactly what's wrong between you and Pauline? After all, Pauline is my sister and—it's trite but true—blood is thicker than water.

HARRY

Well, Fred, it's like this. The fact is that Pauline and I just don't seem to see eye to eye about this question of Jo-Anne's engagement. I mean, that young Wilson boy that Jo-Anne's running around with, Pauline absolutely dotes on him; but me, why, I wouldn't want to have him for a son-in-law. No, sir! Not if he was the last man on earth.

FRED

Sure, I know what you mean, Harry. I went through just exactly the same thing; I mean with Nancy, three years ago. Just exactly the same thing.

HARRY

Is that right? Well, then, Fred, you can understand how I feel. I mean to say, any father would feel the same.

"Now," "well," "the fact is," "sure," "I mean": such verbal pauses are spoken often enough in real life at the beginning of sentences. They give the speaker time to collect and organize his thoughts. But there is no room for such excrescences in stage dialogue: they make the play drag.

Similarly, hesitations, detours, waste words and needless epithets must be cut out of the middle of sentences: "it's like this," "I mean," "just exactly," and so on. Stage dialogue, as a rule, should be crisp, hard-hitting and fast-moving. Consider how the previous passage might be improved:

FRED

Harry, I don't want to stick my nose in, but Pauline is my sister. What's wrong between you and her?

HARRY

It's about Jo-Anne. Pauline likes that Wilson boy that Jo-Anne's running around with. I hate him, the punk!

FRED

I had the same trouble with Nancy.

HARRY

Then you understand how I feel.

This says as much as the first rambling, padded draft, and says it more effectively.

You may be able to use, for comic effect, one character whose speech rambles. Yet that one must be handled carefully; don't let the speeches ramble too far, too often, or the character will turn into a bore.

EXERCISE 6:17

Write a three-scene. Character 1: yourself, in the role of a playwright. Characters 2 and 3: two members of a drama group that is considering performing a play of yours. They are calling on you to discuss some things in your script that they don't like.

They specify their objections (e.g., duplicate cues, lines hard to speak, etc.). You reply to each objection in turn, sometimes agreeing, sometimes declining to make changes. They eventually leave; give each one a good exit line.

SUMMARY

Beware of old-fashioned style in dialogue.

Dramatic dialogue: speech, concentrated and directed.

Stage dialogue has three functions:

1. Creates atmosphere: the environment in which the action takes place.

2. Reveals character: by what each one says, and the way he or she says it. (Be careful with dialects and slang.)

3. Advances the plot: keep moving ahead with a coherent story line.

Dialogue must be enlivened with internal conflict.

One speech, one idea.

For important information, use the three-times rule.

Avoid author-intrusion in style or in matters of fact.

A name at the beginning strengthens a line; a name at the end weakens it.

For a strong line, place the important words at the end.

As often as possible, create suspense within the line.

For best comic effect, place the punch at the end of the line.

Repetition of key words, from line to line, heightens comic effect.

Write dialogue that will aid and please your actors: dialogue should be comprehensible; dialogue should be easy to memorize. Dialogue should be coherent, one line leading naturally to the next, but avoid duplicate cues. Dialogue should be easy to speak.

Write every word that you want to have spoken.

Share the dialogue among all the characters on stage.

Write good exit lines.

Trim dialogue to be concise.

CHAPTER SEVEN

Characters ~III
Action

JOHN HOWARD PAYNE WROTE: "An actable play seems to derive its value from what is done more than from what is said."

Payne (1791-1852) was a famous American actor, playwright and composer. The song "Home Sweet Home" is from one of his operas.

By the remark quoted above he warns against the writing of what are sometimes called "talky" plays, in which characters stand or sit around talking, with little or no significant actions or "business" to do. Many actors dislike such talky plays—understandably, because actors like to *act*, not just talk!

A director will try to cover up the dullness of a talky scene by having the characters stand up and sit down, move upstage or downstage, left or right—anything to vary the picture that the audience sees. But such movements are not real "business," not really significant.

The test is to ask yourself: "Could the spectator follow this scene just as well with closed eyes?" or "Would this scene be comprehensible as part of a radio play?"

If the answer is "Yes," then it's a talky scene and, according to Payne, of inferior value.

Stage actions may be classified as follows:

Dramatic action
- a) To create atmosphere
- b) To create character
- c) To advance the plot

Technical action
- a) To form visually pleasing groups of characters; to provide variety and avoid monotony
- b) To clear the way for movements, entrances or exits
- c) To direct the attention of the audience to a particular part of the stage (e.g., to a character who is going to speak or perform a dramatic action, or to a door through which an important entrance is to be made).

Most details of the technical action can safely be left for the director to arrange in rehearsal. But you, in writing the play, must invent and specify the necessary dramatic action.

You must keep thinking of this all the time, right from the start of your writing. It's no use to write the dialogue of a play first, and then go through it to try to "put in some action." In the very first draft, you must try to combine the action and lines, in order to produce the desired emotional effect on the audience.

CREATE ATMOSPHERE

Study the opening action of *Macbeth*. The brief appearance of the witches, followed by the collapse of the wounded Sergeant, create an atmosphere of supernaturalism and bloodshed.

The locking the shutters in Act I of Shaw's *Arms and the Man* creates the atmosphere of a turbulent, dangerous environment.

The game of lotto in Act IV of Chekhov's *The Seagull* creates an atmosphere of triviality and futility.

Study the opening of *The Miracle Worker* (William Gibson). The action begins in the upstairs bedroom of a house; the characters are Captain Keller, his wife Kate, and the Doctor, who has just finished examining baby Helen. Costumes and furnishings help to set the period and social setting. Then Captain Keller picks up a lamp and leads the Doctor downstairs; this vividly creates the atmosphere of the period before household lighting by gas or electricity became common.

REVEAL CHARACTER

In *The Importance of Being Earnest*, Act I, Algernon reveals his selfish nature by eating the cucumber sandwiches that had been prepared for his guests. Lady Bracknell shows her stern, businesslike temperament by taking out a notebook to record biographical information about Jack, who has just proposed to her daughter.

Let's look at the opening of *Mary, Mary*, one of the most successful plays of this century. The characters we meet in this excerpt are:

BOB MCKELLAWAY, a young independent book publisher in his thirties;

TIFFANY RICHARDS, Bob's fiancée, in her thirties, independently wealthy;

OSCAR NELSON, fiftyish, a tax lawyer and friend of Bob's.

The setting is the living room of Bob's apartment in New York. There are the customary sofa, chairs, liquor cabinet, bookshelves, a fish tank, and so on, plus a cluttered desk, where Bob works when not at the office.

The time: the early 1960s; a Saturday morning in winter. *As the curtain rises, BOB is on the telephone. Several morning newspapers, open to the book page, are spread out in front of him. He dials a number.*

                              BOB
I want to speak to Mr. Howard Nieman.
(The doorbell rings once, perfunctorily)
Okay, I'll hold on.

                            TIFFANY
(Letting herself in at the front door. She carries a jar of wheat germ)
Bob!

                              BOB
Hi, honey.

                            TIFFANY
(Leaving the door ajar and coming into the room apprehensively)
I've read the reviews. How are you feeling?

                              BOB
I'm not exactly dancing with glee.

                            TIFFANY
Well, it's not fair!

                              BOB
(Rising, phone in hand)
Shhhh! This is Nieman. I'm waiting for him to get off the other line.

                            TIFFANY
(Coming to BOB at the desk)
But it isn't fair. You publish books of quality and distinction and you
should get the credit.

                              BOB
You're one hundred percent correct and beautiful besides.
(They kiss)(Into the phone) Hello, Howard! How are you?
(He sits, pulling newspapers toward him)
Yes, sure I read the notices. Well, Howard, we were both hoping for a
better break, but on the other hand there are a lot of good quotes here.
*(Running his finger down a page and having some difficulty finding
a decent quote)*
"A magician with words" and so forth.
*(TIFFANY hangs her coat on the railing, and quietly feeds wheat
germ to the fish)*
And with a book like yours we can hope for something more in the
weeklies. I'm confident we'll go into another printing. What did you
think about the notices? Sure, we all wish Orville Prescott would

write a novel. Look, Howard, please calm down. I hope you're not
going around talking this way. All you do is spead the bad word.
(Rises, fidgeting)
Let me give you some advice from Jake Cooper, in publicity. In his
coarse but memorable phrase, nobody knows you've got a boil on
your behind if you don't tell them.
(BOB listens a second longer, then shrugs and hangs up)

TIFFANY

What did he say?

BOB

He said the boil was not on his behind. *(Picks up a newspaper)* It was
on page 34 of the *New York Times*.

TIFFANY

Why shouldn't he be mad? It's a wonderful book!

BOB

That's what I like. Loyalty. *(Suddenly remembering, picking up a box
of candy)* I have a present for you and I forgot about it.

TIFFANY

A present?

BOB

It's Valentine's Day. *(Bringing her the box)* Did you forget?
To the sweet. Will you be my valentine? *(Kiss)*

TIFFANY

Sure, I'll be your valentine.
*(Pulls BOB down onto the sofa. He is kissing her as OSCAR appears
from the corridor with a briefcase)*

OSCAR

(Pushing the door wider) The door is open. Shall I come in?

BOB

Oh, Oscar—by all means. Tiffany. I want you to meet Oscar Nelson.
My old friend and my new tax lawyer.

TIFFANY

Hello.

BOB

And this is Tiffany Richards. We're getting married next month.

OSCAR

She'll be deductible. *(Comes down to shake hands with* TIFFANY*)*
Congratulations.
(BOB *closes the door)*

TIFFANY

Well, I'm very happy he's got you as a tax lawyer. Don't you think it's
just outrageous—the government investigating his back taxes just
like he was Frank Sinatra?

OSCAR

Under the law we're all equals.

See how action is used to reveal character here. Four actions reveal the
relationship of Bob and Tiffany:
1. She lets herself into the apartment with her own key.
2. She casually throws her coat over the railing. That shows that she is
just a visitor; if she lived full-time in the apartment, she would hang up her
coat properly.
3. They kiss.
4. Bob gives her a box of candy.

EXERCISE 7:1
Identify the actions that indicate Tiffany's character. (Apart
from those mentioned above, that show her relationship with
Bob.)

There is an important reason to have Tiffany leave the door ajar when
she enters: it allows the *surprise* entrance of Oscar, which interrupts the
cuddle on the couch.

Another playwright might have had Bob greet Tiffany right away. But
note how, in this script, Bob's transaction on the telephone *delays* the
greeting between the two lovers. The suspense makes the scene more interesting.

See how the three-times rule is used on "Valentine." The name of the
author on the other end of the phone conversation is given *four* times!

Bob's business as publisher is mentioned, directly and indirectly, at
least *five* times: Tiffany's "I've read the reviews" and "You publish books
. . .," Bob's "I read the notices . . .," " . . . we'll go into another printing
. . . " and "What did you think about the notices?" In addition, there are
his *actions* with the newspapers.

Study this opening minutely: it's a technical masterpiece. It uses four
types of exposition: by special occasion (publication of the new book, and
imposition of the tax investigation); by reunion (Bob and Tiffany); by introduction (Oscar to Tiffany); and by irritation (Bob with Nieman, and
Nieman with the critics).

EXERCISE 7:2
1. How does the opening tell the time of year?
2. How does it establish the location of the action?
3. Why is Tiffany given the action of feeding wheat germ to the fish?
4. Exactly how does the opening set the desired comic emotional tone of the play?

ADVANCE THE PLOT

Well-chosen actions emphasize the lines that accompany them, and unmistakably mark important stages of the plot.

In *King Lear*, Act I, Scene 1, when Lear surrenders his regal power to his sons-in-law, he *hands over the crown*.

In *Death of a Salesman* (Arthur Miller) Act II, when Willy Loman, the salesman, makes his last, desperate appeal to his boss, see how Miller uses action.

(. . . *Howard Wagner, thirty-six, wheels on a small typewriter table on which is a wire-recording machine and proceeds to plug it in. This is on the left forestage . . . . Howard is intent on threading the machine and only glances over his shoulder as Willy appears.*)

WILLY

Pst! Pst!

HOWARD

Hello, Willy, come in.

WILLY

Like to have a little talk with you, Howard.

HOWARD

Sorry to keep you waiting. I'll be with you in a minute.

WILLY

What's that, Howard?

HOWARD

Didn't you ever see one of these? Wire recorder.

WILLY

Oh. Can we talk a minute?

HOWARD

Records things. Just got delivery yesterday. Been driving me crazy, the most terrific machine I ever saw in my life. I was up all night with it.

WILLY

What do you do with it?

HOWARD

I bought it for dictation, but you can do anything with it. Listen to this. I had it home last night. Listen to what I picked up. The first one is my daughter. Get this. *(He flicks the switch and "Roll Out the Barrel" is heard being whistled)* Listen to that kid whistle.

WILLY

That is lifelike, isn't it?

HOWARD

Seven years old. Get that tone.

WILLY

Ts. Ts. Like to ask a little favor if you . . . . *(The whistling breaks off, and the voice of Howard's daughter is heard)*

HIS DAUGHTER

"Now you, Daddy."

HOWARD

She's crazy for me! *(Again the same song is whistled)* That's me! Ha! *(He winks)*

WILLY

You're very good!
(The whistling breaks off again. The machine runs silent for a moment)

HOWARD

Sh! Get this now, this is my son.

HIS SON

"The capital of Alabama is Montgomery; the capital of Arizona is Phoenix; the capital of Arkansas is Little Rock; the capital of California is Sacramento. . . ." *(and on, and on)*

HOWARD

(Holding up five fingers) Five years old, Willy!

WILLY

He'll make an announcer some day!

HIS SON

(continuing:) "The capital . . . ."

HOWARD
Get that—alphabetical order! *(The machine breaks off suddenly)*
Wait a minute. The maid kicked the plug out.

WILLY
It certainly is a—

HOWARD
Sh, for God's sake!

HIS SON
"It's nine o'clock, Bulova watch time. So I have to go to sleep."

WILLY
That really is—

HOWARD
Wait a minute! The next is my wife.
(They wait)

HOWARD'S VOICE
"Go on, say something." *(Pause)* "Well, you gonna talk?"

HIS WIFE
"I can't think of anything."

HOWARD'S VOICE
"Well, talk—it's turning."

HIS WIFE
(Shyly, beaten) "Hello" *(Silence)* "Oh, Howard, I can't talk into this
. . ."

HOWARD
(Snapping the machine off) That was my wife.

WILLY
That is a wonderful machine. Can we—

HOWARD
I tell you, Willy, I'm gonna take my camera, and my bandsaw and all
my hobbies, and out they go. This is the most fascinating relaxation I
ever found.

WILLY
I think I'll get one myself.

HOWARD

Sure, they're only a hundred and a half. You can't do without it. Supposing you wanna hear Jack Benny, see? But you can't be at home at that hour. So you tell the maid to turn the radio on when Jack Benny comes on, and this automatically goes on with the radio . . .

WILLY

And when you come home you . . .

HOWARD

You can come home twelve o'clock, one o'clock, any time you like, and you get yourself a Coke and sit yourself down, throw the switch, and there's Jack Benny's program in the middle of the night!

WILLY

I'm definitely going to get one. Because lots of time I'm on the road, and I think to myself, what I must be missing on the radio!

HOWARD

Don't you have a radio in the car?

WILLY

Well, yeah, but who ever thinks of turning it on?

HOWARD

Say, aren't you supposed to be in Boston?

WILLY

That's what I want to talk to you about, Howard. You got a minute? *(He draws a chair in from the wing)*

HOWARD

What happened? What're you doing here?

WILLY

Well . . .

HOWARD

You didn't crack up again, did you?

WILLY

Oh, no. No . . .

HOWARD

Geez, you had me worried there for a minute. What's the trouble?

WILLY

Well, tell you the truth, Howard. I've come to the decision that I'd
rather not travel any more.

HOWARD

Not travel? Well, what'll you do?

WILLY

Remember, Christmas time, when you had the party here. You said
you'd try to think of some spot for me here in town.

HOWARD

With us?

WILLY

Well, sure.

HOWARD

Oh, yeah, yeah. I remember. Well, I couldn't think of anything for
you, Willy.

WILLY

I tell ya, Howard. The kids are all grown up, y'know. I don't need
much anymore. If I could take home—well, sixty-five dollars a week,
I could swing it.

HOWARD

Yeah, but Willy, see I—

WILLY

I tell ya why, Howard. Speaking frankly and between the two of us,
y'know—I'm just a little tired.

HOWARD

Oh, I could understand that, Willy. But you're a road man, Willy, and
we do a road business. We've only got a half-dozen salesmen on the
floor here.

WILLY

God knows, Howard, I never asked a favor of any man. But I was with
the firm when your father used to carry you in here in his arms.

HOWARD

I know that, Willy, but—

WILLY

Your father came to me the day you were born and asked me what I
thought of the name of Howard, may he rest in peace.

HOWARD

I appreciate that, Willy, but there just is no spot here for you. If I had a spot I'd slam you right in, but I just don't have a single solitary spot. *(He looks for his lighter. Willy has picked it up and given it to him. Pause)*

WILLY

(With increasing anger) Howard, all I need to set my table is fifty dollars a week.

HOWARD

But where am I going to put you, kid?

WILLY

Look, it isn't a question of whether I can sell merchandise, is it?

HOWARD

No, but it's a business, kid, and everybody's gotta pull his own weight.

WILLY

(Desperately) Just let me tell you a story, Howard —

HOWARD

'Cause you gotta admit, business is business.

WILLY

(Angrily) Business is definitely business, but just listen for a minute. You don't understand this. When I was a boy—eighteen, nineteen—I was already on the road. And there was a question in my mind as to whether selling had a future for me. Because in those days I had a yearning to go to Alaska. See, there were three gold strikes in one month in Alaska, and I felt like going out. Just for the ride, you might say.

HOWARD

(Barely interested) Don't say.

WILLY

Oh, yeah, my father lived many years in Alaska. He was an adventurous man. We've got quite a little streak of self-reliance in our family. I thought I'd go out with my older brother and try to locate him, and maybe settle in the North with the old man. And I was almost decided to go, when I met a salesman in the Parker House. His name was Dave Singleman. And he was eighty-four years old, and he'd drummed merchandise in thirty-one states. And old Dave, he'd go up to his room, y'understand, put on his green velvet slippers—I'll never forget—and pick up his phone and call the buyers, and without ever leaving his room, at the age of eighty-four, he made his living. And when I saw that, I realized that selling was the greatest career a man could want. 'Cause what could be more satisfying than to be able to go, at the age of eighty-four, into twenty or thirty different cities, and pick up a phone, and be remembered and loved and helped by so many different people? Do you know? When he died—and by the way he died the death of a salesman, in his green velvet slippers in the smoker of the NEW YORK, NEW HAVEN and HARTFORD, going into Boston—when he died, hundreds of salesmen and buyers were at his funeral. Things were sad on a lotta trains for months after that. *(He stands up. Howard has not looked at him)* In those days there was personality in it, Howard. There was respect, and comradeship, and gratitude in it. Today, it's all cut and dried, and there's no chance for bringing friendship to bear—or personality. You see what I mean? They don't know me any more.

HOWARD
(Moving away, to the right) That's just the thing, Willy.

WILLY
If I had forty dollars a week—that's all I'd need. Forty dollars, Howard.

HOWARD
Kid, I can't take blood from a stone, I—

WILLY
(Desperation is on him now) Howard, the year Al Smith was nominated, your father came to me and—

HOWARD
(Starting to go off) I've got to see some people, kid.

WILLY
(Stopping him) I'm talking about your father! There were promises made across this desk! You mustn't tell me you've got people to see—I put thirty-four years into this firm, Howard, and now I can't pay my insurance! You can't eat the orange and throw the peel away—a man is not a piece of fruit. *(After a pause)* Now pay attention. Your father—in 1928 I had a big year. I averaged a hundred and seventy dollars a week in commissions.

HOWARD
(Impatiently) Now, Willy, you never averaged—

WILLY
(Banging his hand on the desk) I averaged a hundred and seventy

dollars a week in the year of 1928! And your father came to me—or rather, I was in the office here—it was right over this desk—and he put his hand on my shoulder—

HOWARD
(Getting up) You'll have to excuse me, Willy, I gotta see some people. Pull yourself together. *(Going out)* I'll be back in a little while.
(On Howard's exit, the light on his chair grows very bright and strange)

WILLY
Pull myself together! What the hell did I say to him? My God, I was yelling at him! How could I! *(Willy breaks off, staring at the light, which occupies the chair, animating it. He approaches this chair, standing across the desk from it.)* Frank, Frank, don't you remember what you told me that time? How you put your hand on my shoulder, and Frank . . . . *(He leans on the desk and as he speaks the dead man's name he accidentally switches on the recorder, and instantly)*

HOWARD'S SON
"of New York is Albany; the capital of Ohio is Cincinnati; the capital of Rhode Island is . . . ." *(The recitation continues)*

WILLY
(Leaping away with fright, shouting) Ha! Howard! Howard! Howard!

HOWARD
(Rushing in) What happened?

WILLY
(Pointing at the machine, which continues, nasally, childishly, with the capital cities) Shut it off! Shut it off!

HOWARD
(Pulling the plug out) Look, Willy . . . .

WILLY
(Pressing his hands to his eyes) I gotta get myself some coffee. I'll get some coffee . . .
(Willy starts to walk out. Howard stops him.)

HOWARD
(Rolling up the cord) Willy, look . . .

WILLY
I'll go to Boston.

HOWARD

Willy, you can't go to Boston for us.

WILLY

Why can't I go?

HOWARD

I don't want you to represent us. I've been meaning to tell you for a long time now.

WILLY

Howard, are you firing me?

HOWARD

I think you need a good long rest, Willy.

WILLY

Howard—

HOWARD

And when you feel better, come back, and we'll see if we can work something out.

WILLY

But I gotta earn money, Howard, I'm in no position to—

HOWARD

Where are your sons? Why don't your sons give you a hand?

WILLY

They're working on a very big deal.

HOWARD

This is no time for false pride, Willy. You go to your sons and you tell them that you're tired. You've got two great boys, haven't you?

WILLY

Oh, no question, no question, but in the meantime . . . .

HOWARD

Then that's that, heh?

WILLY

All right, I'll go to Boston tomorrow.

HOWARD

No, no.

WILLY

I can't throw myself on my sons. I'm not a cripple!

HOWARD

Look, kid, I'm busy this morning.

WILLY

(Grasping Howard's arm) Howard, you've got to let me go to Boston!

HOWARD

(Hard, keeping himself under control) I've got a line of people to see this morning. Sit down, take five minutes, and pull yourself together, and then go home, will ya? I need the office, Willy. *(He starts to go, turns, remembering the recorder, starts to push off the table holding the recorder.)* Oh, yeah. Whenever you can this week, stop by and drop off the samples. You'll feel better, Willy, and then come back and we'll talk. Pull yourself together, kid, there's people outside. *(Howard exits, pushing the table off left. Willy stares into space, exhausted . . . .)*

Notice how the boss keeps turning away from Willy, in the first part of the scene, to play with his newly bought wire recorder. That action heightens the tension and strengthens the conflict of this climactic scene; it presages the boss' refusal to accept Willy's plea.

The little action where Willy jumps to pick up the boss' lighter and hand it to him vividly symbolizes the master-servant relationship.

The action note on p. 142 *(Howard has not looked at him)* emphasizes Howard's lack of response.

At the top of this page, Willy grabs Howard's arm, hoping that if he can get in just a few more words, he may make his point.

Particularly interesting is the incident on p. 143—the moment where Willy's past intrudes on the present, and he speaks a few words to his old boss, Howard's father: "Frank, Frank, don't you remember what you told me that time? How you put your hand on my shoulder, and Frank . . . . "

To bring him once more into the present, the playwright might have given him a line such as . . . "Ah, I guess there's not much use dwelling on the past" or "Oh, well, bygones are bygones! The practical man has to live in the present." But Miller gives him an *action* that snaps Willy into the present again: switching on the recorder, the machine that so strongly symbolizes Howard, Howard's family, and Howard's refusal of Willy's appeal!

Dialogue

Consider a few technical points about the dialogue of this excerpt. Here is the situation, as the audience knows it from the earlier action of the play. Willy Loman, the salesman of the title, is approaching the end of his career. His health is cracking up, his sales ability is failing, and his circle of business friends and contacts is disintegrating. Willy, in fact, is in a desperate financial situation; but he has been telling his wife that now he will persuade the boss to give him a soft job at headquarters, with no more travelling.

Conflict

Notice the continual sparkle of conflict from start to finish. Willy does begin a few non-conflicting remarks about the recorder and its performance: "It certainly is a . . . ." "That really is a . . . ," but Howard doesn't let him finish them. When Willy says he's going to get a recorder, Howard immediately challenges: "Don't you have a radio in the car?"

Willy's long speech contains bitter internal conflict. He has told how wonderful selling used to be, but "Today it's all cut and dried and there's no chance for bringing friendship to bear—or personality."

Next, Willy's remark, " . . . They don't know me any more." This is the only thing that Howard agrees with!

Howard challenges Willy's claims of the big average sales he used to make.

Eventually, Willy cries: "Howard, are you firing me?" *Even then*, Howard doesn't say "Yes."

One Speech, One Idea

This is consistently carried through. Even Willy's long speech carries one idea: "Selling's not the business it used to be."

The Three-Times Rule

See the main point of the scene, Howard's refusal to give Willy the non-travelling job in town.

"Well, I couldn't think of anything for you, Willy."

" . . . you're a road man, and we do a road business."

"There just is no spot for you . . . "

" . . . I just don't have a single, solitary spot."

"But where am I going to put you, kid?"

"Kid, I can't take blood from a stone."

"I don't want you to represent us."

The idea is put across *seven* times, in seven different ways!

Strong Dialogue

Just as one example, note the growing strength of Willy's appeals for a salary.

The first time: "I tell ya, Howard. The kids are all grown up, y'know. I don't need much any more. If I could take home—well, sixty-five dollars a week, I could swing it."

The proposed wage is near, but not at the end of the speech. The following " . . . I could swing it" makes the request sound somewhat casual.

The second time: "Howard, all I need to set my table is fifty dollars a week." The wage proposal comes right at the end, therefore is strong.

The third appeal (and, of course, this is also an example of the three-times rule): "If I had forty dollars a week—that's all I'd need. Forty dollars, Howard."

The amount is stated *twice*, at beginning and end of the speech: the strongest appeal.

Atmosphere

The action with the wire recorder was contemporary when written. Now it serves to establish the period of the play—a time when the wire recorder was a rare, expensive novelty, before tape recorders were generally available.

Bear this point in mind: "Exactly *when* is my action supposed to be taking place?" Seek vivid means of conveying that information to the audience.

> EXERCISE 7:3
> Look through your Exemplary Dozen to find three examples each of actions that:
> Create atmosphere;
> Reveal character;
> Advance the plot.

> EXERCISE 7:4
> Review three of the exercises you did for Chapter 6. See where you can add actions to clarify or enrich the scenes.

SILENT OPENINGS

A common and useful device is to begin the play, not with dialogue, but with significant action. *The Importance of Being Earnest* opens with action: Lane setting the table for afternoon tea. Chekhov's *Uncle Vanya* opens with action: Marina knitting a stocking and Astoff pacing up and down the garden.

Mary, Mary opens with Bob's arranging his papers and dialing the telephone. (Here, of course, the time taken by dialing is not excessive.)

Death of a Salesman opens with Willy Loman's silent, nocturnal entry to his own home. Linda, his wife, hears him, gets out of bed, puts on a dressing-gown, and listens to him moving around.

A silent opening leads the spectators gradually into the imaginary world of the play. It gives them time to get used to the visual part of the production before they are required to attend to dialogue as well.

> EXERCISE 7:5
> You are constantly judging situations and people by the actions you see performed. For example, you go into an office where the

employees are scurrying about in a seemingly disorganized way, desks are all untidy, and there is constant noise. You see an adult constantly chewing bubblegum and popping it.

Over the next few days, collect by personal observation half a dozen examples of action that serve to:

Create atmosphere,

Reveal character.

Indicate something of what is happening or about to happen, in that situation.

SUMMARY

Don't write "talky" plays: all dialogue and no significant action.

Dramatic action serves (a) to create atmosphere; (b) to reveal character; (c) to advance the plot.

Play and write dramatic action into the very first draft.

Actions emphasize the lines that accompany them.

Silent action, with no dialogue, can be effective for opening an act or scene.

CHAPTER EIGHT

Complications

THROUGH EXPOSITORY dialogue and action you inform your audience about the characters of your play, and about the conflict they are involved with. Yet this is only the first step. You want to heighten and sustain the interest of the audience. You do that by creating suspense—keeping the audience in doubt as to the outcome of the conflict. For that purpose you invent complications, the "delays" that Goethe spoke of in connection with Molière. The basis of every complication is a reversal.

REVERSALS

Imagine a wrestling match, a simple man-against-man conflict, the Good Guy against the Bad Guy. If from the start the Good Guy is obviously stronger and more skillful than the Bad Guy, if he consistently dominates the contest, and rapidly wins in two straight falls, the spectators will lose interest and feel disappointed.

But that's not what happens. First the Bad Guy is on top; then the Good Guy throws him off and gets on top in his turn. That's a reversal. Then the Bad Guy gets on top again: another reversal. The Good Guy seems to have overpowered his opponent; then the referee hauls him off for some imaginary infraction of the rules and lets the Bad Guy get on his feet again. Obviously, the referee favors the Bad Guy: another complication! So the match goes on. As long as the contestants can keep up a varied series of reversals, the outcome will remain in doubt. The spectators will enjoy the sensation of suspense, and their interest will be sustained.

So fascinating is the simple drama (Good Guy versus Bad Guy with complications) that wrestling fans will gladly see it performed several times in one evening by different actors, and will faithfully return, year after year, to watch it over and over again.

A reversal is an abrupt change in the course of events. In *Hamlet*, Act I, Scene 1, Horatio insists that the Ghost doesn't exist, that it was only imagined by Marcellus and Bernardo. Then the Ghost appears, and Horatio is convinced of its existence: a reversal. Horatio commands it to speak, and it vanishes in silence: another reversal.

In Act I, Scene 2, the King and Queen attempt, and seem to achieve, a reconciliation with Hamlet. But as soon as Hamlet is left alone, he reviles them: a reversal.

In Act II, Scene 3, Hamlet finds the King alone, kneeling in prayer. He draws a sword and prepares to kill him:

> Now might I do it pat, now he is praying;
> And now I'll do't. And so he goes to heaven;
> And so am I revenged . . . .

Then he changes his mind, sheathes the sword, and decides to kill the King another time:

> When he is drunk asleep, or in his rage
> Or in the incestuous pleasure of his bed:
> At gaming, swearing, or about some act
> That has no relish of salvation in't. . . .

This is another reversal. (By the way, sheathing of the sword is a good example of an action that advances the plot.)

Willy Loman, expecting to secure the soft job at headquarters, finds that Howard won't let him have it: a reversal. It makes audiences wonder: "What can Willy do now?"

Well-contrived, credible complications, then, will create and heighten suspense by keeping the outcome of the conflict in doubt. As long as you can maintain suspense, you can hold the interest of the audience.

CREATING COMPLICATIONS

Some beginning playwrights find it difficult to develop a sequence of complications that will lead from the initial idea forward to the middle and end of the story. Here is a simple, but successful, technique that will provide enough complications to develop any situation to any desired length. It is the technique of "supposing."

Consider this example. Jackson is told by an old, trusted friend, Swartz, that his (Jackson's) wife, Irene, is in love with Swartz's brother, Fred, and that she has had many secret meetings with him. Here are the characters.

JACKSON, the husband
IRENE, his wife
SWARTZ, his friend
FRED, Swartz's brother, Irene's alleged lover.

Here's how to use the "supposing" technique to develop the situation. Begin with just one aspect of the situation—the possible truth or falsity of Swartz's story.

1. *Supposing* Swartz's story is true, then one of the following developments may occur:
   (a) Jackson refuses to believe the story (although it is true).
   (b) Jackson believes the story but, to save face, will not admit to Swartz that he believes.

(c) Jackson believes and admits that he believes.

(d) Jackson suspends belief, and seeks more evidence.

Each of these possibilities can be developed by the same method.

1 (a) *Supposing* that the story is true, but Jackson refuses to believe it, then one of the following developments may occur:

(i) Jackson calls Swartz a liar and a mischief-maker, and breaks off their friendship.

(ii) Jackson goes home and tells his wife the "absurd" story he has just heard about her and Fred.

(iii) Jackson suspects that Swartz is trying to blame brother Fred in order to cover up his own (Swartz's) interest in Irene.

1 (b), (c) and (d) can be similarly developed. From supposition 1 alone, we could create a dozen different story lines in only two steps. An entirely different group of story lines will arise if we suppose that Swartz's story is untrue.

2. *Supposing* Swartz's story is untrue, then:

(a) Jackson accepts it as truth; he thanks Swartz for the warning, goes home and accuses his wife.

(b) Jackson refuses to accept it and quarrels with Swartz.

(c) Jackson pretends to believe it, in order to lead Swartz on and make him fully show his hand.

The system is simple: at each stage of story development, ask yourself, "Supposing such-and-such a thing happens, what would happen next?" Then write down all the answers you can think of.

EXERCISE 8:1

Suppose someone comes to you with some item of information that threatens to upset the established pattern of your life. Invent such a complication. Use the "supposing" method to find a half dozen ways that the action might continue.

But how do you select for your play one out of all the possible complications at each stage of plot development? Apply three tests.

1. Which complication is the most characteristic? You know the characters of your play. The course of action you choose at each stage will be the one that is most appropriate for the character concerned. For example, Jackson's reaction will depend upon whether he is generous, suspicious, credulous, skeptical, hot-tempered, placid, bold or timid. It will depend, too, on what Jackson knows of Swartz's character, and of Irene's character.

2. Which complication is most appropriate to the tone of the play? For example, in a tragedy you would choose weighty, serious complications; in a comedy, humorous or satirical ones; in a farce, ridiculous ones.

Suppose you need a complication to delay the arrival of a politician. In a tragedy, he might receive word that his only child is seriously ill, and spend time phoning for details. In a comedy, he might be delayed by the chatter of a pompous local dignitary. In a farce, while he was taking a bath at his hotel, you might have someone steal his clothes from the bedroom.

3. Which complication is dramatically most useful? As a rule, the most useful development at any stage is the one that provides the most effective reversal, the one that best maintains or heightens suspense. Howard's piece of business with the wire recorder is a complication, because it temporarily frustrates Willy Loman's attempts to request a job in town. Placed where it is, the complication maintains and heightens suspense. But if Miller had made Howard refuse Willy's request immediately, and *then* play with the recorder, that would have been weak; that would have diminished the suspense of the scene.

The complication you choose must also provide a means of continuing the play. Shakespeare could not have let Hamlet kill the King in Act III, Scene 3, because that would have ended the play. That would have been not a complication, but a conclusion.

Important! Don't sit with all the possible complications tumbling one over another in your head. *Write them all down.* Indeed, the best results will be obtained from this method by *writing down* the appropriate question at each stage (e.g., "Suppose Jackson goes to Fred's house and threatens to beat him up. What will happen then?").

Writing down the questions and answers has a triple advantage:

1. It forces you to *begin writing about the subject.* Most writers know how difficult it is to do that. Any trick that helps the process is welcome.
2. It ensures that any bright ideas you get on the subject *will not be lost.* What writer has not cursed him or herself for thinking of something good and then forgetting it because he failed to jot it down!
3. You often will find that it leads you on to write bits of dialogue and action that can later be incorporated into the script.

> EXERCISE 8:2
> Use the triple test (characteristic? appropriate? useful?) to choose one of the complications you created in Exercise 8:1. Write a short scene based on that complication.

Regular use of the supposing method and the complication-choice procedure will develop your imagination to the point where you can undertake without hesitation to write a play on any subject. You will not need to buy books of plots or mechanical plotting devices; you will develop all the plots you can use with a pencil and some scrap paper.

The number of complications you will need depends upon the type of play you are writing. A serious play should have relatively few complications, each developed in detail. The lighter tone of the play, the more rapid the arrival of complications can be, and the more superficial the development of each.

SURPRISE AND PLANTING

Complications are pleasing to the audience, not only because they maintain suspense, but because they are surprising. There are two stock surprise situations.

In the first, the audience knows what is going to happen, but some of the characters on stage are surprised. For example, Hamlet is surprised at the queen's death after she has drunk from the poisoned cup; Macbeth is surprised to receive the news that Birnam Wood is moving toward Dunsinane.

The ever-popular screen scene is another example of this type: the audience knows character A is hiding behind the screen. They relish the situation as B and C converse in front of the screen, and they enjoy the surprise of B and C when A pops out. Spectators enjoy possessing information of which some of the characters are ignorant. They also enjoy the feeling of suspense in wondering exactly when the surprise will be sprung.

There are few technical difficulties in writing such surprises. The audience is plainly informed in advance: the King tells Laertes about the poisoned cup; Malcolm orders the tree-branch camouflage for the soldiers; character A walks behind the screen. Then, at an effective moment, the surprise is triggered.

In the second type of surprise situation, the characters on stage and the audience are surprised together, as when in *Henry IV, Part II*, Act V, Scene 5, the new-crowned King rebukes Falstaff: "I know thee not, old man; fall to thy prayers."

This type of surprise is more difficult to write. The audience must not be allowed to foresee the event; yet, when it occurs, they must instantly accept it as credible. The effect of the surprise depends upon this *instant acceptance* by the audience. A "surprise" that has to be laboriously explained and justified afterward is useless for the stage.

If the audience withholds this acceptance, the effect of the surprise, and perhaps that of the whole scene, is lost. To guard against that danger, the audience must be prepared for the surprise. This process of preparation is called "planting."

Planting must be done skillfully: if it is overdone, the audience will be led to anticipate the event; if it is underdone, the audience will withhold acceptance of the surprise. Let's look at some examples of planting.

Surprise: *Hamlet*, Act III, Scene 4. Hamlet kills Polonius.

Planting: Act II, Scene 2: Hamlet, speaking to Polonius concerning the players, says, " . . . after your death you were better have a bad epitaph than their ill report while you live." This suggests the idea of Polonius' death.

Act III, Scene 2: Polonius, discussing his own acting experience, says, "I did enact Julius Caesar: I was killed i' the Capitol. Brutus killed me,"—another suggestion of his death.

Act III, later in Scene 2: Hamlet says,

> . . . . now could I drink hot blood
> And do such bitter business as the day
> Would quake to look on.

This shows Hamlet is in a bloodthirsty mood.

Act III, Scene 3; Hamlet is on the point of killing the King. This establishes the possibility of his killing someone at any moment. He is shown actually drawing the sword and preparing to strike.

Act III, Scene 4; Hamlet kills Polonius.

Life With Father (Howard Lindsay and Russel Crouse) portrays a conventionally Christian family in New York, in the late 1880s. Early in Act I, before Father's first appearance, Vinnie, his wife, hears thirteen-year-old Whitney say his catechism. In response to Whitney's questioning, Vinnie explains the crucial importance of baptism in the sight of the church. There's the plant!

At the end of Act I, Scene 2, Vinnie learns that Father was never baptized. Her reaction to this biographical tidbit is the surprise. She declares that Father cannot be a real Christian! He will certainly never, never be qualified to join her and the four boys in heaven! And maybe—oh, horrors!—their marriage is invalid, and the boys all bastards!

EXERCISE 8:3
Find three surprises in your Exemplary Dozen. For each one, identify the plants that the author arranged.

The steps for successful planting are:
1. Introduce the idea of what is to come, well in advance.
2. Supply, by appropriate hints, whichever of the following details are needed (not necessarily in this order, of course):
(a) The motive for the act.
(b) The opportunity to do the act.
(c) The means to do the act.
(d) The person by whom or to whom it is to be done.

Let's create an example. **Surprise:** Goldworthy, a trusted clerk, robs his employer's safe.

Planting: to make the robbery credible, we should place the following information in the script, before the moment of the robbery.
1. The *idea:* Goldworthy, the employer, or someone else in their hearing, talks about robbery, preferably about a robbery occurring somewhere else. (That makes the plant less obvious.)
2. (a) *Motive:* establish that Goldworthy needs money.
   (b) *Opportunity:* Goldworthy is left alone in the office.
   (c) *Means:* Goldworthy has the key or combination to the safe.
   (d) *Person:* establish that Goldworthy has tried other sources for money in vain. The employer is the only possible victim.

EXERCISE 8:4
Here is a surprise that could be used in a play. A married woman, with her children grown and off her hands, feels bored and useless. Her husband won't agree to her getting a part-time job. She suddenly announces that she has bought a dress-shop, and is leaving him the next day to go and live over the store.

Work out how this could be planted, and write the scene. Use whatever other characters you need.

EXERCISE 8:5
You have probably experienced some great surprise in your own life, one that you could scarcely believe at the time. ("No, this can't be happening to me!" "There must be some mistake!" etc.) Suppose that first-person surprise were to be used as a complication in a play. What planting would you provide in order to give it full credibility and instant acceptance by the audience?

A mastery of planting is essential for the playwright. Without it your plays will seem either obvious or incredible. Watch for it when reading scripts or seeing performances. (You also can see the technique used in movies and TV.)

PREPARING FOR ENTRANCES

The first appearance of each character is, in effect, the addition of a new complication. It may sometimes be a surprise, too. It is advisable, when possible, to prepare such entrances by having other characters mention the one who is to come on, and give the audience some information about him.

Study Ibsen's preparation for the first entrances of his characters in *Hedda Gabler*. In Act I the entrances of Tesman, Hedda and Thea are prepared immediately before they come on; preparation for Brack's entrance is spread over the first three-quarters of the act. Note the preliminary and the immediate preparations for Lövborg's entrance in Act II.

Look again at the *Ghosts* excerpt in Chapter 3.

ENGSTRAND
Lots of grand people'll be here—Pastor Manders is expected from town—

REGINA
He gets here today.

These and the five following speeches are advance preparation for the arrival of Manders.

A little later in the scene come the references to young Mr. Alving: preliminary preparation for his entry later on. Regina's *"Here comes Pastor*

Manders" is, of course, the *immediate* preparation for his arrival.

If a character enters without preparation, the audience does not know his name, occupation, temperament, or relationship to other characters. Without that knowledge, the audience may not fully understand what he says and does on stage. Often that information cannot be given credibly at the moment when the character enters. It is more convincing if given in advance, because people always talk more frankly and freely about others in their absence than in their presence.

An unprepared entrance may temporarily puzzle the audience; a well-prepared entrance immediately interests them.

COMPLEX TIME STRUCTURE

Simple time structure, which I've been writing about so far, uses a series of complications in natural, chronological order: the meeting, the courtship, the quarrel, the reconciliation, the engagement, the marriage, etc. Friday the 13th is depicted before Saturday the 14th; 2 p.m. comes before 3 p.m., and so on.

There may be lapses of time between scenes or acts, but every scene occurs some time *after* the scene that precedes it, and some time *before* the scene that follows it, in the script and on the stage.

But there is also complex time structure, which introduces complications *out of their chronological order.* Movies and TV have made audiences familiar with complex time structure by frequent use of the flashback. Flashbacks can be used on stage too. The major technical problem is to *make sure that the audience knows* when you are departing from, and returning to, the simple, chronological order of events.

There is the scene in the *Death of a Salesman* excerpt where Willy envisions his old boss, Howard's father, and speaks to him. Elsewhere in the play are several more detailed scenes in which Willy relives incidents from his past—incidents that help the audience understand the Willy Loman of the present. It's a worthwhile study to work right through this play, and try to assign a date to each of those glimpses of Willy's past.

Here's a flashback from a famous play, *The Miracle Worker.* The play is based on real-life events in the mid-1880s: the education of blind, deaf, mute Helen Keller, six-and-a-half years old. The teacher-to-be, Annie, is just about to leave the Perkins Institution in Boston, where she had been a pupil and a teacher. She is sitting alone, then . . .

(. . . . by a subtle change in the color of the light, we go with her thoughts into another time. We hear a boy's voice whispering; perhaps we see shadowy intimations of these speakers in the background.)

BOY'S VOICE

Where we goin', Annie?

ANNIE *(In dread)*

Jimmie.

BOY'S VOICE

Where we goin'?

ANNIE

I said—I'm takin' care of you—

BOY'S VOICE

Forever and ever?

MAN'S VOICE (Impersonal)

Annie Sullivan, aged nine, virtually blind. James Sullivan, aged seven—what's the matter with your leg, Sonny?

ANNIE

Forever and ever.

MAN'S VOICE

Can't he walk without that crutch? *(Annie shakes her head and does not stop shaking it.)* Girl goes to the women's ward. Boy to the men's.

BOY'S VOICE (In terror)

Annie! Annie, don't let them take me—Annie!

ANAGNOS (Offstage)

Annie! Annie?
(But this voice is real, in the present, and ANNIE *comes up, out of her horror, clearing her head with a final shake; the lights begin to pick out* KATE *in the* KELLER *house, as* ANNIE, *in a bright tone, calls back.)*

ANNIE

Coming!

This scene, obviously, is a powerful way of presenting the information. Much weaker would it be to have Annie say to someone in the present, "I was very much upset when my little brother and I were separated," or something like that.

SUMMARY

Interest, aroused by conflict, is sustained and heightened by suspense.

Complications create suspense.

Reversals create complications.

The reversal: an abrupt change in the course of events.

Develop complications by the "supposing" method.

Choose complications that are characteristic; choose complications of appropriate tone.

Choose complications that will most effectively sustain your play.

Write down complications as you think of them.

Complications often create surprises; surprises should be well prepared by "planting."

Prepare for the entrance of new characters.

Complex time structure (events out of their natural order) can sometimes be effective.

CHAPTER NINE

Crises

IN CHAPTER 3, I POINTED out that the playwright's basic unit is the French scene. Although French scenes are seldom, if ever, marked off and numbered in modern playscripts, you need to recognize them. The reason is that each French scene must be plotted *to build toward a crisis.*

The audience, of course, does not think about this structural feature. But if you let some of your French scenes slip by without crises, the the audience begins to feel that the play is just drifting, "not getting anywhere." Some of them begin to feel bored.

Re-examine the *Death Of A Salesman* scene in Chapter 7. Feel it from Willy Loman's point of view. He begins quietly, calmly; but his desperation keeps building to the point where he finally pounds his fist on the boss's desk: "I averaged a hundred and seventy dollars a week in the year of 1928! And your father came to me—or rather, I was in the office here—it was right over this desk, and he put his hand on my shoulder. . . ." Here was the very peak—real or imagined—of his success and influence in the firm.

In the following one-scene, he starts low, reproaching himself for shouting at the boss, but he rapidly builds up to an even more dramatic enactment of that scene of bygone glory. There is the crisis of the one-scene.

So every French scene has its crisis. Correct construction and placement of these crises will contribute much towards the total emotional impact of the play.

EXERCISE 9:1
Check the scene from your own life that you wrote for Exercise
3:4. Analyze the crisis. Is it the strongest part of the scene? See if
you can find some way to make it even stronger.

HOW MANY CRISES?

The average length of the French scenes (and the frequency and number of crises) depends on the type of play you are writing. As a general rule, the lighter the play, the shorter the French scenes will be and the more numerous the crises. In a farce the characters are likely to be rushing in and out all the time: crisis follows crisis at a rate limited only by the audience's power to grasp the new ideas and situations. In more serious plays, the French scenes tend to be longer—there is more information, and a weightier kind of information, to be conveyed to the audience—so the crises are fewer.

MAGNITUDE OF THE CRISES

Have you ever seen a magician at work? He does not reveal the full scope of his ability at once. He begins with a fairly simple effect, goes on to something a little more elaborate, and so builds by degrees to his last and most impressive illusion.

A playwright should arrange crises in the same way, building toward the last, which, according to the nature of the play, will be the most comic, the most dramatic, or the most tragic.

In a one-act play, the arrangement is simple: a steady growth from beginning to end. You are carrying the audience right along with you. But there's a problem with multi-act plays. The spectators, during the intermissions, have lost some of their emotional involvement with the play. You have to recapture their attention, and work up their feelings again. So you have to begin the second and third acts at an emotional level only a little above that in which you began the first.

But there is a great advantage: dividing a play into acts lets you use more crises at a high emotional level, and distribute them more evenly through the play than you could in a one-act play of the same length. The crises of Act I can range from 1 to 8, on an emotional-intensity scale of 10. The crises of Act II can range from 2 to 9; and those of Act III from 3 to 10.

> EXERCISE 9:2
> Analyze the crises from one of your Exemplary Dozen. Score each one on the 10-point scale of emotional intensity.

DURATION OF CRISES

Edgar Allan Poe wrote in "The Poetic Principle:" ". . . . all excitements are, through a psychical necessity, transient." What Poe said of poetry applies to plays. Beware of trying to sustain crises too long. There is a limit to the length of time that people can laugh at a comic crisis. If the limit is exceeded, laughter turns into tears. At the other end of the scale, people are unable to endure too much grief or pity. After a short time, they seek relief in the opposite emotion, mirth.

So keep your crises fairly short; between them put material of lesser emotional intensity.

CONSTRUCTION OF CRISES

It is not a bad idea, when planning a play, to construct your last crisis first, and work backward from it. You can then make sure that the last crisis is the strongest; you can avoid the serious weakness of rising to a peak too soon and trailing off toward anticlimax at the end. Playwrights often fail to take this precaution. That is the reason for the stock question, "How's your third act?" The commonest cause of a weak third act is a crisis at the end of Act II so strong that nothing within the limits of the story line can overtop it.

How can you construct the last, strongest crisis of the play? Simply set the main character and the opposition in the most vigorous conflict possible (consistent with the style and tone of the play) for the highest stakes possible.

At the final crisis of *Hamlet*, the main character is physically fighting Laertes, the King's proxy swordsman. This is the most vigorous conflict possible in the framework of the play. Hamlet is fighting for his life—the foil and wine are poisoned—the highest stake possible.

In the final crisis of *Ghosts*, Oswald reveals the nature of his congenital disease and tell his mother that, when the next attack comes, she must kill him. Here is the strongest possible conflict of man against nature in the form of heredity.

In the final crisis of *Arms and the Man*, Bluntschli makes a definite proposal of marriage to Raina. In a romantic comedy like this, the heroine's hand is commonly the highest possible stake.

To construct the earlier crises, proceed by graduated steps from the initial conflict, building toward the final crisis of each act. Study well-written plays to see how the author has built and arranged his crises. Here, for example, are the concluding crises of Acts I through IV of *Hamlet*.

Act I: Hamlet swears to avenge his father's death.
Act II: Hamlet curses himself for not having carried out his oath.
Act III: Hamlet reproaches his mother, the Queen.
Act IV: The King and Laertes plot Hamlet's death.

Take pains over your crises. Playgoing is primarily an emotional experience for spectators, and the crises are the most intense parts of that experience.

OBLIGATORY SCENES

Depending upon the nature of the conflict and the characters involved, the audience will expect to see certain scenes. Suppose you have a mother-in-law conflict: husband, wife, and wife's mother, with the husband as the main character. He tells other characters what he thinks of the mother-in-law, what he would like to say to her, and so forth. The mother-in-law similarly reveals her hostility towards the husband.

Now suppose that, without any open quarrel, the problem is solved—say by the mediation of a clergyman, an old friend of the family. That would be credible; in real life, it would be an excellent solution. On stage, however, it would not be satisfying. You have aroused in the audience the expectation of an onstage clash between husband and mother-in-law, with the daughter present, torn between her love for her mother and her husband. This is called an "obligatory scene": you must include it somewhere before the resolution of the conflict.

The fight between Macbeth and Macduff is an obligatory scene: a physical clash between the tyrant and a representative of his victims.

Romeo's finding Juliet in the tomb is an obligatory scene: the lovers must have a final, tragic meeting.

The runthrough of the play-within-a-play in *The Play's the Thing* (Ferenc Molnar) is an obligatory scene. To have let Turai merely *tell* the audience that his stratagem has succeeded would have been intolerably weak; they want to *see* it succeed.

Obligatory scenes like these are created by the author, by the plot he has devised, and by his manner of handling it. There is another category that crops up when you are dramatizing some historic or legendary event, or some well-known piece of fiction.

Certainly not all plays will have obligatory scenes but many plays do have them. So, keep alert to this requirement. Remember that the audience will not be satisfied with a narration of the obligatory scene; it must be enacted before their eyes.

> EXERCISE 9:3
> See if you can identify some obligatory scenes from your Exemplary Dozen.

> EXERCISE 9:4
> Review your Exercise 6:12 and 6:13 (the visits to me, first alone and then with a friend). Develop each scene so that it builds to a good, strong crisis. Include unmistakable implications of some obligatory scene to follow later.

Maybe a few hints on that last exercise would be helpful. I've suggested above that *vigorous conflict* for *high stakes* leads to a strong crisis.

(a) Exactly what were your motives (or your friend's motives) for wanting to make a deal with me? Can you strengthen those motives, or add new ones?

(b) Exactly what were my motives for taking the line that I did in the original scene? Can you now strengthen those motives, or add new ones?

(c) What means of persuasion did you (or your friend) use? Can you now strengthen them, or come up with some new ones? Can you think of *ten* possible means of persuading me, a freelance writer, to devote *my* time and *my* skill to *your* affairs? (By the way, that's exactly what I'm doing as I type these words! Why do you think I'm doing it?)

> EXERCISE 9:5
> Review the scene you planned in Exercise 5:8 (girl shows that she doesn't fit into boyfriend's social circle). Write it in full,

with dialogue from at least four characters. Use actions that create atmosphere, reveal character, and advance your plot. Build the scene to a powerful crisis, either comic or dramatic, according to the style you have chosen.

SUMMARY

Every French scene must build to a crisis.
Crises come more frequently in comedy than in tragedy.
Graduate your crises with the most powerful last.
Plan you last crisis first, to make sure it is the strongest.
Don't try to sustain crises too long.
Vigorous conflict for high stakes makes a strong crisis.
Don't omit the obligatory scenes.

CHAPTER TEN

Catastrophes

EVERY FRENCH SCENE, then, builds up to a crisis: "Mr. Hull, if only you will help me write my book, I'll pay you ten million dollars, and give you my beautiful, nineteen-year-old twin daughters as your mistresses!"

But things cannot be allowed to stop there. A crisis, no matter how minor, requires a catastrophe—the "downward turn," the change, the new factor, that leads on to a conclusion.

When the pain of toothache rises to an intolerable intensity (crisis), the sufferer phones the dentist (catastrophe), and has the tooth pulled (conclusion). When the shy lover's desire becomes more powerful than his timidity (crisis), he proposes marriage (catastrophe), and the couple lives happily ever after (conclusion). When Argan's suspicions about his older daughter reach their very peak (crisis), he receives good news (catastrophe), and his mind is relieved (conclusion). When Bob McKellaway says, "Will you be my valentine?" (crisis), Tiffany says, "Sure, I'll be your valentine" (catastrophe), and pulls him down on the sofa (conclusion).

The catastrophe, the turn of events, is essential if the conclusion is to be satisfying. Imagine a wrestling match in which, after half an hour's struggling, the Good Guy simply stops struggling, lies down and lets himself be pinned! This is an unsatisfactory outcome. Much more satisfying to the spectators will be the Bad Guy's unleashing some new and superlatively effective piece of dirty business (a turn of events, a catastrophe) that gives him the victory.

The catastrophe, in fact, is a special kind of complication, and it usually takes the form of a reversal. Each earlier reversal/complication has raised the conflict to a higher level, like the switchbacks of a road ascending a mountain. The catastrophe is like the crest of a hill: in passing it, the directon of travel is changed.

DEUS EX MACHINA

I mentioned the ancient Greek and Roman technique of *deus ex machina* in Chapter 2. No one nowadays would think of using a god-character to resolve a tricky crisis, but playwrights sometimes fall back on the same principle. Suppose the hero and his family are hopelessly in debt. The mortgage on the old homestead is due, Mother needs a hernia operation, Father needs a new team of horses, the young hero needs cash in order to marry the girl he has gotten into trouble, and a hailstorm has just destroyed the wheat crop upon which all their hopes were staked. The son goes into the yard and angrily kicks at the ground. He stubs his toe on a nugget, and they find that the house was built over a gold mine. That is a *deus ex machina* catastrophe.

The fine, upstanding young author is just about to yield to temptation, allowing himself to be lured away from the gruelling course of work and study that he had planned, in order to write something that he knows has no lasting artistic value.

Ring! Ring! It's the mailman, with a special delivery letter from Writer's Digest Books, offering him fame and fortune on his own terms.

"Keep your ten million dollars, sir, and your twin daughters! I don't need them now!"

Thrilling, but scarcely credible!

I saw a play whose hero was wrongfully accused of murder. For two-and-a-half acts he vainly struggled to clear himself. Then suddenly there appeared a new character never mentioned before, an old hermit who lived in the swamp where the murder took place. He had seen the crime committed, and proved the hero to be innocent. This was a *deus ex machina* catastrophe, and it failed to convince the audience.

Any *favorable* turn of events that is based purely on luck, or that occurs at *too precisely the right moment* will usually be rejected by a present-day audience. True, in real life people sometimes do get lucky breaks to help them out of their troubles; but such "miracles" seldom satisfy us in the theatre. Strangely enough, we readily accept a chance turn of events that is unfavorable to the main character. We have come to think of luck or fate as being mainly malignant.

CATASTROPHES—ACCEPTABLE AND UNACCEPTABLE

The ideal catastrophe should, in Aristotle's words, seem inevitable, yet unexpected. The spectator must be made to feel: "I didn't foresee that development; yet, after all, that's exactly the way things would have turned out."

What are the elements that make the catastrophe seem inevitable?

As a surprise, it will be well planted. It will seem appropriate to the characters who are concerned with it. It will be in keeping with the tone of the play.

Here is a classic example of a well-planted catastrophe. In *Othello*, Act V, Scene 2, Othello stabs himself.

Planting:

Act V, Scene 2, line 192: Emilia says, "I'll kill myself for grief." This suggests the idea of suicide.

Line 252: Othello, whose sword has been taken away, has another sword in reserve.

Line 287: The second sword is taken from him.

Line 290: Othello says, "In my sense 'tis happiness to die." The idea of death is repeated, applied to Othello himself and motivated.

Line 356: He produces a dagger and stabs himself. It is instantly accepted and that he may well have a second reserve weapon, and may use it on himself.

This catastrophe has proved thoroughly acceptable to audiences. It is appropriate to the character of Othello, a professional soldier, who might well be expected to choose death before dishonor; it is in keeping with the tragic tone of the play.

Let us look at an unacceptable catastrophe. The play is a comedy. Jack is in love with Jill and wants to marry her. Jack's father approves of the match, but his mother strongly disapproves. (She is not on speaking terms with Jill's mother, and so would not want to associate with her at the wedding.) The plot moves on through complication after complication, with many humorous situations. Finally the mother threatens suicide unless Jack breaks with Jill. Jack refuses. Mother kills herself, then Jack marries Jill.

What's wrong with this? Suicide is uncharacteristic of a petty snob; moreover, it destroys the comic tone of the play.

EXERCISE 10:1
Write an opening scene based on the plot above.
See if you can strengthen Jack's motives for wanting the marriage; say, three extra motives besides young love.
See if you can strengthen Jack's father's approval by giving him two or three definite motives.

EXERCISE 10:2
Write a closing scene for the play, with an acceptable catastrophe.

EXERCISE 10:3
Write a different opening scene, treating the story line as a drama, and giving Jack's mother a serious motive for disapproving of the Jack/Jill match.

The catastrophe of a French scene has a specific function, coming as it does toward the end of the scene: it must put an end to the internal suspense of the scene. The main line of suspense, of course, continues right up to the last scene.

It is unacceptable to *prolong* the catastrophe; the thread of suspense should be cleanly cut, not gradually chewed off. Any unnecessary delay, once you begin the process of destroying the suspense, may weaken the interest of the spectators. Some of them will begin to think, "Yes, yes, we understand that! Let's get on with the show."

Look back at the *Uncle Tom* scene in Chapter 6. Shelby says, "I'll think the matter over and talk with my wife." It is obvious that Shelby has weakened; he can't quite make himself come right out and say "yes," but Haley sees that he had made his point, and promptly withdraws. The technical feature of the line is that it is *short*, and yet unmistakable. Snap! the thread of internal suspense has been cleanly cut.

The catastrophe of a scene is not always in dialogue; it may sometimes be an action: a slap, a shot, the pouring of a poison dose, a kiss, etc. Such nonverbal transactions can serve very well to lead on to a conclusion.

A few notable catastrophes: in *Ghosts*, Oswald's line, "Mother, give me the sun." In *The Importance of Being Earnest*, Jack's line: "Christian names, Ernest John." In *Macbeth*, Macduff's entrance, carrying Macbeth's head. In *Hamlet*, Hamlet stabs the king.

> EXERCISE 10:4
> Review the scenes that you have already written; see if you can improve the catastrophes. Are they all inevitable, unexpected, characteristic and compatible with the tone of the scene?

SUMMARY

Catastrophe: the turn of events, the new factor, that leads on to a conclusion.

The catastrophe is usually a reversal.

Bits of good luck seldom yield satisfying catastrophes.

A good catastrophe seems surprising, and therefore must be well-planted.

A good catastrophe must be fitting to the character(s) involved.

A good catastrophe maintains the emotional tone of the play.

A good catastrophe acts quickly, to cut the internal suspense of a French scene.

Actions may serve as catastrophes.

CHAPTER ELEVEN

Conclusions

THE CONCLUSION OF A French scene has two functions:

1. It depicts the new state of affairs brought about by the catastrophe. The playwright should not slide from a catastrophe straight through into the next French scene, trusting that the audience will deduce the significance of the catastrophe. That significance must be spelled out. Doing this, the conclusions are like a series of guideposts leading the spectator through the play. Let each conclusion be made clear and decisive; then each step of the action is well understood before you move ahead to the next.

In the scene from *The Imaginary Invalid* quoted in Chapter 3, the catastrophe is Louison's "And then my stepmother came to the door, and he ran away." Argan's bit of comic business with his finger demonstrates unmistakably that he accepts Louison's story; that is the conclusion.

2. The conclusion provides a transition to the next French scene. Look at the last two speeches of *The Drunkard* excerpt in Chapter 15. They prepare for the coming scene, in which Cribbs plies young Edward with liquor.

EXERCISE 11:1
Review the scenes you have already written, and revise the conclusions, if necessary, to meet these two requirements.

CURTAIN SCENES

The French scene immediately preceding each curtain drop (except the last) of a long play is called a curtain scene. The conclusion of a curtain scene differs somewhat from the others in the act.

Like those others, it must quickly sum up the results of the catastrophe that has just occurred. But instead of providing a bridge to the next French scene, it must provide the audience with something interesting to think and talk about during the intermission.

The usual way of fulfilling that second function is to give the audience a strong reminder of the play's main line of conflict, stating or restating some aspect of the conflict that will create suspense.

The curtain scenes of *Ghosts* are highly dramatic. The conclusion of Act I is Manders' realization that Regina is Oswald's half-sister. (By the way, it is an interesting study to search out and mark the plants for this surprise: they extend as far back as the opening scene between Regina and Engstrand.) The audience can now spend the intermission in a pleasurable state of suspense as to the likelihood of an incestuous relationship between Oswald and Regina. The conclusion of Act II is Manders' cry that there is a divine judgment on the corrupt Alving household. The audience now has the pleasure of speculating how this judgment will work out wth respect to the proposed Oswald-Regina marriage and to the philanthropic plans of Mrs. Alving and Manders.

In Chapter 4, I described the Act I curtain scene of *Uncle Tom's Cabin*. At the risk of their lives, Eliza and Harry have escaped—*for now!* Haley, Loker and Marks know where she is, and they will be hot on her trail.

The Act I curtain scene of my *The Drunkard* takes place in a New England village in the mid-nineteenth century. Mrs. Wilson and her 18-year-old daughter, Mary, are about to be thrown out of their cottage for nonpayment of rent.

Mary has received marriage proposals from Cribbs, the mean old lawyer, and from Edward, the rich young hero. Unfortunately Edward has shown himself as a drunkard. Cribbs and Edward have just gone out.

MRS. WILSON
Mary, dear, I repeat my question—what do you say?

MARY
(Distracted) What can I say? To save us both from destitution I am forced to marry. But *which* am I to marry? That old man whose very touch makes me shrink in horror or . . . or . . . . merciful heavens! The drunkard! *(She bursts into tears and runs sobbing off Left.)*

MRS. WILSON
Mary! Mary! My child! My child! *(She runs off Left after MARY.)*

N.B. The double exit would not normally be necessary. This version was specially written to leave a clear stage after every scene and act, for use in theatres that have no curtain. If a curtain is available, the better way to play this scene would be to keep both women on stage, and have Mrs. Wilson embrace Mary on her last line.

CLOSING SCENES

The conclusion of the last scene of a play has only one function: to clarify and consolidate the final state of affairs—the resolution of the main conflict.

The conclusion of *Macbeth* is a short acclamation of the new king, Malcolm.

The conclusion of *Ghosts*, which takes less than a minute to play, consists of Mrs. Alving's acceptance of Oswald's final seizure.

The conclusion of *Arms and the Man* plays about forty-five seconds: Bluntschli sets a date for his wedding and departs.

SUMMARY

French scene conclusion:
1. Clarifies the results of the catastrophe.
2. Leads on to the next French scene.

Curtain scene conclusion provides strong suspense for the intermission.

Closing scene conclusion winds up the main conflict.

CHAPTER TWELVE

The Stage and Its Equipment

A NOVELIST MAY WRITE successful books without ever seeing a printing press or a book bindery. But the playwright *must* know something (the more, the better) about play production, acting, stage management, makeup, costuming, set construction and the psychology of actors and spectators.

Some famous writers (e.g., Robert Louis Stevenson and Alfred Tennyson) have failed as playwrights because they lacked that knowledge.

So make yourself familiar with the stage and its equipment. Work backstage as often as you can. You will find that the experience helps you write more easily and more effectively.

STRUCTURE OF THE STAGE

The stage we are most familiar with is the proscenium stage, a raised platform at one end of a rectangular hall. The spectators sit in front of the stage, and it can be concealed from them by the closing or lowering of a curtain. The arch or opening across which this curtain moves is called the "proscenium," and gives its name to this type of stage.

The "platform stage" is simply a raised platform without a proscenium or curtain. If the platform is at one end of the theatre, all the spectators sit in front of it. Alternatively, the platform may jut out from one of the long sides of the room; then the audience sits on three sides of it.

For "theatre-in-the-round," the audience sits all around the platform, something like the audience at a boxing match. Alternatively, the actors may perform at floor level, and the seats are raised in tiers all around it. This arrangement is called "arena theatre."

There is no particular standard of mechanical equipment. Some stages have hydraulic lifts that can raise heavy scenery and groups of actors up from below; many big theatres have not even a trap door in the stage. Some proscenium theatres are equipped with fly lofts above the stage; pulleys and ropes can hoist pieces of scenery and properties up out of sight of the audience. A fly loft may sometimes be useful, but not all theatres have them, so you had better not write scripts that absolutely demand the flying of sets or properties.

You want your play to have the best possible chances of success. Then don't write it so that for one reason or another, it is barred from many stages.

To write a play that must have a revolving stage is a waste of effort—unless it is specially commissioned—because not one theatre in a hundred can put it on. A play that must have a full box set—say a bedroom farce that requires five doors and two large closets—can only be played on a proscenium stage.

One property, even, may be decisive. Suppose your play centers around a large, old-fashioned upright piano; it is barred from the arena stage because, no matter where you put the piano on that stage, it blocks the view of one segment of the audience.

Observe carefully, in your theatre-going, what can and what cannot be done on different types of stage.

THE STAGE: WHAT DOES IT REPRESENT?

There is a convention in most plays that the stage represents some definite place: a tenement room in New York, a cabin on an ocean liner, a barroom, the living room of author Raymond Hull, or anything else that the playwright can imagine and the scene painters depict. The stage is fitted up with appropriate sets and properties to look approximately like the chosen place. This is representational staging.

So each time the action moves to a new location, there must be a curtain drop or blackout while the set and properties are changed to give the appearance of the new location. All this takes time and costs money, so one-set plays have become increasingly common in recent years.

There is another convention under which the stage represents no definite place. It might be compared to a movie screen—a blank area upon which various actions are portrayed. This was the convention in Shakespeare's day. There were no curtain drops or intervals between scenes. As characters A and B finished one scene and walked off right, characters X and Y entered left to begin the next scene—which might be located in another room of the castle, in another part of the city, or on the other side of the ocean.

Many playwrights use this convention nowadays. Audiences easily adapt to it, and it allows great flexibility of plotting, because you can have as many locations as you like. It reduces production costs, because you need no sets. Changing of such properties as are needed (chairs, tables, etc.) can be done by a stagehand in full view of the audience. (See Thornton Wilder's *Our Town* for a good example of this style.) On a proscenium or platform stage, when no sets are used, it is customary to play in front of plain drapes, dark for tragedy, light-colored for comedy.

STAGE GEOGRAPHY

Left and *Right* in stage directions are identified from the *actor's* point of view as he or she faces the front of the stage. *Up* is toward the back of the stage; *Down* is the area nearest the audience. Theatre stages used to be sloped slightly upward, away from the audience, so the actor who moved toward the back of the stage did physically move uphill: toward the audience, downhill.

For describing actors' movements in your scripts, divide your stage into the six areas marked in the diagram.

Back of Stage

	Up Right (UR)	Up Center (UC)	Up Left (UL)	
Right Wings				Left Wings
	Down Right (DR)	Down Center (DC)	Down Left (DL)	

Audience

If there are several doors in your set, you may need to indicate which door a character must use for each entrance and exit. Usually it is sufficient to write *Exit UR, Exit DL, Enter UC*, etc.

In some old playscripts you will find a different system of describing entrances and exits. Before the box set came into use, a common arrangement was to provide three fixed openings on each side. These were numbered from front to back. So *Exit 2L* means that the actor goes out by the middle opening on the left. Another notation for the system is *RLE* for *right lower exit, RSE for right second exit,* and *RUE* for *right upper exit.* These old stages often had a door (a regular hinged door, not just an opening) in the upstage wall. This would be called *CD*, for *center door.*

Read all the old scripts you can; there's much to be learned from them. But remember one point: they were written at a time when actors, musicians, singers, dancers, scene painters and materials were much cheaper than they are today. So don't imitate the lavishness of these old-time productions.

EXERCISE 12:1
From one of your Exemplary Dozen, diagram a stage plan for the set up of sets and properties. Mark where the entrances should go.

EXERCISE 12:2
Draw similar plans for two of your own scripts. Carefully consider the actions that will be done on stage; allow for the timely, convenient entrances and exits of the various characters. Take pains over this: you are now beginning to see these works as performances, not just as words on paper.

SETS

I read the script of a one-act play that opened in the library of an English country house. There were to be panelled walls, heavy furniture and hundreds of books. After five minutes' action in the library, the script called for a thirty-second blackout, during which the scene was to be changed to the realistic interior of a night club, with patrons dining at tables, waiters hurrying to and fro, a band playing and a floor show in progress. There was one minute's action in the night club, then another thirty-second blackout and a change back to the library. The whole play would have run about eleven minutes.

The author asked for my frank opinion of the script. I pointed out that the set changes described could not be made in thirty-second blackouts: each of them would take about ten minutes behind a closed curtain. I added that, even if the set changes could be made more quickly, two such costly sets were not justified for a one-act play, and, there is very little demand for eleven-minute plays. The author, apparently wounded by the mention of practicalities, never spoke to me again.

An experienced semi-professional actor recently praised a certain play as being "easy to travel with." That simply means that the sets and props could be easily transported from one performance location to another. Many theatre groups do not want to stay home all the time, playing to the same limited audience. They like to visit other communities for more performances, more fun and more revenue from their effort in putting together a production. So, if your play is "easy to travel with," it is likely to be performed more often, and earn more money for you.

Bear in mind that even the most elaborate theatre sets cannot rival the spectacular potential of the movie screen. So ask yourself when planning your sets: "Are the cost and trouble of a certain piece of scenery *really* justified by what it will add to the play? Could I find a simpler, cheaper way of achieving the same effect?"

The set for *Mary, Mary* is the realistic living room of Bob McKellaway's apartment—nothing difficult or expensive about that. And the entire action takes place in that one room.

Often your set can be symbolic, rather than realistic: you can make a door and a window frame represent a house; a sundial and a rose trellis can suffice for a garden scene.

Look at the set description for *The Miracle Worker*.

TIME: *The 1880s*
PLACE: *In and around the Keller homestead in Tuscumbia, Alabama; also, briefly, the Perkins Institution for the Blind, in Boston.*
THE PLAYING SPACE *is divided into two areas by a more or less*

diagonal line, which runs from downstage right to upstage left.
THE AREA *behind this diagonal is on platforms and represents the Keller house; inside we see, down right, a family room, and up center, elevated, a bedroom. On stage level near center, outside a porch, there is a water pump.*
THE OTHER AREA, *in front of the diagonal, is neutral ground; it accommodates various places as designated at various times—the yard before the Keller home, the Perkins Institution for the Blind, the garden house, and so forth.*
THE CONVENTION OF THE STAGING *is one of cutting through time and place, and its essential qualities are fluidity and spatial counterpoint. To this end, the less set there is, the better; in a literal set, the fluidity will seem merely episodic. The stage therefore should be free, airy, unencumbered by walls. Apart from certain practical items—such as the pump, a window to climb out of, doors to be locked—locales should be only skeletal suggestions, and the movement from one to another should be accomplished by little more than lights.*

Study good play productions. Look at them not with a spectator's eye, but with the playwright's eye, asking at every turn, "Why was this done? How was that done?"

See how little scenery some of them use. Remember that some drama festivals—valuable training grounds for the playwright—bar the use of sets altogether, so as to avoid giving an unfair advantage to wealthier competing groups and to those that don't have far to travel.

LIGHTS

The playwright is concerned with three qualities of light: **color, intensity** and **direction.**

A yellowish tinge to the stage lighting suggests sunshine and gives a cheerful effect. A reddish tinge suggests danger and can be used in scenes of anger. Greenish light suggests jealousy and is traditionally used on sinister, villainous characters.

A decreasing intensity of light suggests nightfall; it also tends to produce in the audience a feeling of gloom and sadness. An increasing intensity of light has the opposite effect.

Light from above gives a normal appearance to the characters: in everyday life we see people illuminated from above. Light from below gives characters a ghastly, supernatural appearance. (In a dark room, try shining a flashlight on your face from below your chin.)

An ideal lighting system would give full control of color, intensity and direction for the light on every part of the stage, variable from moment to moment. That ideal is costly; it requires a lot of equipment, and skilled technicians at the switchboard. Theatres vary widely in the range of lighting effects they can provide. If you are writing to order for a particular theatre, you should find out exactly what can and cannot be done with its lighting system.

Otherwise, the best rule is to be cautious and modest in your calls for lighting effects. That way, you improve the play's prospects of being performed.

SOUND EFFECTS

The golden rule for sound effects is to *keep them simple.* They should be easily recognizable by the audience. For example, when William Gibson wants to use that "neutral ground," (downstage left) as a railroad depot, he prescribes railroad sounds. At another part of the play, to suggest the passing of a long period of time, he calls for belfry chimes, slowly increasing in loudness, and then fading. That sound effect is accompanied by a dim-out of the lights, then a brightening to show the state of affairs several years later.

Simple sounds that can be produced mechanically behind the scenes (knocking on the door, ringing doorbells, gunshots, etc.) are fairly easy to produce exactly on cue. Recorded sounds are less reliable: you can never be sure that they will come in exactly on time.

PROPERTIES

Properties—usually called props—are movable articles, not a part of the set. Chairs, tables and books are props; so are cups, plates, bread, cheese and beverages. The same advice holds good for props as for sets and sound effects: be reasonable and modest in your requirements.

1. Remember that someone has to procure the props. I saw one script that called for a dead moose to be wheeled on, lying over the saddle of a bicycle. Now a dead moose is not easy to find. It's true that an efficient properties department, given enough time and money, can find or make anything. But a playwright should constantly bear in mind the question of cost. How much will a dead moose, or a live boa constrictor, or a full-size working guillotine cost to buy, rent or simulate?

2. Remember that, when procured, the props have to be gotten on stage. To be sure, there is no difficulty finding stoves, sinks, kitchen cabinets and refrigerators. But they are big and heavy. It would be troublesome for an amateur drama company to truck such things to the theatre and haul them on and off stage in order to show, say, the renovation of a kitchen in a one-act play. The script would stand a better chance of performance if the action were in a living room. A few chairs and a coffee table are easy to move.

3. The actors have to use the props. The dead moose mentioned above could weigh half a ton. Even a moosehide stuffed with sawdust might weigh several hundred pounds. An actor would have quite a time wheeling

that mass around the stage on a bicycle.

Props serve not only to dress up the stage; a well-chosen item can serve important dramatic functions. Study the uses of the pistols in *Hedda Gabler*. They offer an excuse for giving information about Hedda's father, who formerly owned them. The pistol shots at the opening of Act II scare Brack. The shooting demonstrates Hedda's unusual character—after all, very few women blaze away with pistols in their back gardens. A pistol provides the big surprise in Act III, when the audience expects Hedda to give Lövborg the manuscript and she gives him instead the pistol with which he later shoots himself. In Act IV that pistol becomes the means by which Brack blackmails Hedda. Its mate serves as Hedda's suicide weapon.

When reading *The Miracle Worker*, carefully analyze the functions of the doll with the eyes that open and shut that the tutor Annie brings as a gift for little blind Helen.

There is little point in cluttering the stage with a multitude of props. They distract the audience's attention. It is better to choose a few and make each one serve some significant purpose: e.g., the newspapers, the desk, the telephone, the fish tank, the sofa, in the *Mary, Mary* scene.

EXERCISE 12:3

For the two scripts of Exercise 12:2 make lists of requisite lighting changes (if any), sound effects (if any) and portable properties required for production.

STAGE DIRECTIONS

Keep stage directions as brief and simple as you can. Complicated descriptions of sets and lighting are useless, because you can't tell what facilities will be available in any theatre. Minute descriptions of costumes and actions are not needed, either. Even if you put them in, directors will ignore them. Put in only the entrances, the exits, and the essential, significant movements and business.

SUMMARY

Make yourself familiar with stage equipment.
Write scripts that can be played on any stage.
Learn and use the conventions of stage geography.
When specifying sets and props, consider cost and convenience.
Avoid complicated lighting and sound effects.
Properties should be easy to obtain, simple and safe to use.
Make properties serve some dramatic function.
Keep stage directions simple.

CHAPTER THIRTEEN

Actors, Directors, and Spectators

I'LL EMPHASIZE AGAIN that a playscript is not a self-contained literary work, but a *set of directions* for a *performance*. You, as playwright, are telling the director and actors to say and do certain things that will—you hope—produce a desired effect upon an audience.

So do your best to understand the human instruments through whom you are working (actors, directors) and the human instruments upon whose emotions you intend to play (audiences).

DRAMA GROUPS

If you want to write good plays, get to know some actors. You need not go to New York; there are actors in every town, school, church or community center that has a drama group. Join the group and study its members. Here's how to proceed.

Don't march in and announce, "I'm a playwright, and I'd like to have you stage a few of my plays!" That will likely arouse hostility right away.

It's better to announce that you are not an actor, and don't want to perform, but would like to help with some of the offstage work. You'll be welcomed.

To help you get best value from this experience, with the minimum of delay and embarrasssment, I offer this outline of drama group organization.

Executive Committee

Like other clubs and societies, the drama group has administrative personnel consisting of a president, vice president, secretary, treasurer, and other officers whose number and function will depend upon the size and aims of the group.

Play Selection Committee

This committee's business is to choose plays that will suit the aims and resources of the group. By "resources" I mean:

(a) The number and abilities of actor/members.

(b) The performing space available.

(c) The funds available for such expenses as play royalties, costumes, sets, publicity, rentals, etc.

(d) Time available for rehearsals and performances.

The Play Section Committee reports to the Executive Committee.

Casting Committee

This committee should include the Director. They read and discuss the chosen play, then hold auditions to select an appropriate cast and, if necessary, understudies. They report to the Executive Committee.

Producer

The Producer coordinates all arrangements for the performance, supervising these people and departments: Accounts, Box Office, Director, House Manager, Publicity and Promotion. The Producer reports to the Executive Committee.

Accounts

This department has to check all expenses and receipts connected with the production, filing appropriate documentation. They control issuance of cash and the writing of checks. They prepare a final accounting after the production closes. They report to the Producer.

Box Office

The first duty of Box Office is to see the printing and to keep custody of appropriate numbers of tickets for all planned performances. They sell and check tickets at each performance. They report to the Producer.

House Manager

The House Manager is responsible for overseeing the auditorium and lobbies at performances. He recruits the ushers and assistants—who check tickets, show ticket holders into the auditorium, and distribute programs and other promotional material.

He arranges for appropriate music before the show and during intermissions. He supervises refreshment service during intermissions. He should be present in the auditorium or lobby at all times to answer queries from the public and to deal with emergencies. He reports to the Producer.

Publicity and Promotion

This department designs, prints and distributes posters and advertising leaflets. They design and place newspaper ads. They notify newspaper theatre critics well in advance. They try to get radio or TV interviews and local newspaper coverage for the Director and cast members and—if it's your play being performed—for you, as the local author.

They design and print programs for the show. The program not only gives technical details of the present production, it should also be an advertisement for the company, plugging its past and future activities. Paid ads, if they can be obtained, are helpful.

Alternatively, leaflets describing the company and its activities can be prepared for distribution at performances.

(N.B. Here, amid all this writing and printing, could be a congenial niche for a writer like you.)

This department may also provide an emcee to make announcements to the audience. Publicity and Promotion reports to the Producer.

Director

The Director takes part in casting. He supervises rehearsals to create a technically and artistically sound performance. He supervises the costume and makeup departments to obtain the desired appearance of the cast. He controls, via the Stage Manager, the Lighting, Properties, Set Design and Sound Effects departments. He chooses and rehearses a Prompter.

The Director reports to the Producer.

Costume

This department rents, buys, borrows or makes appropriate costumes for all characters. It reports to the Director.

Makeup

Makeup has to create the desired physical appearance of all characters (age, youth, beauty, ugliness, deformities, etc.). Makeup reports to the Director.

Prompter

The Prompter attends rehearsals and performances to prompt whenever actors forget their lines. Also, if convenient, the Prompter may give cues for Sound Effects and Cast Call. The Prompter reports to the Director.

Stage Manager

The Stage Manager coordinates all physical arrangements for the stage, supervising these people and departments: Cast Call, Lighting, Properties, Set Design and Construction, and Sound Effects. The Stage Manager reports to the Director.

Cast Call

This department uses a messenger, or messengers, to call cast members from dressing rooms in ample time for their entrance cues and, in general, to transmit instructions and messages to and from backstage. Cast Call reports to the Stage Manager.

Lighting

The Lighting staff, in consultation with the Director, work out lighting effects during rehearsals and execute them in performance. Lighting reports to the Stage Manager.

Properties

The Properties department, in consultation with the Director, obtains all movable objects:

(a) used to give scenic effects on stage: e.g., chairs, tables, pictures, books, fish tanks, etc.

(b) used as significant items in the action: e.g., cups, coffeepots, bottles, food, guns, telephones, etc.

Their work usually requires one or more members standing by throughout all rehearsals and performances to check such materials, hand them to actors when required, reposition them as necessary between acts, and put props into safe storage after the closing curtain. Properties reports to the Stage Manager.

Set Design and Construction

In consultation with the Director, this department designs and builds sets appropriate for the play. If required, they attend backstage to change sets between scenes or acts. Set Design reports to the Stage Manager.

Stage Crew

The Stage Crew attends backstage for opening and closing the curtain, to cooperate with set and property changes, and any other necessary backstage functions. They report to the Stage Manager.

YOUR PARTICIPATION

Not every group will be organized exactly like this; titles of some departments may be different; chains of command may be differently linked. All the same, these are the essential functions for putting on a play and, under one heading or another, they must be carried out.

In a small group, all these functions may be handled by just a few people (e.g., one member is Director, Producer and Stage Manager; another handles Sound, Lights and Properties). In a big group the duties will likely be spread around, so that every member has something useful to do.

EXERCISE 13:1
Join a drama group. Draw up a written chart showing how it is organized and who carries out the various functions.

Watch, listen, think about what you see going on in your group. Why does it, and umpteen thousand more, keep going?

Nowadays many people feel powerless in their working and political functions, like chips of wood swept along by currents they cannot control. But through theatre, some people find means of creating and controlling an orderly, important event: backstage, onstage and front-of-house staff will work together; hundreds or thousands of spectators will attend; money will flow. It's deeply satisfying, as anyone knows who has done it. The social and economic conditions that favor this particular kind of group activity are likely to continue, so the market for plays is likely to keep growing.

ACTORS

Right from the start of your involvement in a theatre group, study and try to understand the actors. Most of them are talkative. That's natural; the voice is part of an actor's stock-in-trade. He or she has taken trouble to develop and control it, and likes the sound of it. So draw out the experiences of actors; they may not know much about writing plays, but they know much more than you do about performing them. Listen closely; make notes. Any actor will be pleased and flattered to see you do that.

In some amateur companies you will find people who are aiming at a professional acting career. Some may be part of the way there already, doing an occasional day's paid work—acting in a TV commercial, substitute teaching at a dramatic or elocution school, or maybe acting as hold-up artist for a practice class at the police training academy. Such people are likely to be very earnest. They (like writers) are struggling for success in a competitive business and they realize the unmatched value of the amateur theatre as a training ground.

What parts of the actors' advice are you to accept, and what to reject? Here is a rough guide. An experienced actor can tell you fairly accurately which lines and actions will be easy to perform and which will go well with an audience. But actors, of necessity, have their minds concentrated on their own roles and on the particular scenes in which they appear. So an actor may not be a sound judge as to the overall relationship of the characters, or the plot structure of the play as a whole.

You can volunteer to help actors learn their lines by giving them their cues in private run-throughs. If there are some lines that the actor keeps saying wrong again and again, discuss with him or her *why* there is trouble just there.

You cannot know too much about actors, since you are writing for *actors*. Some authors write as if for a cast of playwrights or literary critics. Such work cannot succeed, because actors will not perform it effectively.

Become a performer of some kind yourself. This need be no more than a sideline to your writing. You might act bit parts in plays; you could sing, dance, play a musical instrument, or do conjuring tricks. You might want to take a course in public speaking. Such methods will give you firsthand knowledge of what it feels like to face an audience; you will acquire a better understanding and appreciation of actors.

DIRECTORS

The director has a complex, delicate task. Always bearing in mind the abilities of the company, and the apparent meaning of the script, he or she works to produce the best possible emotional response from the audience.

The director serves as intermediary between playwright, players, and public.

Successful directing calls for broad theatrical knowledge (acting, lighting, sound effects, sets, etc.), plus large measures of firmness and tact to deal with the often temperamental people of the stage. You can learn a lot from a good director.

But you may occasionally run into a director who goes beyond what I've described above. The poor playwright—to hear such a director talk—provides only a rough, bungling sketch from which the director will create a masterpiece.

Steer clear of such people, if you can. Try to find a director who understands and likes your work as it is; then cooperate with him or her. Such cooperation will do much to develop your skill and build your reputation.

After gaining some experience with successful scriptwriting and cooperation with good directors, you may want to try directing a play of your own. Bernard Shaw recommends this course, and his treatise *The Art of Rehearsal* gives concise instructions on directing.

The author-director combination is a good one; but don't go too far and try to be author, director and actor all at once. It's exceedingly difficult to properly direct a play in which you are performing.

YOUR PLAYS

You may get the chance to write a play for your own group, perhaps on some special occasion. Or, when they get to know and like you, they may want to put on one of your already-written scripts. Attend all the rehearsals you can; they are highly instructive. Some actors and directors dislike having an author present at rehearsals of his or her own play. That is because some authors behave badly. Here is the *right* way to behave:

1. Don't interrupt! Never interrupt an actor or the director; never offer suggestions or criticism while the rehearsal is in progress. Sit quietly, some distance from the stage, with pen and notebook handy. When you see something questionable, *don't speak*, but make a note of it. When the director orders a pause, tell him or her, *out of hearing of the actors*, what you have noted, ask your questions, and make your suggestions.

2. Don't deal directly with the actors. Some of them may come to you with suggestions, criticism, or disputes for arbitration. They may try to use you as a lever to move the director. Say something like, "Monica, I'm only the author. You'll have to take that up with the director."

3. For a new, unpublished play, even if you can't go to all rehearsals, try to be at the first, in order to check the scripts. Typed or duplicated copies may contain errors, such as the alteration of words, the placing of character A's name against a line that belongs to character B, the omission or transposition of sections of the script, etc. Such errors need correcting before they become fixed in the actors' minds. Take your master copy to the first rehearsal, follow closely as the actors read through, and report every error to the director.

4. Prepare yourself for the fact that the first few rehearsals will sound and look horrible. Remember that you have lived with your characters for weeks or months; you know how you want them portrayed. The actors have no such ideas; they must start from scratch.

Moreover, many actors are bad readers; but remind yourself that they will do better when they have memorized the lines. Don't pester the director with criticisms and suggestions at this stage. He or she knows how bad it sounds, and will only think you amateurish if you point it out.

5. Be patient during the blocking process, when actors carry their scripts and write down the moves and actions that the director gives them. If the director has minutely prepared moves and actions in advance, blocking may not occupy many rehearsals. If he or she prefers to work out the blocking during rehearsals, it will take longer.

During this blocking you may see some of your own stage directions altered. Don't be hasty in protesting. If you have confidence in the director, wait and learn the reasons for the change.

6. Be prepared for a bad slump in rehearsals immediately after scripts are put down. The actors are now under great mental strain, trying to remember all the notes the director gave them, plus their lines. Bear with the confusion: it will pass.

7. Prepare for alterations. Rehearsals may reveal weaknesses in the script: lines that are hard to speak, bits of action that are not time-matched to the accompanying dialogue, and so on. Don't be stubborn and insist on keeping your original script untouched. Take such alterations as a chance to learn more about your trade.

But don't sit down and try to rewrite with cast and director looking over your shoulder! Better say, "All right. You go ahead with the next section, and I'll have this rewritten in ten minutes" (or by the next coffee-break, or by tomorrow, depending on the work involved). Then sit in a corner and get on with it by yourself.

8. Don't expect perfect accuracy. Don't nag over trifling departures from the script. Some actors have the knack of memorizing quickly, and reproducing the lines perfectly every time. Others memorize with difficulty, and never achieve perfect recall. Bear with it patiently.

9. Give praise. Without treading on the director's toes, you can still, at the conclusion of a rehearsal, make a few congratulatory remarks. Many actors feel insecure and nervous during rehearsals. Your praise will help them gain confidence.

AUDIENCES

Emile Augier, the great French nineteenth-century dramatist, made some significant remarks about audiences. "There are a large number of people assembled by design but without any selection; people of differing intelligences, yet united by the occasion that has brought them together. The performance must appeal instantly to all those levels of intelligence from the highest to the lowest: excessively complicated situations and overly subtle dialogue will no more be understood by the audience than tiny gestures will be seen or faint sounds will be heard by them."

The theatre is a mass entertainment. A play must appeal, not to an individual reader, but to a large number of people crowded together in one place.

The reactions of a large group will be more intense than those of a few. A line or action that draws a smile from an individual can raise a roar of laughter from an audience. A tragic situation that evokes a "Hm! Too bad!" from an individual can reduce an audience to tears. That is because emotions are infectious. A's laughter sets B and C laughing. B's and C's laughter confirms A's judgment that the situation is funny, and thus makes A laugh harder.

The reactions of the audience are *slower* than those of the most perceptive members. The transmission of emotion through the audience is not instantaneous; it takes a certain time. Long after the people who first caught a joke have finished laughing, others are still laughing because they started later.

Audience reactions depend not only on the number of people present, but on the degree to which they are crowded together. Five hundred people in a 500-seat theatre will react vigorously; the same number in a 1,500-seat theatre will react feebly, because they are spread out thinly.

The spectators communicate, not only with each other, but also with the actors. When a show is going well, the audience/cast interaction becomes very strong. It spurs the actors on to greater efforts, and provides the audience with a keener emotional experience. This mutual stimulation may be effected without laughter or applause; it cannot very well be described in words, yet when once experienced it is unmistakable. This emotional interaction is the principal advantage of live theatre over movies and TV.

Credulity of the Audience

At the beginning of Act I, the audience knows nothing about your play. They are in a credulous mood, willing to accept any situation, ready to believe any information.

But their credulity dwindles as time passes. Having accepted your incredible premise, they will expect faultless logic in the development of your plot. Also, the later in the play new information is given, the less readily they will accept it.

So make your exposition interesting and convincing; capture the attention and exploit the acceptance of the audience at the time when they are most willing to believe.

The Attention of the Audience

When the audience is interested, its attention is narrowly focused—so narrowly that not one person in a crowded theatre will notice anything but the common object of attention. Directors sometimes use this phenomenon to introduce a ghost. Something interesting is going on DR while the ghost, unnoticed by the audience, walks on UL. One of the characters shrieks and points to the ghost; it seems to have materialized out of thin air.

The sense of hearing, as well as that of sight, can be focused by attention. (You know how, at a noisy party, you can shut out all voices except that of the one person you are talking to.)

So suppose you have three characters on stage: A, B, and C. A and B have been talking together for some time while C sits apart. Now you want C to deliver a line; but if C speaks without preparation, he or she will not be understood. So you must direct the audience's attention to C. It could be done by movement: e.g., you make C stand up and move toward A and B so A and B look in C's direction. It could be done by a line: let A say, "Now C, old friend, let's hear what you think."

Such direction, necessary when actor C is on stage, is particularly important if C is off. To direct the audience's attention to an offstage line, you can make someone on stage say, "Listen! What's going on out there?" An action will do just as well: a character gestures for silence, and points to the quarter from which the offstage voice will come.

Learning from the Audience

A live audience passes immediate and accurate judgment on a performance. To be sure, bad acting or bad directing can kill a good play, but, given a fairly competent performance, a playwright can learn a lot by studying audiences.

Suppose it's your play being performed. Don't hang around backstage, getting in the actors' way. Don't sit in the front row, thinking to get the best possible view. Sit right at the back, to watch the *audience*; have a pen handy, and a copy of the script.

If the play is a comedy, listen for laughs. Note which laugh lines get a laugh every time, which ones get a laugh only occasionally, and which ones fail completely. Such a study, repeated over a number of nights, will help you write sure-fire laughs.

Watch for what are called "bad laughs," unintended bursts of laughter. A crisis sustained too long—say a dragged-out death scene—can produce a bad laugh. If a bad laugh occurs more than once at the same place, consider rewriting or redirection.

When no laughs are expected, watch the audience for signs of interest. Is every head directed to the actor who is speaking, or to the part of the stage where significant action is going on? If so, the play is going well. Are some people staring around the theatre, reading their programs, coughing or shuffling their feet? They have lost interest in the play. Note where such signs of inattention occur. If they occur repeatedly at the same place, rewrite.

Such loss of attention usually means that people are bored. They understand the situation, yet the characters go on and on talking about it, and the plot stands still. The remedy is to cut.

The spectators will unconsciously analyze your play for you. This in-show analysis is more accurate, more honest, than anything they may say to you afterward.

If you are in doubt about any aspect of your play, trust the average spectator rather than the professional critic. Moliére got his cook to criticize his plays. Would your plays pass a similar test?

SUMMARY

Mix with actors, study them, learn from them.
Study the organization of your drama group.
Behave properly at rehearsals.
Cooperate with directors, but don't worship them.
Crowds react more slowly, but more intensely, than individuals.
The audience is most credulous in the first few minutes.
Direct the attention of the audience.
Study audiences and learn from them.

CHAPTER FOURTEEN

Writing the Play

NOW FOR THE PRACTICAL process of putting a play on paper.

COLLECTING IDEAS

Begin a file of play ideas and continually feed it. Keep yourself "tuned in." Radio, TV, newspapers, magazines, conversation, etc. produce an inexhaustible supply of themes and plots. The prolific Victorien Sardou was forever taking notes, jotting down ideas for scenes, dramatic situations, themes for plays. As a result he always had in reserve more or less complete plots for fifty plays!

TITLES

A title can be an important element in the success of a play. Here are some pointers:

The title may indicate the subject of the play (e.g., *The Drunkard, The Doctor's Dilemma, Julius Caesar)*; but it should not give away the ending. It may set the tone of the play (e.g., *Mourning Becomes Electra* [tragic], *Guys and Dolls* [comic]).

Your title should be fairly short, for convenience in advertising. It should be comprehensible and easily pronounceable. (*Les Misérables* is a title that has handicapped more than one film and stage version of the novel.) Word-of-mouth publicity is important; if people can't remember—or can't pronounce—the title, they won't talk about it.

PLANNING

The "planner" creates and develops all his characters, works out the plot, divides it into French scenes, and contrives all the action before he begins to write the script. One such planner, asked how his new play was coming along, replied quite seriously: "It's practically finished. Tomorrow I start writing the dialogue."

This method obviously requires a great deal of thought before the script itself is begun. Bronson Howard used to draw on a 4x6-inch card a stage plan for every French scene. He sketched in the furniture and major properties, and diagrammed movement of the characters. You can try this: use coins to represent your characters; shift them to and fro as necessary.

This procedure avoids the risk of leaving a character on stage long after his business there is finished. It reminds you which characters are on stage at any moment, so you can share the lines and action among them. (Actors appreciate that; none of them likes to be left standing too long, silent and inert, like a post.)

After some trials with the coins, you can permanently mark up your scene plan with crayons (one color for each character), and go ahead to the next scene.

No Plan

The "no-plan" author starts out with only a slight foundation—maybe one character, one telling scene, a fragmentary plot, or just a title. He puts Act I, Scene 1 at the top of the page, and writes a detailed script as he goes along. He may complete Act II before beginning to think about Act III. George Sand, who wrote her novels like this, remarked that each new page was as much a surprise to her as it was to a reader of the published book.

If you choose to be a no-planner, and you find yourself bogged down, use the "supposing" technique described in Chapter 8. Write questions about the development of the plot, and write all the answers you can contrive. Or skip over the obstacle. Ignore the line that is bothering you, and jot down bits of dialogue and action from farther on in the scene.

You can also begin *in the middle* of a scene or act, and work backward as well as forward. For working backward, ask yourself such questions as, "How could he have got into this position?", "What information must she have received to make her do so-and-so?" etc.

You can perhaps tap the judgment of some friend. Summarize the story line you already have, and ask, "What do you think so-and-so would (or should) do next?" If the friend's idea is obviously good, accept it; if it's not good, you are stimulated to think and say why it won't work. Then you can discuss what would be better.

Whims and Fancies

Experiment to find which writing method works best for you, the planned or unplanned. Experiment also with different ways of putting the first draft on paper. Some writers use the typewriter, some use a pen, others speak into a tape recorder. Some walk around the room saying each line of dialogue and evaluate how it would fit the character who says it. No particular method is right or wrong; you must find which method works best for you.

Many writers have found that changes in furniture, clothing, timing or other details can turn failure into productivity. Turning the desk to face another way, sitting in a different chair, working at a different time; playing some particular kind of background music; repainting the workroom, wearing some particular kind of clothing—any of these might work for you.

One man told me he never writes except when wearing a heavy silver ring set with a massive gemstone. When stuck for ideas, he finds them by prolonged gazing into the depths of that red stone. One woman I know has to wear a man's undershorts, socks and shoes in order to get started and keep going.

Talk to other writers; swap hints on what they and you have found effective in this line. Believe me, this personal search for stimulative work procedures and surroundings is by no means the least important element of success in writing.

WRITING TO LENGTH

In the late nineteenth century, people went to the theatre expecting a full evening's entertainment. They would see a one-act curtain raiser and then the main play, likely in five acts. Then, to wind up the evening, an afterpiece—usually a farce or pantomime. The whole show would last five hours.

Now, audiences tend to get restless if the play drags on beyond two-and-a-half hours, but some of them would feel cheated by a play that ran only one-hour-and-fifty minutes. So, with a full-length play, aim at a running time of two-and-a-quarter hours, including intermissions. Don't bother writing four-hour plays; they will never be performed.

As for one-act plays, usually two or three are played in one evening; preferred lengths are about thirty-five to fifty-five minutes each. Much shorter or longer one-acts stand less chance of performance.

A two-act play may be written to make an entire evening's performance (although, as I mentioned elsewhere, there are physical and economical reasons for having two intermissions); or it may serve as two-thirds of an evening, being accompanied by a one-act play. In either case, Act II should be the shorter, perhaps thirty-five percent to forty-five percent of the whole.

No one can tell you how many pages of script you must write to fill thirty-five minutes, or any other chosen length. That depends on the kind of dialogue you write, and the kind of actions you describe. Quickfire dialogue, with lots of short speeches, may run thirty seconds per page. A page containing a few long speeches may play for two minutes.

Check the timing as you go. When you have a rough draft of a scene, read it aloud, delaying where necessary for business, and time your reading. Stand up and move around the room as you read—that helps prevent you from rushing over the lines.

A good proportion for the acts of a three-act play is 45/40/30; with two intermissions, this gives the right length. This is not a cast iron rule of proportion, of course, but the third act should certainly be the shortest.

Dumas père's rule for playwrights was: "Let your first act be clear, your last act brief, and the whole interesting."

SCRIPTS

There is a conventional way of presenting your script, either to a drama group or to a publisher. A neat-looking script, in correct format, makes a good impression on your behalf, before the potential buyer or producer has even read the first page. I cannot over-emphasize the importance of this point! If you neglect it, you risk wasting all the effort you have put into the rest of this book.

For playwriting you must have a typewriter. If you are buying a used machine, make sure that the tabulator is in good working order, because the different components of the script are inset at different distances from the left side of the page.

As for type size, pica is best: that prints ten characters to the inch. You can get away with elite type (12 characters to the inch). But don't use fancy type faces; only the square, print-style letters known as "Roman type" are wanted.

Use black ribbons; and for scripts that are to be sent out, change ribbons often enough to give clear, black impressions.

Paper

The required size for script paper is 8½x11 inches. For final copies of scripts, and for letters to publishers or producers, use plain white, and type only on one side of the sheet. A 500-sheet box is a good size to buy; that should serve for several plays. It's called "White Typewriter Paper," "Typing Paper," or some such name. It comes in several different qualities called "bonds"; the higher the bond number, the thicker and more costly the paper. Somewhere in the range of fourteen to twenty-pound is best for this work.

Don't buy special paper from which typescript can be erased as easily as pencil marks; such paper is next to impossible for editors to write on. And don't use thin "onionskin" paper; it reduces the bulk of a script, and your cost of mailing, but it would not stand hard handling at publishers' offices or in playreading committees.

Don't waste that good white paper for all your notes and rough drafts. For disposable work, use a cheaper yellow paper of the same size; it's called "Canary Newsprint," "Yellow Second Sheets," or something like that.

Format

A serviceable playscript format must make perfectly clear which character speaks which line and it must clearly distinguish stage directions from dialogue. The New York format, commonly used on this continent, sets the character's name in the middle of the page, typed in capitals. A line of space separates the name from the speech below. If the speech extends

(CAPTAIN <u>is sitting at his desk,</u>
<u>head on hands.   Knock on door.</u>)

CAPTAIN: Come in.

(<u>Enter</u> MESSENGER.)

MESSENGER: Captain Ahab, sir?

CAPTAIN: Yes; what is it?

MESSENGER: Message from Northern Lights Lumber, Hardware and Frozen
   Fresh Foods, sir. No more paint until you pay for the last batch.

(MESSENGER <u>hands</u> CAPTAIN <u>a paper.</u>)

CAPTAIN: But I must have that paint. My show opens in three days,
   and we've got to paint the set.

(MESSENGER <u>gives another paper.</u>)

MESSENGER: And no more lumber till you pay for those last two loads.

CAPTAIN: But that lumber's urgent: I have sets to build.

(MESSENGER <u>gives another paper.</u>)

MESSENGER: And no more fresh frozen food till you pay for those last
   three sowbellies.

CAPTAIN: But...but...my crew has to eat!

MESSENGER: Sorry, sir; that's how the cookie crumbles: no money,
   no merchandise.

(<u>Exit</u> MESSENGER. CAPTAIN <u>paces</u>
<u>the floor.</u>)

CAPTAIN: Holy heavens above! Who'd want to produce a show? Short
   of talent, short of money, short of everything!

(<u>Enter</u> CLOBBER, <u>dressed as a</u>
<u>lawyer, carrying a briefcase.</u>)

CLOBBER: Captain!

CAPTAIN: Ah, Mr. Clobber! More bad news?

(CAPTAIN <u>sits down and gestures</u>
CLOBBER <u>to a chair.</u> CLOBBER <u>sits,</u>
<u>opens his briefcase and takes out a</u>
<u>legal-size document.</u>)

CLOBBER: Bad news, Captain? That's for you to decide. I have here a
   proposal from a company to...etc.

beyond one line, the extra lines are single spaced. There is a double-space between speeches.

Stage directions are inset 2½ inches farther than the speeches, enclosed in brackets, and underlined, to indicate that, when printed, they will go in italics. Character names occurring in stage directions are typed in capitals, not underlined. Brief stage directions occurring within a speech are bracketed and underlined.

Here's a sample of what it looks like. This is a page from my forthcoming musical comedy *Mounting the Show* (Bud Harris, composer). The action takes place on a showboat on the Yukon River, about 1900—during the Gold Rush. This scene: the Captain's cabin.

Don't crowd too much material on the page: leave margins of 1½ inches at sides, top and bottom.

Number pages straight through from start to finish, with figures in the top right-hand corner.

[Note: when submitting scripts to play contests, watch the rules! Some contests call for unusual formats; follow the rules if you want a chance at the prize. For example, the so-called London Format puts the characters' names in a wide left-hand margin. (You will see many published plays printed in this format because, for the typical script with many short speeches, it saves space.)]

Multiple Copies

Never mail out, or lend out, your only copy of a play. You also need to keep copies of letters written about your plays. So buy and use some carbon paper.

For informal readings of your play at home, a few carbon copies will serve (two people can share each copy). But if you want the play to have trial performances by a drama group, you'll need several more copies of the script than there are people in the cast. For making those copies, use a duplicator or photocopier.

Folders and Binders

Buy some manila filing folders to hold notes and partly finished scripts. For sending out complete scripts you need three hole binders. Buy assignment covers or thesis holders at a large stationery store; they have built-in metal clips. Punch holes in the sheets, fasten them into the binder, and glue a neat label bearing the title and your name on the cover.

TEST READINGS

To check your play when it's in near-final form, get a group of people together. Invite as many people as the play has speaking parts. Have them read the script aloud, with the best emphasis that they can give it at first sight.

Don't take a part yourself; you read the stage directions aloud, allocating roughly the amount of time that the action would take in performance. Note on your script where laughs occur—planned or unplanned. Mark places where you had expected laughs but didn't get them. Note where the script seems to drag. Note where readers falter, or where they give false emphasis to a line. Those are danger spots; if someone finds them difficult reading from a script, then spectators in a theatre might also find them difficult. Remember, in a play, each sentence must be *instantly* understood. There's no pausing to think it over; the play keeps moving on.

Also time each scene; compare the length to your estimate. Give the readers a break wherever an intermission would occur in performance. Afterward, try to get the readers to say what they liked or disliked about the play. Note what they say. With luck, this test reading will give you material for another rewrite.

REWRITING

Here is a list of points to check when rewriting:
1. Structure.

    Does Act I (or the opening of a one-act play) properly introduce most or all of the characters?

    Is the main conflict briskly moving within the first few minutes?

    Is each French scene complete and satisfying in itself?

    Is the first curtain scene strong enough to occupy the spectators' minds during the intermission?

    Does Act II vigorously move the conflict ahead?

    Is the second curtain scene stronger than the first?

    Does Act III raise the conflict to maximum level before resolving it?

    Have you omitted any obligatory scene?

    Have you included any superfluous scenes?
2. Conflict.

    Have you maintained unity of action? Does everything in the play relate, directly or indirectly, to the main line of conflict?

    Does the conclusion of the play really resolve the main conflict?
3. Characters.

    Have you maintained the dominance of the main character or characters?

    With which character(s) do you expect the audience to sympathize?

    Are all characters credible and consistent in speech and action?

    Is all dialogue easy to memorize and speak?

    Have you introduced your own prejudices or speech habits into the dialogue?

    Are all actions reasonably safe to perform?

4. Time.

Could the time lapse from start to finsh be shortened by begin-ning later in the action, or ending sooner?

Have you allowed time for performance of on-stage and off-stage actions?

After doing a rewrite based on these questions, *lay the script aside* for a few days and reread it, looking for more errors. Correct any that you find.

SUMMARY

Systematically collect and file ideas for new plays.
Take pains to find a good title.
Playwriting may be either planned or unplanned: whatever works.
Experiment to find suitable working methods.
Stick to conventional lengths.
Check the timing of the script as you write.
Use proper script format, on the right kind of paper.
Keep copies of your scripts and correspondence.
Scripts should be neatly bound for submission.
Test nearly finished plays by informal readings at home.
Rewrite thoroughly and repeatedly.

CHAPTER FIFTEEN

Special Forms

I WILL DESCRIBE in this chapter three special playforms that are in steady demand by drama groups and audiences and therefore that offer good prospects for playwrights.

MELODRAMA

Melodrama is a word compounded of *melody* and *drama*. A melodrama used to be a dramatic script with songs and music intermixed, the dramatic equivalent of a musical comedy. Nowadays the typical melodrama has no musicians or singers, only actors. Yet it still retains something of the unrealistic tone of the old format.

The modern melodrama is a mock drama. The characters are simplified, far simpler than people in real life. The hero is noble; the heroine is sweet; the villain has no redeeming quality; the assistant villain is the sneak, the toady, *par excellence.*

The audience, even if they don't already know the plot, are sure from the start that everything is going to turn out right. The drunkard *will* reform; the widow's cottage *will* be redeemed from the grasping mortgageholder, the lovely heroine *will* be saved from the clutches of the villain and so on.

The melodrama is interesting to write. It requires a well-constructed plot, plunging right at the start into a brisk conflict of good against evil. It further demands ingenious complications, intense crises, daring catastrophes (even the occasional *deus ex machina* is acceptable in this form), and, of course, the essential happy ending. Particularly important is that you think always of the audience—how to keep them strongly involved, clapping, cheering, booing, hissing, laughing. With a melodrama, strong audience reaction is considered to be the hallmark of success. (I recently saw a crossword puzzle clue: "Gripping plays." The solution: "Melodramas.")

Here is a French scene from my adaptation of *The Drunkard*. Cribbs is the villainous lawyer, Stickler, his clerk and assistant; the scene is Cribbs's house.

(CRIBBS *and* STICKLER *enter L.* STICKLER *carries a law book.)*

STICKLER

Yes, sir, Mr. Cribbs, that's a most interesting hypothetical case. The party of the first part is due to obtain a splendid inheritance, conditional upon the death of the party of the second part.

CRIBBS

Right, Stickler. Good! I'll make a lawyer of you yet! Now, Stickler, in these circumstances, how would you advise the party of the first part to act?

STICKLER

(Looking in book) Hm! Now, let me see . . . Why, the party of the first part should act so as to remove the . . . er . . . obstacle—namely, the party of the second part.

CRIBBS

Stickler, you have a mind like a steel trap. I shall take you into full partnership . . . er . . . someday! Now, *how* would you achieve the removal of the . . . er . . . obstacle?

STICKLER

(Pulling out a pocket knife) Cut his throat?

CRIBBS

No, no, no, no, no! How often must I warn you against *direct* methods? My dear Stickler, you must learn to be *devious*, always devious, *semper deviosus* as Homer puts it.

STICKLER

You mean hire someone else to cut his throat?

CRIBBS

No, no, no, no, no! Still more devious than that.

STICKLER

You tell me, then.

CRIBBS

I will tell you. I shall work . . . ahem . . . I mean the party of the first part must work on the weakness of the party of the second part so as to make him destroy *himself*.

STICKLER

But suppose the party has no weakness.

CRIBBS

There is one weakness common to every young man.

STICKLER

What is that?

CRIBBS

The weakness for alcoholic stimulants. Once young Edward Middleton . . . I mean the party . . . has taken the fatal first glass, his ruin is assured.

STICKLER

But can we be sure that he *has* taken that fatal first glass?

CRIBBS

He must have taken it. He has been three years at college.

STICKLER

Ah!

CRIBBS

So I'll lead him on to the second glass, the third, and on, ever on, down the road to debauchery, degradation and death. Then, heh-heh, the rich Middleton estates will belong to the aforementioned party of the first part.

STICKLER

And what, Mr. Cribbs, will that party do with the aforesaid rich estates?

CRIBBS

He will retire to a life of elegant ease and connubial bliss at the side of a certain fair young party.

STICKLER

Retire! But what about the practice? You'll not abandon the practice?

CRIBBS

I shall make over the practice to you, my dear Stickler—the active work, that is! I shall remain as a sleeping partner, with a fifty percent interest.

STICKLER

Full partnership! Ah! I can see the brass plate now: Cribbs and Stickler!

CRIBBS

No, no, my dear fellow. It shall be Stickler and Cribbs.

STICKLER

Stickler and Cribbs! Oh, sir, how can I ever express my gratitude?

CRIBBS

Save your gratitude until the business is completed. In the meantime, study, work, and be zealous to serve me.

STICKLER

Oh, I will, Mr. Cribbs, sir. I will.

CRIBBS

Listen, then, I am momentarily expecting young Edward Middleton. Give me a few moments alone with him and then bring in the liquor!

STICKLER

Very good, sir. Thank you sir. I shall never forget your kindness, Mr. Cribbs. You are indeed a good employer, sir.
(CRIBBS impatiently waves him away. Exit STICKLER)

Compare this dialogue with the sample from the W.H. Smith version (itself an adaptation, probably from W.M. Thackeray) in Chapter 6. There are still touches of the old-fashioned style, but the speeches are quite short, and there is a continual sparkle of internal conflict.

EXERCISE 15:1
This scene comes early in the play, and is partly expository. Note down five bits of information about characters and situation that an audience could gather from the scene.
The W.H. Smith version of *The Drunkard* calls for such a large cast of actors, so many singers, dancers and musicians, and so much scenery, that scarcely any present-day company could afford to produce it. My object, with this adaptation, was to put *The Drunkard* story within reach of just about every drama company. This effort has proved successful.

FARCE

Farce is a form of comedy in which all the constituents are exaggerated to the limit, or even *beyond* the limit of credibility. Its one purpose to to make the audience laugh. (Comedy, though it, too, aims to arouse laughter, often has some serious underlying message or theme.)

Farce usually portrays extremes. Characters extremely strong, extremely weak, extremely clever, extremely stupid, extremely suspicious, extremely credulous, and so on, will be useful in farce writing.

Repetition is another useful technique for farce; repetition far beyond what's needed for the three-times rule and repetition very obvious, to the point where the audience can foresee each new speaking of the words, or performance of the action.

Here is a potentially farcical situation. The scene is a party, beginning with the host (or hostess) and Guest A. Guest A is obsessed by one subject: slot machines. "I've played on the same machine as the guy who broke the world's record—fifty-four million, nine hundred thousand. I drove fourteen hundred miles to play on that machine. I scored seventeen million myself."

EXERCISE 15:2
Elaborate this slot machine story a bit; have Guest A tell it over and over again as each guest arrives and is introduced. The host, and various guests, try to change the subject, in vain. The last guest finds some means of squashing Guest A.

The simplified, exaggerated characters tend to grow monotonous after a time; and the repetitions, funny for a while, will eventually become boring. So, it is neither easy nor desirable to stretch the farce form to full 2½-hour length. It's better to stick to one acts for farces.

Some fine·examples of the form are the one-act farces by Anton Chekhov: *The Proposal*, *The Bear*, and *The Celebration*.

Chekhov is often thought of as gloomy and pessimistic; but I have seen these farces draw howls of laughter from a packed house. One important feature of these little plays; they can be performed with no sets—just a table and a couple of chairs on the bare stage. There's a lesson from the old master for the would-be playwright!

THEATRE OF THE ABSURD

Absurd is generally understood to mean "contrary to reason, nonsensical, impossible." Absurdity has long been an accepted style of writing for the printed page, as well as for the stage.

Aesop's fables are absurd, with their talking animals and plants; *Reynard the Fox* is absurd, with his political conspiracies and his all-seeing globe of glass; Jonathen Swift's Yahoos and Houyhnhnms are absurd. *Peter Pan* (J. M. Barrie, 1904) is absurd, with its pirates, crocodile and alarm clock. In modern drama, Eugéne Ionesco is the playwright most closely associated with the theatre of the absurd, but Samuel Beckett's *Waiting for Godot* is probably the best-known absurdist play. Harold Pinter and Edward Albee have both written absurdist plays.

Some plays, mainly realistic, incorporate absurd passages: the Gravediggers' scene that opens Act V of *Hamlet* is absurd. Every farce, of course, is absurd in the exaggeration of character, action and plot that create its farcical style.

In fact, it is difficult to draw a hard line between what is absurd theatre and what isn't. It is possible, however, to see that certain pieces are definitely in the absurd category.

THE CLOSE SHAVE

> *(A bedroom. A man is using an electric shaver. He continues shaving for twenty minutes. Curtain.)*

This is bad absurdity—bad because, even for ten minutes, it would not interest an audience. It has only one of the six C's.

I saw a report of a "play" produced in a twenty-room mansion. There was no cast; the audience was expected to roam around the house and "create" its own play. But this idea is hopelessly impractical: very few drama groups have twenty-room mansions at their disposal. Moreover, I suspect that most audiences would feel swindled at being asked to take part in this kind of theatrical jamboree. Again, we see only one of the six C's—not enough to provide a satisfying theatrical experience.

Here is a section, near the beginning, of my absurd one-act play, *The Washing Machine*.

The scene: the laundry room of a shabby old apartment building: a washing machine bearing the name of SWILLWELL.

The characters: Mrs. Watson, the middle-aged manageress, and Mr. Cummings, a new tenant, a mild-looking bachelor of fifty.

WATSON
. . . . I was in the middle of telling you about the late Mr. Watson. See this brass plate set into the floor, here?

CUMMINGS
My, my! That's interesting.

WATSON
Read it. Read the inscription *(Takes broom and dusts off the plate.)*

CUMMINGS
(Reading) "The foundations of this building were poured with Watson Doubleset Cement." *(Looks up)* Watson Doubleset Cement?

WATSON
Another of my husband's inventions.

CUMMINGS
(Reading) "With Watson Doubleset Cement into Watson Warpless Forms." *(Looks up)* Warpless forms?

WATSON
My husband developed a whole new system of building.

CUMMINGS
Indeed! *(Reading)* "Warpless forms. This building designed, owned

and operated by Watson Universal Enterprises Incorporated." (*Looks up*) Watson Universal Enterprises! Oh, I've heard of them.

WATSON

Watson Universal represented the height of our achievement. Ah! It was a glorious height! But then (*sigh*) we fell!

CUMMINGS

Fell?

WATSON

Yes, Mr. Watson was betrayed by his own partner.

CUMMINGS

Betrayed? How very unpleasant!

WATSON

Yes, betrayed by a man named Lewis. (*Indicates machine*) You see Swillwell is a perverted form of Lewis spelled backward.

CUMMINGS

Tut-tut-tut! There's obviously no depending on a man who can't reverse his name in a straightforward way.

WATSON

You're so right. And everytime I see the machine, I'm reminded of it all over again (*sniffs*), and of the late Mr. Watson.

CUMMINGS

Too bad, really too bad, that Mr. Watson's reputation is . . . er . . . obscured.

WATSON

It's my life's work to restore Mr. Watson's reputation to full glory. That's why I must keep up my strength. I still have some of his plans, you know . . . plans not yet revealed to the world. For example, the Watson Sin-Eliminator.

CUMMINGS

Sin-Eliminator! That would be a kind of a lie-detector?

WATSON

More than that, much more than that. The Watson Sin-Eliminator not only detects a liar, but it destroys in him the power . . . even destroys the desire to tell a lie.

CUMMINGS

A sort of spiritual washing machine, heh-heh!

WATSON

In fact, it eliminates all sin, completely wipes it out: pride, avarice, lust, envy, gluttony, anger and sloth, all seven of them.

CUMMINGS

Well now! That is something! A real soul-conditioner, heh-heh!

WATSON

(*Suspicious*) Mr. Cummings, You don't really believe me, do you? You think I'm mad.

CUMMINGS

I didn't say I disbelieved you, Mrs. Watson.

WATSON

But you didn't say you do believe.

CUMMINGS

(*Pause*) Oh, I do! I do believe you.

WATSON

Unfortunately, no one else does. How can I raise the capital I need? I do my best, (*sniff*) I work and slave here as manageress, a glorified janitor, in the apartment that we built and owned. I try to make a little extra money . . . this laundry concession for example, and a small-scale catering operation.

CUMMINGS

Catering! Mighty slim pickings there, I'm afraid, Mrs. Watson.

WATSON

Slim pickings indeed, Mr. Cummings. (*Sniff*)

CUMMINGS

Ah, yes, it must be quite a struggle. (*Pause*) But this sin-eliminator . . . that was just a plan, I suppose . . . never built.

WATSON

Not at all. A trial model was built.

CUMMINGS

And where is it now?

WATSON

I destroyed it personally, to save it from Lewis and his gang. But while Mr. Watson lived, the machine was used. Once!

CUMMINGS

(*Looks at her with a new interest*) But Mrs. Watson, I'm honored to know you . . . the perfect woman.

WATSON

Perfect?

CUMMINGS

Free from sin.

WATSON

Oh, that's not me.

CUMMINGS

No?

WATSON

No. For his supreme test, Mr. Watson chose our daughter, Evelyn.

CUMMINGS

Indeed! And was the experiment a success?

WATSON

Unqualified. Evelyn is the living proof of Mr. Watson's methods. She is free from sin: from the seven deadly sins, the twenty-eight intermediate vices, and the sixty-four minor faults.

CUMMINGS

And you say today is her laundry day?

WATSON

Yes.

CUMMINGS

I should be most honored to meet your daughter, then, Mrs. Watson. (*Footsteps and the sound of whistling approach.* CUMMINGS *straightens his necktie.*)

N.B. This short passage, I know, contains little significant action; but there was some in the early part of the French scene, and there is plenty more after the other two characters (one male, one female) arrive.

The Washing Machine has a well-developed six-C's structure. Cummings is the main character, who wants to get his laundry done; his conflict is with the malfunctioning machine. Th complications are with the other characters, who, in one way or another, delay and divert him. The crisis is when, at last, the machine is restored to action, open, ready to receive his wash. The catastrophe and conclusion . . . . well, read the play, or see it, and find out for yourself. *The Washing Machine* has been published, and performed many times. Audiences have enjoyed it. Some people have seen in it a profound symbolic meaning. So, as absurd plays go, it's successful.

So, *absurd* as we use it in connection with the stage, does not (at least *should* not) mean "purposeless" or "meaningless." A good absurd play, like a good comedy, may be written with a serious purpose and may convey a significant message.

EXERCISE 15:3
From some seemingly absurd situation in your own life, develop an absurd one-act play. Define your main line of conflict; select characters—absurd, yet not incomprehensible. Create French scenes—dialogue absurd, yet not incomprehensible; actions absurd, yet not impossible. Build to a crisis, then outline catastrophe and conclusion—absurd yet emotionally satisfying.

SUMMARY

Melodrama: a mock drama, unrealistically simple.

Good melodrama needs strong plot, and characters unnaturally good or bad.

Successful melodrama aims to produce lively audience reaction.

Farce: comedy with all constituents incredibly exaggerated to produce laughter.

Absurd: plays nonsensical beyond the limits of comedy or farce.

Good absurd theatre may yet convey a serious message.

CHAPTER SIXTEEN

Production and Publication

I PUT *PRODUCTION* before *publication* in this chapter title, because playwrights must proceed in that order. Play publishers, as a rule, won't even read a play that has not been produced.

GETTING PRODUCED

In Chapter 13, I emphasized the importance of joining and working through a drama group. How to find one? Watch your newspaper for advertisements, reports, and reviews of local play productions. Watch the bulletin boards of community centers, public halls, and any such places where performances are likely to take place. Look for notices in the Arts section of your public library, on the bulletin boards in supermarkets, stuck up in laundromats, and on telephone or power poles. Tune yourself in, and you will probably discover that information abounds. If you live in a good-sized city,there may be a dozen or more amateur drama groups; find one that produces the kinds of plays you're most interested in.

First, become recognized as a hard-working, cooperative member of a compatible group. Then is the time to reveal your ambitions and accomplishments as a playwright. Invite a few members to your home for a play-reading party such as I described in Chapter 14. As part of the entertainment, hand out copies of your script, and have the guests read it over.

Try to get a director interested in your work. He may like the idea of directing the premier production of a new play: it makes him feel creative.

If full-scale public productions of your scripts do not seem forthcoming, there's an alternative. "Workshop productions," in which plays are performed simply and cheaply (i.e., no sets, no costumes) to small audiences, are instructive. They show you the effect of your play upon actors and spectators.

Contests

Play contests can be useful to the unknown writer. There are local and regional contests, held by various theatrical or artistic organizations. They are announced through local newspapers, and through bulletins that circulate among arts organizations in the constituent territory. (You will be seeing such notices when you become active in the theatre.) There are nationwide contests, announced in theatrical and writers' magazines. In all contests, study the rules closely and be sure to follow them explicitly.

I would not recommend entering any contest that demands large entry fees, or any contest where you have to sign away rights to your play, win or lose.

It is reasonable for the contest sponsor to reserve first-performance rights of prize-winning plays, for a limited time—say six months. But an unconditional grant of first-performance rights can tie up your play forever, if, as sometimes happens, the sponsor gives it a prize, but does not produce it. No contest sponsor should be given any rights at all in a play that wins no prize.

Producers' Listings

A few producers announce in writers' directories and magazines that they will read new plays. The competition in those markets would likely be more intense, and the production delays longer, than with a local group. Moreover, even if one of these producers selects your play, you are liable to miss the instructional benefit of being personally involved with the production. Think matters through carefully before you go this route.

Evidence

So, by one means or another, your play is produced. Be sure to gather evidence of that production: e.g., photographs of the action on stage; photographs of posters; copies of programs; photocopies of reviews.

PUBLISHERS

Now you are ready to approach a publisher. Publishers who accept freelance material are listed in the "Scriptwriting: Playwriting" section of *Writer's Market*. The safest procedure is to submit to one publisher at a time (producers, too) unless you find an advertiser who specifically says he will accept "multiple submissions."

The typical publisher prints playscripts and issues a yearly catalogue. Theatre groups look through the catalogue, choose plays that interest them, and buy copies from the publisher. The most important feature, from the writer's viewpoint, is that the publisher also collects the performing fees or "royalties"—so many dollars for each performance.

Most play publishers specialize: i.e., they want only certain kinds of plays, aimed at certain kinds of performing groups and audiences. Note their requirements and save yourself wasted postage and time. Choose the right publisher, and send off your script, with some of that evidence of production.

A typical playwright-publisher contract will give the writer 5 percent to 10 percent of receipts from sale of copies, plus 25 percent to 50 percent of royalties. Payments may be higher for playwrights whose previous work has succeeded in publication but the beginner is not in a strong bargaining position.

I would not recommend selling your play outright: i.e., for one flat fee at the time of sale, and no royalties. This is not your best deal. With a good play, the royalty contract will earn you more in the long run. A piece that proves successful with amateur groups, or that becomes a popular contest entry, can go on earning money for ten, fifteen, twenty years and more.

In your writing, and in selling negotiations, bear in mind that a play focused on one day of the year (Christmas, New Year's, Easter, etc.) is going to be limited in its earning power. You're better off writing scripts that can be played any week out of the fifty-two.

PATIENCE

When you begin sending scripts out to publishers, agents, theatre groups, contests, etc., you must be patient while awaiting replies. Some of them admit that they take six months or more to make a decision!

SUMMARY

"Production before publication" is the general rule. In contests, don't give away your rights unconditionally.

Gather, keep, and use evidence of your productions.

Publishers sell scripts and collect royalties.

Study publishers' special requirements.

Outright sales are not usually best for the playwright.

A seasonal theme limits a play's earning power.

Response to submissions may be very slow.

CHAPTER SEVENTEEN

How To Build a Writing Career

IF YOU WANT TO BECOME a successful professional writer, the following suggestions will save you time, and spare you some disappointments.

THE PLACE WHERE YOU LIVE

Many a would-be playwright, with sights set fixedly on Broadway (where, to be realistic, the chance of success is minute), overlooks open doors of opportunity close to home.

Subjects of special local interest—local historical events, celebrated characters, legends, notorious crimes, centennials and such things—offer scope for dramatic treatment.

Keep your feelers out. Track down such special local subjects and the people who might be expected to produce plays about them. In this specialized market, you are not facing competition from famous New York writers, or from the umpteen-hundred-thousand other playwrights scattered around the continent. On your home turf, you have an advantage.

Adaptations

Local drama companies performing published plays by established writers often want the scripts adapted:

(a) To meet the interests, understandings and prejudices of local audiences;

(b) To fit the abilities and preferences of the local director and actors. For example, one or two minor roles, originally for men, may have to be rewritten for women, because the company is short of men. Nothing mysterious about that, of course! But it calls for careful attention to detail throughout, and a good ear for dialogue, since some masculine turns of speech may need feminizing.

Another example: just about every Shakespearian production nowadays is done with an adapted script. The famous speeches: "Is this a dagger . . .," "Friends, Romans, countrymen . . .," and such are retained; but many other speeches will be abbreviated. Characters may be eliminated, combined, transsexed, aged, rejuvenated, or what have you. Whole scenes will be cut out.

The play *must* be made to fit the resources of the producing company;

it *must* be cut to a currently acceptable length; it *must* be made to fit the tastes and pocketbooks of its potential audience. Adaptation is an interesting and highly instructive exercise for the playwright who happens to be on the spot.

Writing to Order

By utilizing contacts with actors, directors and producers, you can eventually build the reputation of one who can write to order. You can take a subject, a character, or a group of characters suggested by someone else, and create from that material a technically sound, artistcally pleasing play. Then you are really on the road to success; then you find customers coming to you.

WATCH FOR OPPORTUNITIES

Study markets continually. Look particularly for the opening of *new* markets: these may offer opportunities for little-known writers.

Be content to start with small sales—likely to some of the local markets I mentioned earlier. Each transaction leads to more publicity and improves your chances for further success. But always be practical in the search for those sales. Ask yourself bluntly, and try to answer realistically, "Why would my play be acceptable and significant to them?" *Them* means the people who will read your script. Recognize that play rejections and acceptances are usually committee decisions. Those committee members will be considering (quite rightly) not only their own artistic tastes, but also the financial resources and the political and ethical standards of the people they want to have in their audiences.

An example: a director recently told me about an organization that refused a play because one character, whose mother and father were unmarried, was described as "a bastard."

If your clue to the marketing opportunity comes about in a conversation, promptly ask questions that will give you the information you need. As for printed market announcements, they usually offer information that will help you determine a particular market's needs.

Misdirected submissions—the wrong material to the wrong markets—make your writing look amateurish, and injure your reputation.

INSTRUCTIVE PLAYGOING

Whenever you can, study the script before you see the play. Make scene cards, *à la* Bronson Howard. Take them to the theatre with you, and see how well your concept of the performance agrees with the director's.

Even when seeing a play whose script you have never read, don't be a passive spectator. Here are some ways to combine education with entertainment.

(1) Study the program well, to familiarize yourself with the list of char-

acters that you are going to see.

(2) When the curtain rises, pay close attention to the exposition. Observe how the author handled it—what's clever, what's clumsy. How does he or she establish time, place, atmosphere, emotional tone, and general line of conflict? Are there any points in which the playwright failed, any parts of the situation or story line that remain incomprehensible or unconvincing?

(3) Note how the author defines each character: preparation (if any) before he or she enters; the character's own speech and actions; other characters' words and behavior toward him or her; costume, etc.

(4) What about the actors? How well does each one portray the character? How well do they deliver the dialogue? Can you hear and understand every word? Analyze any faults of characterization: do they seem to result from the actors' incompetence? Or is the material hard to memorize, hard to speak?

(5) Analyze set design and construction. Exactly what functions was it supposed to serve (physical and emotional)? How well does it do so?

(6) Now, a very important and interesting exercise: as the play moves on, set your playwright's imagination whirring; try to anticipate minor and major turns of the plot. What is Character A going to do and say next? When and how is Character E going to be introduced? What characters will be on stage, and what will be the action for the close of the first and subsequent acts? Etc., etc.

(7) How does the audience react to the show? Are they interested? Where, and how loudly, do they laugh? Why? Exactly what line or action produced this magical explosion?

Are they ever bored? Why? Does part of the audience disappear during intermissions? Can you figure out why? Such lessons from the audience cannot be learned at the desk or in the library.

(8) Maybe you can't cover all these points at one session. So invest the time and cash to see the same production several times over, before different audiences. (Or become an usher; most big theatres and arts organizations cut costs by using volunteer ushers who arrive early, hand out programs, help people to their seats—and thus get to see the performance *free*.) Note how widely the performance and audience differ from one night to the next.

Edgar Allan Poe saw *Fashion* (the 1845 play by Anna Cora Mowatt excerpted in Chapter 6) no fewer than ten nights running! He was a keen student of the theoretical (as well as the practical) aspects of writing.

DIVERSIFIED CONTACTS

Don't be content with joining a theatre group. You'll benefit, too, from joining a writers' club or society. There you can meet other writers interested in the stage.

Make a point of attending writers' conventions and conferences.

There you can meet, and discuss your problems with, playwrights who have already succeeded. There you can hear lectures from, and consult with, producers, publishers, editors, agents—people from the other side of the writing business whom you would never get to meet by staying at home. Success in play writing, more than in most other fields of writing, depends upon personal contacts. Such conferences are unsurpassed for making those contacts. You can find ads for them in writers' and literary magazines.

WRITE COPIOUSLY

Don't be a "one-script writer" with all your hopes riding on one play, biting your nails while it is out with a producer or publisher, and utterly dejected when it comes back. Keep hammering out scripts and keep submitting them. By the time you have twenty or thirty scripts out, a single rejection won't unduly depress you.

It's said that you must write a million words before you can really call yourself a writer: so write that million as fast as you can, and proceed at once to the second million. It's only by doing a great deal of writing that you attain the technical skill, the backlog of finished work, and the speed of production that you will need when success does come.

From time to time, exhume old scripts and rewrite them. When you find yourself detecting and correcting flaws in your old work, you know you are progressing, technically and artistically.

SUMMARY

Watch for opportunities close to home.
Adaptations: often in demand.
Try writing to order.
The script must suit the market at which you aim it.
Playgoing, a means of technical instruction and exercise:
Study exposition;
Analyze characters and how they are played;
Try to predict the course of action;
Study audience reactions;
See the same production several times over.
Make contacts with other writers.
Attend conferences for wider contacts, including publishers, producers, etc.
Write copiously; much new material, and some revision of old.

GLOSSARY OF THEATRICAL TERMS

Angel: An investor who advances money to finance production of a play.

Apron stage: an area of stage projecting some distance forward of the proscenium; this allows parts of the performance to take place in front of the closed curtain. It may be useful for playing one scene while sets for the next are changed behind the curtain.

Arena stage: an open stage set in a saucer-shaped theatre, with the audience in rising tiers of seats on three sides. Actors enter and leave around the ends of the backdrop, or from tunnels beneath the audience.

Aside: a speech, or part of a speech, made by one character to reveal what he is thinking, or to give a bit of information to the audience; it is supposedly not heard by the other characters on stage. At one time, a standard dialogue technique; but by no means so commonly used nowadays. (Although there have been some signs of a revival.)

Backdrop: a curtain or set that forms the back of the visible stage. The backdrop preferably is some distance away from the back wall of the stage house, so that actors can move from wing to wing behind it.

Boards: the stage. A play that "holds the boards" is being more or less regularly performed.

Broadway: a group of theatres, and a style of production—often large-scale and lavish—centered on Broadway, New York City.

Business: actions used to reveal character or to help advance the story: e.g., pouring tea, drawing a sword, opening a safe.

Cast: the group of actors and actresses who perform a play.

Casting: the process of choosing actors and actresses to perform a play. Physical characteristics (sex, age, height, weight, and general deportment) will generally be important. In a small theatre group, only one member may fit the physical requirements of a certain part. If several applicants are physically suitable, they will compete by reading, singing, dancing, or demonstrating whatever performing skills are required for the role.

Commedia dell'Arte (Italian for *Comedy of the Arts*): a form of comedy using a small number of stock characters: i.e., the same characters appear over and over in different story lines, like comic strip characters. Among them were Harlequin, a clown; Pantaloon, a silly old man; and Columbine, an artful, pretty girl. The male characters wore masks. The cast improvised their own dialogue, while hewing to a prearranged plot.

The Commedia flourished from the sixteenth to eighteenth centuries, and is seldom seen nowadays, except as a historical revival.

Credits: the list of names in programs, posters, advertisements, etc., telling the public who is responsible for various functions in connection with a play: e.g., producer, director, actors, stage hands, prompters, house manager, writer, adapter, translator, etc.

Cue: the last few words of a speech by Actor A, which signal to Actor B that it's time to deliver the next speech. In studying their parts, actors carefully memorize the cues preceding each of their own lines. Cues must be delivered accurately.

Director: the director usually has the main responsibility of casting a play. Then he or she supervises all rehearsals as described in Chapter 13.

In the eighteenth and nineteenth centuries, star actors often directed their own plays; nowadays the director normally does not perform in a play.

(N.B. In British theatrical writings, the director is usually called the "producer.")

Dress rehearsals: the final rehearsal(s) before opening night. Actors rehearse in full costume; sound and lighting effects are applied, just as they will be in the public performances.

Exit: Latin for "he goes out." We use the English *enter* when a character comes on stage, but *exit* when he or she leaves. The conventional way is to put the verb first and the name after: e.g., *enter* JACK, or *exit* MACBETH.

Exeunt, meaning "they go out," is used for the departure of two or more characters.

In some old scripts you will see *Exeunt omnes,* meaning "they all go out"—as might happen at the end of a scene.

Extras: subordinate characters, with nothing specific to say or do, who can be added or omitted, according to the resources of the producing company: e.g., extra couples for a ballroom scene; extra soldiers for a battle, etc.

Farce: a kind of comedy in which the characters, situations, dialogue and actions are exaggerated, for humorous effect, close to the limits of credibility.

Flats: flat, lightweight scenic units that can be easily moved and fastened together to build the set. A set representing a room, for example, might have one flat containing a door, one flat with a fireplace, two flats containing windows and four, six or more depicting plain wall.

The height of a flat will be determined by the height of the stage on which it is used; it will probably not be more than six feet (two meters) wide, narrow enough for one stagehand to pick it up by the sides and carry it onto the stage, or into the wings.

Flies: scenic units designed to be lifted up, out of sight of the audience. The fly loft is a hollow tower above the stage, fitted with hoisting gear for raising and lowering the flies. Flying is the quickest way of making elaborate set changes; but many theatres and halls don't have the equipment to do it.

Floods: short for floodlights, arranged to cover a wide area, or the whole stage, with light of uniform intensity and color.

Footlights: in the days of candle, oil and gas lighting, a row of lights placed across the front of the stage at floor level, shielded so that the audience could not see them, but with all their light reflected up at the actors. (This strong illumination from below necessitated a special style of heavy make-up to make actors' faces look natural.)

Footlights are seldom used in theatres with electric lighting but the word is often used as symbolic of theatrical activities and people.

Ham: over-acting, with excessive, insincere variation of voice and facial expression, and extravagant, unrealistic gestures.

Intimate theatre: a small-scale style of production, designed to utilize small casts and simple properties and sets. Such intimacy usually implies the absence of a high stage, proscenium arch and curtain. The actors may perform on an open floor, at the same level as (and at times almost within touching distance of) the front row of spectators. A common arrangement is to have one back wall for the acting area (to give the cast cover before entrances and after exits), and to have the audience in curved rows of seats on three sides.

Lines: the actor's name for his or her part of the script. In some productions, each actor is given a special script containing only that character's own lines, plus the cues that lead into them.

Makeup: articles and materials used to change the appearance of actors before performance: e.g., cosmetics, wigs.

Mime: a style of silent theatrical performance. Actors use facial expression, gestures, body movements and props to tell the story, but no words. Mime obviously offers little scope for the playwright.

Open stage: a stage with no proscenium and no curtain. (See *Arena stage.*)

Producer: in professional theatre, the person who has overall responsibility for a theatrical venture. He or she chooses the theatre, the play, the director and technical staff; supervises all functioning committees/personnel; and oversees payment of all expenses.

Sometmes a company or partnership raises the money for a play production; they will likely appoint one person as producer, to handle all the details for them.

For the function of the producer in amateur theatre, see Chapter 13.

Prompter: a backstage worker who holds a script during rehearsals and performances, ready to read a few words to any actor who forgets his or her lines.

Props (the customary abbreviation for properties): movable objects used (a) to give a scenic effect on stage (e.g., chairs, tables, pictures); or (b) to be used as significant items in the action (e.g., teacups, wine bottles, food, typewriters, telescopes, telephones, etc.).

Proscenium: the rectangular opening that in the conventional theatre divides stage from auditorium. Usually the proscenium can be opened or closed by a movable curtain.

Repertory company: a theatre company that employs a fixed group of actors and actresses to perform a number of different plays, acting one play while they are rehearsing the next.

In pre-movie times a touring repertory company would have several plays always ready for performance. They played some or all of these in rotation at each theatre where they were booked.

Sets: items, other than properties, used to create scenic effects on stage: e.g., walls and doors of a building; a city skyline; the deck and superstructure of a ship; the bars of a prison cell.

Good sets help to create the proper emotional tone for a performance, and also give important background information about the play (the period at which the action occurs, the social status of the characters, etc.)

Sound effects: sounds produced by offstage apparatus, mechanical or electronic, to help create dramatic illusion in a play: bells, railroad trains, wind, thunder, gunfire, etc.

Stage directions: the printed description of actions to be performed by characters (e.g., *She slaps his face; Henry rushes out the door*, etc.), or of the manner in which a speech is to be delivered (*Tenderly, Sarcastically*, etc.).

In published playscripts, stage directions are sharply differentiated from the spoken words, usually by brackets and/or italics. Be sure to make the clear distinction in your script. (See Chapter 14.)

Stage house: the part of a theatre that contains the stage. For convenient operation, there should be plenty of space in the wings and behind the backdrop. A desirable extra feature is ample space overhead, fitted with hoisting gear so that sets, props—even actors—can be quickly lifted from or lowered to stage level. (See *Flies.*)

The stage house will also contain many of the lights, mounted overhead and in the wings. A few stage houses include trapdoors in the stage floor, with mechanisms for lifting and lowering platforms beneath.

Many old playscripts include frequent, rapid set-changes that could not be made without an elaborately equipped stage house.

Stage manager: supervises the making and movement of sets, and the procurement, movement and safe storage of properties. The more elaborate the play (with regard to sets and properties), the heavier the stage manager's work. During rehearsal and performance, the stage manager also supervises lighting and sound effects.

Stock company: (See Repertory company.)

Understudy: an actor who learns and rehearses a role in order to play it if the original actor is sick, or otherwise unable to perform.

Upstaging: any maneuver by Actor A to draw the audience's attention to himself when, by rights, they should be concentrating on the speech or movements of Actor B.

Wings: the space at the sides of the stage where actors can wait, out of sight of the audience, until it is time to go on. Some members of the stage crew also work in the wings: e.g., prompter and sound-effects and lighting control personnel.

RECOMMENDED READING

PLAYS

Across the Continent: James J. McCloskey
Arms and the Man: George Bernard Shaw
The Bear: Anton Chekhov
The Cassilis Engagement: St. John Hankin
The Celebration: Anton Chekhov
The Cherry Orchard: Anton Chekhov
Death of a Salesman: Arthur Miller
Desire Under the Elms: Eugene O'Neill
The Doctor Despite Himself: Molière
The Drunkard: Raymond Hull
The Drunkard: W. H. Smith
Everything in the Garden: Edward Albee
Fashion: Anna Cora Mowatt
The Glass Menagerie: Tennessee Williams
The Glory of Columbia: William Dunlap
Ghosts: Henrik Ibsen
Hamlet: William Shakespeare
Hedda Gabler: Henrik Ibsen
Henry IV, parts 1 and 2: William Shakespeare
The Imaginary Invalid: Molière
The Importance of Being Earnest: Oscar Wilde
Life with Father: Howard Lindsay and Russel Crouse
Macbeth: William Shakespeare
The Madwoman of Chaillot: Jean Giraudoux
Mary, Mary: Jean Kerr
The Miracle Worker: William Gibson
Othello: William Shakespeare
Our Town: Thornton Wilder
The Play's the Thing: Ferenc Molnar
Po-Ca-Hon-Tas or *The Gentle Savage:* John Broughton
Prometheus Bound: Aeschylus
The Proposal: Anton Chekhov
Roast Pig: Raymond Hull
Saratoga: Bronson Howard
Secret Service: William Gillette
A Streetcar Named Desire: Tennessee Williams
Uncle Tom's Cabin: George L. Aiken
The Washing Machine: Raymond Hull
Wedded to a Villain: Raymond Hull

Bibliographical information is given for books still in print. But many of these books—in print and not in print—are available in numerous editions. The essays are included in anthologies. So check at a book store—particularly a good used book store—or at your public library.

BOOKS

Going to the Theatre. John Allen.
The Complete Play Production Handbook. Carl Allensworth, et al. Thomas Y. Crowell, 1973.
The Old Drama and the New. William Archer.
Dramatic Technique. George Pierce Baker. R. West, 1975; reprint of 1919 edition.
On Directing. Harold Clurman. Macmillan, 1974.
My Memoirs. Alexandre Dumas. (Craig A. Bell, translator and editor) Greenwood, 1975; reprint of 1961 edition.
The Art of Dramatic Writing. Lajos Egri. Touchstone Books, 1960
Play Directing: Analysis, Communication, and Style. Francis Hodge, Prentice-Hall, 1981 (2nd edition).
Play Directing: Analysis, Communication, and Style. Prentice-Hall, 1982 (2nd edition).
The Writer's Encyclopedia. Kirk Polking, ed. Writer's Digest Books, 1983.
The Dramatist's Sourcebook. James Leverett & David Izakowitz, eds. Theatre Communications Group, 1981.

ESSAYS & PERIODICALS

"Essay on Comedy." Emile Augier.
"The Poetic Principle." Edgar Allan Poe.
"The Art of Rehearsal." Bernard Shaw.
Writer's Digest. Monthly.

ANNUALS

Literary Market Place, R.R. Bowker Company.
Writer's Market, Writer's Digest Books.

INDEX

A

Abraham Lincoln, 90
"Absurd" theatre, 213
Accounts department of drama groups, 188
Across the Continent, 19
Action, 45, 64; and characters, 131-148; dramatic, 131-148; technical, 131; types of, 131; unity of, 47
Actors, 187, 191; and dialogue, 120-124
Acts, 31-34
Adaptations, 225-226; as source of ideas, 61-62
Adding Machine, The, 115
Aeschylus, 10, 58, 61
Aiken, George L., 51, 113
Albee, Edward, 21, 55, 213
American theatre, 18-21
Amphitryon 38, 61
Anderson, Maxwell, 59
Animals as characters, 84
Anouilh, Jean 61
Appearance of characters, 88
Arena theatre, 179
Aristophanes, 10
Aristotle, 170
Arms and the Man, 70, 132, 165, 177
Articulateness of characters, 82
Art of Rehearsal, The, 192
As You Like It, 108
Atmosphere: and dialogue, 99-100; and dramatic action, 132, 147
Attention of audience, 194-195
Attire of characters, 88
Audience, 193-196, 209; attention of, 194-195; credulity of, 194; learning from, 195-196; relationship between playwright and, 17-18
Augier, Emile, 83, 193
Author intrusion, 115

B

Bad laughs, 195
Bad Seed, 59
Barrie, J. M., 213
Bear, The, 213
Beckett, Samuel, 21, 213

Block, 200-201
Blocking process, 193
Box office of drama groups, 188
Brecht, Bertolt, 21
Brighton, 4
Broadway, 20, 103
Broughton, John, 19

C

Cassilis Engagement, The, 51, 54-55, 85
Cast call department of drama groups, 189
Casting, 19; committee on, 188
Cast list, 87-88
Catastrophe, 31, 169-172
Celebration, The, 213
Characters, 31, 79-93, 95-128, 205; and action, 131-148; animals as, 84; appearance of, 88; articulateness of, 82; attire of, 88; deformed, 84; depicting of, 88-89; exaggeration of, 83; friends of, 89; habits of, 88-89; judgment of, 89; kinds of, 82-85; lists of in programs, 88; main, 62-63, 90-91; minor, 91; names of, 69, 85-87; number of, 80-82; occupation of, 89; reputation of, 89; revealing of through dialogue, 100-102; revealing of through dramatic action, 132-136; secondary, 91; simplicity of, 83; sketches of, 89-90; telephones as, 83-84; temperament of, 89; with unusual skills, 84; young children as, 84
Chekhov, Anton, 56, 70, 132, 147, 213
Cherry Orchard, The, 56, 75
Children, 84
Chorus, 9, 64
Closeups, 48
Closing scenes, 176-177. *See also* Conclusion
Coherence in dialogue, 122
Coleridge, Samuel Taylor, 17
Color of lights, 183
Comedy, 11-12; and tragedy, 13-15
Comic dialogue, 117-120
Comic relief, 15
Complex time structure, 158-159
Complications of, 31, 151-160; creation of,

152-154; entrances as, 157-158; and planting, 155-157; and surprise, 155-157
Comprehensibility of dialogue, 120-121
Conciseness in dialogue, 126-128
Conclusion, 31, 175-177
Conflict, 31, 51-76, 163-167, 205. *See also* Crises: and dialogue, 103-106; and dramatic action, 146
Construction of sets, 190
Contacts, 227-228
Contests, 221-222
Contracts, 222-223
Conversation vs. dialogue, 97-98
Copies of script, 204
Corneille, Pierre, 13, 58, 61
Costume department of drama groups, 189
Credulity of audience, 194
Crises, 31, 163-167
Crouse, Russel, 156
Cues, 123
Curtain scenes, 175-176

D

Death of a Salesman, 136-147, 152, 158, 163
Deformed characters, 84
De la Barca, Calderon, 13
Delany, Shelagh, 91
Design of sets, 190
Desire Under the Elms, 52, 53
Deus ex machina, 12, 169-170, 209
De Vega, Lope, 13
Dialects, 101
Dialogue, 64, 95-128; and actors, 120-124; coherence in, 122; comic, 117-120; comprehensibility of, 120-121; conciseness in, 126-128; and conflict, 103-106; vs. conversation, 97-98; creating atmosphere through, 99-100; and dramatic action, 145-146; duplicate cues in, 123; ease of speaking, 124; for exits, 125-126; functions of, 98-103; memorizability of, 122-124; names in, 116; revealing character through, 100-102; strong, 116-117, 146-147; tennis analogy for, 106; weak, 116-117
Diamond, 3
Direct exposition, 64-66
Direction: of lights, 183; stage, 185
Directors, 189, 191-192
"Disbelief, willing suspension of," 17
Dithyrambs, 9
Doctor's Dilemma, The, 199
Doctor Despite Himself, The, 90, 103-106, 118-120

Don Juan, 89
Don Sebastian, King of Portugal, 2
Drama groups, 187-190, 221
Dramatic action, 131-148; vs. technical action, 131
Drunkard, The, 19, 95-96, 126, 175, 199, 209-211
Dryden, John, 2, 61
Dumas, Alexandre, 97, 202
Dunlap, William, 18, 19
Duplicate cues in dialogue, 123

E

Ease of speaking and dialogue, 124
Effects, 18-19
Electric lighting, 18
Elephant Man, The, 59
Entrances, 102-103; as complications, 157-158
Equipment, 179-185
"Essay on Comedy," 83
Euripides, 10
Everything in the Garden, 55
Evidence of production, 222
Exaggeration of characters, 83
Executive committee of drama groups, 187
Exits, 80
Experience as source of ideas, 60
Exposition, 63-75

F

Fables, 213
Famous names, 86
Farce, 212-213
Fashion, 96-97, 100, 102, 227
Fatalism doctrine, 58
Fate vs. man, 58-60, 61
Father, The, 53
Favorable Balance, A, 120
Files of ideas, 62, 199
Films, 19-20, 47-48
Flashbacks, 158
Folders, 204
Foote, Samuel, 122
Format of scripts, 202, 204
Free will, 58
French scene, 32, 163, 169, 171, 175; structure of, 34-35
Friends: of characters; 89 as source of ideas, 61

G

Ghosts, 35-44, 75, 157-158, 165, 172, 176, 177

Gibson, William, 59, 132, 184
Gillette, William, 99
Giraudoux, Jean, 61, 70
Glass Menagerie, The, 63, 89
Glory of Columbia, The, 19
Goal, 62-63
Goethe, Johann Wolfgang von, 25, 30, 151
Goldoni, Carlo, 89
Gossiping-servant technique, 68
Great Divide, The, 99
Great Train Robbery, The, 20
Guys and Dolls, 199

H

Habits of characters, 88-89
Hamlet, 51, 90, 91, 108-109, 125, 151-152, 154, 155-156, 165, 172, 213
Hankin, St. John, 51, 54
Hazlewood, C. H., 109
Hedda Gabler, 75, 157, 185
Henry IV, 64
History, 9-22
House manager of drama groups, 188
Howard, Bronson, 3-4, 200, 226

I

Ibsen, Henrik, 35, 54, 75, 157
Ideas, 60-62, 199; adaptation as source of, 61-62; files of, 62, 199; friends as source of, 61; newspapers as source of, 60-61; one per speech, 106-109, 146; personal experience as source of, 60; sources of, 60, 61-62
Imaginary Invalid, The, 25-30, 175
Importance of Being Earnest, The, 32-34, 118, 126, 132, 147, 172
Indirect exposition, 67-68
Inevitability of catastrophes, 170
Intensity of lights, 183
Interchangeable lines, 115
Interlude, 13
Intermission, 31, 175
Introduction, 70-74
Intrusion of author, 115
Involvement, 1-2, 4
Ionesco, Eugene, 213
Irritation, 75

J

Judgment of characters, 89
Julius Caesar, 91, 199

K

Kerr, Jean, 51
King Charles II, 16
Kopit, Arthur, 21

L

Lady Audley's Secret, 109
Lamb, Charles, 65
Laughs, 195, 212. *See also* Comedy
Le Gallienne, Eva, 35
Length, 201-202
Les Miserables, 199
Life with Father, 156
Lighting, 18-19, 183-184; color of, 183; department of, 189; direction of, 183; electric, 18; intensity of, 183
Lilian's Last Love, 3
Linday, Howard, 156
Little Theatres, 20-21
Livius Andronicus, 11
London format, 204
Lyly, John, 13

M

Macbeth, 15, 56, 58, 132, 155, 166, 172, 177
Macklin, Charles, 122
Madwoman of Chaillot, The, 70-74, 116
Main characters, 62-63, 90-91
Makeup department of drama groups, 189
Managers: house, 188; stage, 189
Man vs. fate, 58-60, 61
Man vs. himself, 56-58
Man vs. man, 53-54, 61, 151
Man vs. nature, 51-53, 165
Man vs. society, 54-56, 61
Man Who Came to Dinner, The, 90
Marlowe, Christopher, 13
Mary, Mary, 51, 84, 132-136, 147, 182, 185
McCloskey, James, J., 19
Melodrama, 209-212
M+G+O=C, 62-63
Miller, Arthur, 136
Minor characters, 91
Miracle plays, 13
Miracle Worker, The, 59, 132, 158-159, 182-183, 185
Miser, The, 67, 90
Miss Julie, 90, 91
Molière, 13, 25, 30, 34, 61, 91, 103, 104, 118, 119, 151, 196
Molnar, Ferenc, 166
Moody, William Vaughn, 99

Moorcroft, 3
Morality plays, 13, 47
Motion pictures, 19-20, 47-48
Mourning Becomes Electra, 199
Movies, 19-20, 47-48
Mowatt, Anna Cora, 96, 227
Mystery plays, 13

N

Names: of characters, 69, 85-87; in dialogue, 116; famous, 86; variety of, 86
New York format, 202-204
New York Times, 21
'Night, Mother, 80
Norman, Marsha, 80
Number of characters, 80-82
Number of crises, 163-164

O

Obligatory scenes, 165-167
O'Casey, Sean, 101
Occupation of characters, 89
Odets, Clifford, 61
Oedipus story, 58
Off Broadway, 20-21
Off Off Broadway, 21
O'Neill, Eugene, 52, 59
One speech, one idea, 106-109, 146
Openings, 69; silent, 147-148
Opposition, 62-63
Othello, 170
Our Town, 65, 180

P

Parting, 74-75
Patrick, John, 32
Payne, John Howard, 131
Personal involvement, 1-2, 4
Peter Pan, 213
Peter Stuyvesant, 3
Pillars of Society, 54
Pinter, Harold, 21, 213
Place, 45; unity of, 47
Planning, 199-201; of catastrophes, 170; and complications, 155-157
Plants, 57
Platform stage, 179
Plautus, 11, 61
Playhouses, 15-17. *See also* Theatres
Play selection committee of drama groups, 187-188
Play's the Thing, The, 166
Playwright-audience relationship, 17-18

Plot advancing through dramatic action, 136, 147
Poe, Edgar Allan, 164, 227
"Poetic Principle, The," 164
Pomerance, Bernard, 59
Presentation of scripts, 202-204
Producers: of drama groups, 188; listings of, 222
Production, 221-222
Programs, 188; character lists in, 88
Prologue, 64
Prometheus Bound, 10-11
Prometheus story, 58
Promotion, 188
Prompter in drama groups, 189
Properties, 184-185; department of, 190
Proposal, The, 56-57, 213
Proscenium stage, 179
Publication, 222-223
Publicity and promotion department of drama groups, 188-189
Publishers, 222-223
Punch in comic dialogue, 117-119

Q

Queen Mary, 81

R

Racine, Jean Baptiste, 13
Readings, 204-205
Regional theatres, 21
Rehearsals, 192-193
Religion, 9, 12-13
Renaissance, 13
Repetition, 212. *See also* Three-times rule
Reunion, 74-75
Reversals, 151-152
Reviews, 3
Rewriting, 205-206
Rice, Elmer, 115
Riders to the Sea, 52
Roman theatre, 47
Romeo and Juliet, 51, 53, 90, 166
Royalties, 222-223

S

Sand, George, 200
Saratoga, 3, 4
Sardou, Victorien, 199
Scenes, 31-34; closing, 176-177; curtain, 175-176; French. *See* French scenes; obligatory, 165-167
Scripts, 202-204

Seagull, The, 132
Seating capacity, 17
Secondary characters, 91
Secret Service, 99
Seneca, 11
Set design and construction department of drama groups, 190
Sets, 182-183
Setting, 45, 47
Shakespeare, William, 13, 15, 34, 61, 91, 154, 225
Shaw, George Bernard, 61, 70, 132, 192
Shelley, Percy B., 58
Shot, 47-48
Silent openings and dramatic action, 147-148
Simplicity of characters, 83
Six C's, 30-31, 218
Sketches of characters, 89-90
Skills of characters, 84
Slang, 101
Smith, W. H., 95, 212
Sophocles, 10, 58
Sound effects, 184
Sources of ideas, 60, 61-62
Special forms, 209-218
Special occasion, 68-70
Stage, 179-185; Greek, 9; Roman, 12
Stage action types, 131
Stage crew of drama groups, 190
Stage directions, 185
Stage manager of drama groups, 189
Stowe, Harriet Beecher, 113
Strange Interlude, 59
Streetcar Named Desire, A, 75
Strindberg, August, 53, 91
Strong dialogue: and dramatic action, 146-147; vs. weak dialogue, 116-117
Structure, 205
"Supposing" technique, 152-154, 200
Surprise, 194-195; of catastrophes, 170; and complications, 155-157
Suspense, 25-49, 151, 155
Swift, Jonathan, 213
Synge, John Millington, 52

T

"Talky" plays, 131
Talley's Folly, 65, 80
Tartuffe, 91
Taste of Honey, A, 91
Teahouse of the August Moon, The, 32
Technical action vs. dramatic action, 131

Telephone as character, 83-84
Television, 21, 47-48
Terence, 11
Test readings, 204-205
Theatre of the absurd, 213
Theatre-in-the-round, 179
Theatres, 15-17; arena, 179; Little, 20-21; regional, 21
Thespis, 9
Three Sisters, The, 70, 90
Three-times rule, 109-116, 212
Three unities, 45-47
Time, 206; complex structure of, 158-159; unity of, 45-47
Titles, 199
Tongue-twisters, 124
Touring companies, 19
Tragedy and comedy, 13-15

U

Uncle Tom's Cabin, 51-52, 113-115, 172, 176
Uncle Vanya, 147
Unity, 45-47
Unusual skills of characters, 84

V

Valency, Maurice, 70
Variety of names, 86
Victoria Regina, 90
Village Voice, 21
Voltaire, 58

W

Waiting for Godot, 213
Washing Machine, The, 214-218
Weak dialogue vs. strong dialogue, 116-117
Wedded to a Villain, 68-69
Wilde, Oscar, 32, 34, 118
Wilder, Thornton, 65, 180
Will, 58
Williams, Tennessee, 63, 75
"Willing suspension of disbelief," 17
Wilson, Lanford, 65
Workshop productions, 221
Writer's block, 200-201
Writer's Market, 222

Y

Young children as characters, 84